LOST PROPERTY

MEMOIRS &
CONFESSIONS
OF A BAD BOY

BEN SONNENBERG

SUMMIT BOOKS

NEW YORK · LONDON · TORONTO
SYDNEY · TOKYO · SINGAPORE

SUMMIT BOOKS
Simon & Schuster Building
Rockefeller Center
1230 Avenue of the Americas
New York, New York 10020

SUMMIT BOOKS and colophon are trademarks
of Simon & Schuster Inc.

Designed by Deborah Thomas
Manufactured in the United States of America

1 3 5 7 9 10 8 6 4 2

Library of Congress Cataloging in Publication Data

Sonnenberg, Ben.
Lost property : memoirs & confessions of a bad boy / Ben Sonnenberg.
p.   cm.
Includes index.
1.Sonnenberg, Ben.   2.Authors, American—20th century—Biography.
3.Editors—United States—Biography.   I.Title.
PN4874.S5753A3   1991
818'.5409—dc20
[B]   91-2545   CIP

ISBN 0-671-70188-6

For Dorothy

&

for Susanna, Emma and Saidee

And the soul seems to say: *How true, but I missed it!*

Aristotle, Rhetoric

CONTENTS

PREFACE

I am a Collectors' Child.

I was born in New York City, on the thirtieth of December, 1936, and was brought up in a very grand private house, 19 Gramercy Park. It was crammed with servants, furniture, art.

My father and mother were famous for the "fabulous" parties they gave there. Names of the famous, and once-famous, are inscribed on the walls of this book. I grew up in a sort of *Arabian Nights*, with extreme attributes being given to all the adults and objects around, which then (and this to me was the most truly fantastic thing) disappeared.

Until his death in 1978, my father was one of the best-known public relations men in America. He described his business as "making giant plinths for little men to stand on." In fact, his clients were often large powerful corporations, and his services to them were different from the flackery which his description implies, more commonplace, more corrupt. For his services he was paid, as he said, "*scandalously* well," and we all lived in a showy, extravagant public way.

Lost Property is a story drawn from fifty-four years of my life. The story is truthful: so far anyway as is consistent with entertainment, or art. My favorite autobiographers in this century are Vladimir Nabokov, Theodor Adorno and Walter Benjamin. My favorites in the last century are Baudelaire, Berlioz, Stendhal and Herzen.

I'd like to have told my story in anecdotes, like Robert Burton in *The Anatomy of Melancholy*, or in aphorisms, like Adorno in *Minima Moralia*, or in captions to photographs, like my friend Edward Said in *After the Last Sky*. But the consecutive narrative (despised linear!) is often hard to resist, and sometimes for its sake I've compressed time and relocated event. I've also gotten things wrong now and then and let them stand that way, and I've changed people's names, always noting where. The reader will want at all times to recall the old man who in the 1890s claimed to have seen the burning of Moscow in 1812. "I remember the Emperor Napoleon well. He was very tall and had a long white beard."

The first part of *Lost Property* is about sex, money, politics and art. The second part is about them too, as well as marriage and debt and disease. The title *Lost Property* comes from one of the books by Sebastian Knight, in Nabokov's first English novel, *The Real Life of Sebastian Knight* (1941). The subtitle, *Memoirs and Confessions of a Bad Boy*, is meant to evoke *The Private Memoirs and Confessions of a Justified Sinner* (1824) by James Hogg. From *Justified Sinner* to *Bad Boy* is a comedown, I know; and it may be that Booth Tarkington in *The Magnificent Ambersons* has told the story once and for all. The main trouble with *Bad Boy* is that at the end it offers no eminence for a Pisgah-sight of Truth.

My thoughts on autobiography are pretty much those set out in the Symposium on page 158 of this book, except that I don't do justice there to how unruly an art it is. Its characters, even its narrator, stand up and talk back to the author, and in that respect autobiography tends most to be like fiction. Autobiography is also more autoerotic than I knew before I began, not masturbatory exactly, but as in Auden's "Eros, builder of cities."

•

I am grateful to Elizabeth Pochoda, who first published parts of *Lost Property* in the *Nation*, and to Ileene Smith, my editor at Summit Books, who called for this book ten years ago.

I am grateful to Deborah Thomas, who designed this book and its cover. I am grateful to Helene Pleasants for copyediting it. I am grateful to Allison Prete for her help with the final changes. A list of other acknowledgments comes after the index.

I am most specially grateful to Lori Toppel, to whom much of *Lost Property* was spoken. She called my attention to "Sacrificial Lamb" in *Minima Moralia*, where Adorno writes:

> . . . But thanks are due to the person taking down the dictation, if at the right moment [s]he pulls up the writer by contradiction, irony, nervosity, impatience and disrespect. [S]he incurs wrath, so diverting it from the store of bad conscience with which otherwise the writer would mistrust his own work and therefore dig in his heels all the more defiantly over supposedly sacred text.

PART ONE

RICHES

THE POLISH RIDER   I've always had a fondness for books like *The Top Drawer* "By One Who Was Born In It," and in my worst recurring dream I'm cut at a party by Henry James. This is because of where I grew up, 19 Gramercy Park.

A grand house, for me it was not grand enough. One Christmas vacation I came up from school with a senior boy. He had two or three hours before his next train. "We always hear tell of your house, Sonnenberg. Why don't you take us there?" I took him instead to Seventieth Street and Fifth Avenue.

"You live *here*?"

"We let in the people sometimes. Morning, Packard," I said to the guard. "It's called the Frick Collection because my mother was born Frick."

"His name is Packard?"

"We have another inside named Rolls. . . . Morning, Rolls."

I loved armed guards. Not only because museum guards body forth riches and fear, but also because, as at the Frick, their courtesy made me an heir. At home, by contrast, I was a kid at the mercy of angry help. (My mother's maiden name is Caplan, by the way.)

"I'd show you upstairs where we live except my parents are giving a luncheon for Folke Bernadotte."

"*Count* Bernadotte?" The Swedish diplomat Folke Bernadotte, the United Nations mediator in Palestine, had been much in the news the year before.

"You won't want to miss your train," I said. "But first come and look at the Rembrandt. We bought it for one hundred thousand, today it's worth—"

"I say, thank you, Ben. Sorry I've got to rush. . . . See you at the Jigger Shop, Ben."

A better-known liar, Ford Madox Ford, used this same technique. Ford was looking after the young son of friends visiting Paris one day. " 'Wait here on the corner while I go ask that policeman a question,' Ford said. Well, you know how French policemen salute on being approached in public," the son told me in later years. "Returning, Ford said, 'Did you see? He saluted me. Yes; and why? Because I'm a Papal Count.' "

Stories like these always make me glad, their theme being dissatisfaction with given measures of truth. My own story announces, "the flight into sabotage and anarchy that later makes it so difficult for the intellectual to see things clearly" (Walter Benjamin's words) if he grows up where money is "ruinously" at the center of all.

That was also the way being shown me by Rembrandt's *Polish Rider* (allegedly Rembrandt's son): both in its gorgeous subject, overarmed and ready for flight, stupid but with the promise of reason in savage action; and no less in its domestication to the wall of a rich museum, once a home, like the Frick.

THE TOWN HOUSE   Looked at from the street, my house wasn't much: large, but just to the standard of wealthy post–Civil War New York, more "Murray Hill" than "Washington Square," and too sheerly ample for good design. Except for being a corner building, at Twentieth Street and Irving Place, it was like all those bland New York mansions which always are being converted from misuse or dilapidation into monuments to individualism understood as earning-a-fortune.

Inside, however, our house was of a class of singular dwellings. Typically rural, these often are dandyish as well. Baudelaire saw with the dandy himself that the need to be odd, at whatever the cost, is finally a heroic shape taken in their decadence by leisure and inherited wealth. *"Le dernier éclat d'héroïsme dans les décadences,"* Baudelaire wrote. So it may be with houses, in twilights of other sorts. Nineteen Gramercy Park was quaint, self-conscious, a "mad" expense. But its finally heroic shape was due to its being in town: that is what made it conspicuous and expressive as an excess.

Room after comfortable, colorful room: various, orderly, studied, profuse: devoted to what Henry James defined "the mysteries of ministration to rare pieces"; all brought together, and made to cohere, through force of furnishing, so to speak, in a sumptuous, costly, luxurious style. It made a unique impression. Not, as with Frick and the subtle Duveen, of a wedding of riches to expert taste, but of something much more peculiar. In "Louis-Philippe, or the Interior," Benjamin says: "For the private individual the private environment represents the universe. In it he gathers remote places and the past. His drawing room is a box in the world theater." My home gripped the imagination as wholly a fiction, a play, a dream: formal and yet almost overcharged with personal emblems and feelings.

I was puzzled when, in the 1960s, my home turned out not to substantiate a historical revolt. Inwardly, many like we must have cried, *Oh, for a Winter Palace! Oh, for an Escorial!*

COLLECTORS' CHILDREN My parents conspired well in the house. They lived there for forty-eight years. My father had a compulsion to buy, my mother to decorate. Together they made a fetish of antique furniture. At first they collected like children, to renew the world. Later, with money, acquiring things was very far from naïve. The justifications, the reasons. Good business was one. Well might it have been. Still, like all of the genus Collectors' Child, while I was jealous principally of my parents' unstinted passion, I hated worse their profession of a practical purpose. And why? Their passion suggested only that I was subordinate to Sheraton, second to George the Second, and not so much fun as a cheerful chintz: which a seven-year-old would of course resent but could nevertheless comprehend. But their tacit profession that all was not in fact what it so clearly seemed: that to me was trumped up, arrant make-believe. And it was typical of adults.

OVER THIRTY-FIVE ROOMS, MORE THAN THIRTEEN IN STAFF The house was ruled more with reference to the wishes and expectations of its large, exceedingly specialized staff than with thought (as *I* thought) of my own childish good. The atmosphere was officious. I had status, the servants had power. We had fights and they always won. *Real* English butlers and *real* Irish maids, they afflicted me with the moral zeal of the disciplined but disenfranchised, avid to show where I failed.

With what literal force I later read, in "The Love Song of J. Alfred Prufrock," *And I have seen the eternal Footman hold my coat, and snicker.* I acted towards them vengefully, in turn, consoling myself by reflecting upon their replaceability. That was the ultimate fact, wasn't it? A wretched result has been that I still think status of more worth than power.

And yet how replaceable were they? The English butlers, one formerly with H.R.H. the Duke of Windsor, another with Myron T. Herrick, our ambassador to France: a butler who, moreover, on May 21, 1927, had loaned Lindbergh a pair of pajamas? The servants were truly needed. It showed in the numerous valuable plates they presented at even family meals, ceremonially, not to be eaten from; in the deference of silence to which they appeared, and which to me from an early age made a paradox of the then common ideal of unobtrusive service; and in their great importance as topics of conversation.

They were needed besides as mirrors, implicated thereby in the purchasing of vast amounts of shoes and clothes, of dishes and linen and silver and glass, all of which they had also to care for. This will account for the strong link I made between home life and restaurants and retail stores, where service, appearance, consumption, excess are comparably important.

HEARTBREAK HOUSE   All was phantasmagoric. To me at least, the house stood for taste and culture in an era of mass fright (the 1940s) quite as if these were enough armament, together with making money. For the house to succeed, it had to exclude. And with exceptional force. Decoration was in, but poetry and music had no place. Talk of people was in but not of ideas; of Democratic electioneering but not of politics. Biographies, table talk, memoirs, "characters" crowded the shelves; portraits and "conversations" were everywhere on the walls.

It was more a venue for parties than ever an actual home. Like the Dedlock mansion in *Bleak House*, "Fairyland to visit, but a desert to live in." If a home, however, then Heartbreak House, so far as Shaw's play does indeed represent "leisured, cultured Europe" before the First World War. Only, alas, by the time I was nine, *two* world wars had occurred, and my mother and father had lived through both.

DISRAELI'S BRACES   I had a German governess during the
Second World War. She was openly pro-Axis after the Allied
bombing of Metz in her home region of Moselle. In fact she went
off her head. She started telling me what I could do when the
Nazis took over New York. "Just don't mention you're Jewish."

I was Jewish? I knew and I didn't know. It wasn't exactly a
secret. My parents spoke Yiddish fluently; two grandparents
lived on the Lower East Side; Bernard Baruch, Albert Einstein,
Leslie Howard made us proud.

Yet to look at the walls with their portraits of Millicent, Duchess of Sutherland, of Lady Ottoline Morrell, at the Queen Anne
this and the Charles the First that, at the bust of Pope and the
braces that had once belonged to the sometimes "Hebrew"
Disraeli—. . . . Surely I wasn't Jewish? Or if I was, then so
what? To ask of the Duchess's portrait, or of my father's still
more ducal "man," was to invite the answer, *You are as Jewish as
you want to be.* That was the answer I got.

Little wonder that then it was left to one in a lunacy of sorrow
to bring the effect of my question well and truly home.

THE RENT TABLE   I have an older sister, dearer than our
parents to me. But in spirit, at least, I felt more like the younger
son in a family of great English furniture. My eldest "brother"
was a big round-topped piece of mahogany called the Rent Table. I knew him best when I was eleven. The Rent Table (late
eighteenth century) stood in the capacious room at the top of the
house: "the red room," "the big room," "the movie room": kept
dark except when there were parties. The Rent Table had a frieze
of twelve drawers in its wide circular top. Each drawer was inlaid
with letters of bone. The rents of some vast estate were deposited
there by the tenants (submissively, no doubt). At the center of
the table was a shallow circular drawer. Opening this well (so-
called), I heard the sounds of England in the eighteenth century:
aristocrats and highwaymen, laws and resentments, murmurs
and yells.

For my father also each such piece spoke of the world it was
made for. But for me each such piece, in every room, had another
ghost.

In a story by the Japanese mystery writer Edegawa Rampo

(his name a transliteration of Edgar Allen Poe) a furniture maker
goes to live in an armchair he's made. The chair is bought by a
hotel; the furniture maker feels nothing but disgust for the common people who sit in the chair, but he tells himself, *I can always
escape.* Then the chair is bought by a young woman; the furniture
maker falls in love with her but finds he can no longer escape. He
has become the chair.

For my father, the owners before him were important. For me,
the maker was.

SEX

A PRINCE IS VEXED   The first pleasant words I remember are, *Louise is going to give you your bath.* To which I say, *God bless the hand that makes me stand.* The first unpleasant words I remember are, *Your father is coming.* I was frightened of my father, yet I wanted to be as much like him as I could.

My father was born in Brest-Litovsk, Russia, in 1901, the only son of Ida Bedder and Harry Zonnenberg. He had two sisters, Mary and Belle (born in 1899 and 1903). His father left Russia for New York in 1905 and found himself living on the Lower East Side. Now with an *S* instead of the *Z*, Harry Sonnenberg sold clothing from a pushcart on the street. He sent for his family in 1910. They all lived together on Grand Street. My father went to P.S. 62, then to DeWitt Clinton High School. All this was narrated to me on long walks, from when I was ten to when I was in my thirties. He narrated the city to me as well, often referring to people and events beyond my ken. "Your mother lived there," he said, pointing to 519 Grand Street. (The little house still stands.) "We heard the noon whistle every day from R. Hoe and Company, the printers on Grand Street. People still spoke of the *General Slocum* disaster. My family lived on Suffolk Street. Read *Jews Without Money* by Mike Gold."

In the *New Yorker* profile of him that came out in 1949, when my father was forty-eight, his friend Geoffrey Hellman wrote, "He got most of his recreation at the Henry Street Settlement House. . . . He made such a model-boy impression on Lillian D. Wald, the organization's founder and director, that when he was in his late teens she gave him board and lodging there in exchange for his services as boys'-club leader. She also helped him get a scholarship at Columbia, which he entered in 1919." He showed me the settlement house. "Lillian Wald lived as *I* wanted to: with antique furniture and works of art." And with a social purpose? "I'm no reformer," he said to me. "I am a realist."

My father stuck to college for less than a year, got a job on the *Brooklyn Eagle*, got a job as a traveling salesman in the Middle West, got a job back East on the Joint Distribution Committee, a post-World War One relief agency. ("Read *A Raw Youth* by Dostoyevsky.") In 1922 Lillian Wald recommended him to Lewis L. Strauss, head of the American Relief Administration, formed by Herbert Hoover to send food and medicine to the famine-stricken Ukraine. He spent six months over there. And there he was first acquainted with opulence; there he first heard the oriental, the *Vathek* note. He told Hellman, in the *New Yorker*, "Incongruous as it was, . . . I lived in a villa outside Odessa with a chef and five other servants." He was driven around in a limousine: the heir of the grandson of Haroun-al-Rashid!

Speaking to Hellman, he also sounds the Arnold Bennett note.

I got a salary of two hundred dollars a month and a perdiem allowance of six dollars. Practically all our expenses were taken care of, so I was able to save a couple of thousand dollars. After my mission was completed, I went to Rome, and later in the fall of 1923, to Paris, and then to London. You could live like a lord in Europe for thirty or forty dollars a week then. I stayed at first-class hotels, bought books, went to the theatre and the ballet, had some suits made to order, and acquired a cane, a black Homburg, and a Burberry. The significance of having a man draw your bath and lay out your clothes burst upon me like a revelation. I realized for the first time what it was to be rich. . . . I think it was while feeding the people of Odessa, paradoxically, that I first decided to become a cross between Condé Nast and Otto Kahn.

The *significance* of a man drawing your bath! That to him was the bolt of lightning on his road to Damascus.

My father returned to New York in the fall of 1923, and, in March 1924, he married my mother, whom he had met at a Henry Street Settlement dance when he was sixteen and she was fifteen. Pointing to the Bowery Savings Bank at the corner of Grand Street and the Bowery, he told me, "That's where I first saw her. I was standing on the steps of the bank and she walked by with a girlfriend. The building is by Stanford White." And then he told me about Evelyn Nesbit and her husband, Harry K.

Thaw, and how Thaw shot Stanford White to death in his apartment in the old Madison Square Garden, which White had designed and built. Thaw was tried but never convicted. "The saying on Broadway at the time was, *You can't electrocute a million dollars.* . . . And that is where we courted," he said, pointing to the French-Roumanian, a restaurant on Delancey Street.

He and my mother lived for a time in a basement apartment on West Twelfth Street. They hung out at the Lafayette, the Brevoort, where he once saw Ford Madox Ford, and at the Neighborhood Playhouse. "Read *The Golden Spur* by Dawn Powell," he said. "That was our milieu." He spoke of the poets Maxwell Bodenheim and Harry Kemp ("Read his *Tramping on Life*"), and of Benjamin De Casseres, who had been in love with my mother. My father's best friend, Jack Tworkov (his family name was Bialiastok), had been in love with my mother, too; made a pass at her anyway. "We never spoke after that. Jack's sister, Janice Biala, was Ford Madox Ford's last wife." Why did Jack change his name to Tworkov? Why had my father changed his?

He answered me with a story from a book by Louis Adamic. A man goes before a judge in Boston and petitions for a change of name. Your name is Lowell Cabot? says the judge. Yes, the man says (thick middle-European accent), and I want to change it to Louis Kabotnik. The judge says, But Lowell Cabot is a name uniting two of the most distinguished families in American history. Why do you want to change it? Because, says the man, when I tell people my name is Lowell Cabot, they say, What was it before you changed it? So now if I tell them my name is Louis Kabotnik and they ask— . . . My father saw no advantage to changing his name. "It wasn't as if I wanted to join the Maidstone Country Club," he said. No, being a Jew had a certain *cachet*. And here he quoted Disraeli, about the "splendor" of descending from King Solomon in a noble line longer than that of the Queen of England's.

After his marriage to my mother, my father was a press agent for theaters, nightclubs, hotels. He tried writing for the *Smart Set*. He and my mother were always going to lectures and plays. St. John Ervine, Rabindranath Tagore. He became a "first-nighter." One evening Irving Berlin set up chairs in the aisle of the Music Box Theatre for them. No one moved more featly than he between uptown and down. "Unless it was Walter Winchell," he said.

By the time my sister, Helen, was born, in 1926, my father was no longer a flack but was working earnestly for a different class of client. He tried writing again: a play, *The White Dove*, about one of his clients, Elizabeth Arden. He took a lease on an office at 247 Park Avenue. By the time I was born, ten years later, he was living at 19 Gramercy Park. Other public relations men were happy if they got a mention for their clients somewhere, anywhere! in a newspaper; he was able to get whole stories printed in the *Times* just as he had written them and to get his clients onto the covers of *Fortune* or *Time*. The money they paid him, in "scandalous amounts," went to support an elaborate life of ceremony and grandeur. "The only life *you* ever knew," he liked saying to me, ruefully.

Our walks often ended at Ratner's on Second Avenue. He was recognized there but not warmly, as contrasted with the bowing and scraping at Voisin or the Colony, the restaurants he went to uptown.

"Is this your boy?" said the waiter.

"Klein will tell you how he loaned five dollars to Leon Trotsky in 1917."

"Or Trotsky would never have gotten back to Russia," Klein said and went to the kitchen.

"You didn't know Trotsky, did you?" I said.

"No, but I know twenty waiters who loaned Leon Trotsky five dollars. And," he said, "I arranged for *Life* magazine to send Margaret Bourke-White to Mexico in 1939 to take his picture."

The secondary name-drop! How well he did it. Once I said to him, George Gershwin! Did you know George Gershwin, too? "*Know* him? I used to play gin rummy with his mother."

•

An impressive man, he was certainly that: in the mode of the late nineteenth century; a "new" man to the dons and peers he loved to entertain, an "aristocrat" to the company heads he was hired by. His snobbism was the same as Morel's in Proust's *Le Temps retrouvé*: that Anglomania and cult of stylized living found less among aristocrats than among those aspiring to rise. It led to peculiar locutions ("My man will show you out"), as well as to the fairyland air of 19 Gramercy Park.

Our home, *my* home, was a stage for his work; when he was home, he was changed by whatever role he was playing. He wasn't the same as he was on our walks. Giving the provenance of a painting was different from telling the story of a city building. And the stories of uptown buildings: how impersonal. "That is where Joseph Pulitzer lived. A tunnel runs under the street from his house to that of his mistress. . . ." He narrated a different city. "That is the Brook Club. They don't let in Jews. . . . The Racquet and Tennis Club: no Jews. . . ." I came to know much of uptown New York, in terms of whether the buildings there were or were not "restricted."

His way of walking when he was uptown was nimble, on the balls of his feet. In and out of restaurants, galleries, shops, fleetly, sometimes impolitely, he was always a patron, a customer. Downtown, by contrast, his progress was that of big man in a small village, slow and a little flat-footed, hands down by his sides, awaiting obeisance, tribute, petition. There he was what he was. Not that he wanted for deference uptown. Once, in fact, in the 1960s, in Central Park, we crossed paths with a young policeman who saluted my father, "Good afternoon, sir." Even then, New York City Policemen weren't so civil, as a rule.

Self-made, self-taught and self-assured, on the whole he shared little of his self with others. I used to think he shared most with me. On our walks, and then when he was angry. He got angry with me about money. I stole money from him from when I was six to when I was in my twenties. He carried only new bills. A stack of these, to the thickness almost of a building brick, lay on the marble counter of his dressing table, along with his keys and pocket watch. As a rule, I was careful never to take more than a couple of bills, none larger than a ten. Once, though, early in my life of crime, I took six five-dollar bills. I was found out. Tell your father, my mother said. You have something to tell me? my father said. *Never!* I said, Prometheus preparing his defiance of Zeus. He'd taken off his jacket and was pulling off his shirt before lying down for his afternoon nap. Tell me, he said. My mother said, Tell your father. He took off his pants and underpants.

Never! Naked, he hit me in the face. I said nothing. He hit me again, I was knocked to the floor. His belly swayed with the force of his blow, so did his balls. Ben, said my mother.

From this time on, I began to expect only the worst from my parents. I loathed them, and so overvalued even the least show of kindness.

•

Impressive as my father was, my mother was impressive, too: in the mode of Joan Blondell. Her favorite locution was the wisecrack. "People open up to your mother," my father said.

"Clams open up. People break down," she said.

People *did* open up to her, though. She was funny: when high, hilarious; and people trusted her. It is also true that she broke people down. The more impregnable they acted, the more efficient she was at breaking them down. She called it *telling truths*. "Let's tell truths," she said to me sometimes, smelling of drink, before a big formal party: important clients, rich men and women. She enjoyed her reputation for outspokenness.

But her great gift was to meet sadness with story and calamity with anecdote. I can still hear her saying, "You know, sad as it was, I couldn't help thinking of when— . . ." And I could imagine her saying to the SS man on her way to Auschwitz, "I always hate changing trains, don't you?" I know that to this habit of hers I owe my own of cutting away to a story or joke when faced with strong feeling.

My sister wasn't impressive, not to our parents at least. Helen's favorite locution seemed to be the yawn. "Be impressive," our father berated her. "Don't sell yourself short. [Yawn.] Look at Mary McCarthy. [Yawn.] Stop selling yourself short. Let them know you went to Vassar. [Yawn.]"

Our mother berated her: "Get more fun out of life. Be happy. [Yawn.] Let boys know you like luxury. Look at Gene Tierney. [Big yawn.]"

"Don't cry. Please don't cry," I'd say to her. (Did she think I was berating her, too?) "You're impressive to me." Never more so than when you're crying, I might also have said. Depression, menstruation, breasts: these were impressive to me. But how to console her? I used to get into trouble just so she could speak up for me and forget she was sad. Yet only our mother and father could make her truly happy. Theirs was the power of memories of a close family life ten years before I was born, and of money.

The first of many sad: sad, sad, oh! uncannily sad: women in my life, Helen was also the first older woman I wanted to take me into her bed. I was four and she was fourteen. I lay close against her. All of a sudden, she made me get out of bed. What had I done? Premonition of a lifelong bafflement.

I was most impressive. At seven years old my favorite form of expression was the epigram. Did you do that? they'd ask of some naughtiness. How could you? And I'd reply, "My virtue is too exalted for the vulgarity of words." I used to stammer if asked to explain. Once I said, "An imposing character like mine is built on reserves, not on revelations." As I grew older, I got fat. By the time I was fifteen I weighed almost three hundred pounds. The fatter I got the more insolent I was, and the more insolent the more avid for someone weak to push around. Servants were good for that, some of them. My favorite activities were masturbating, eating and reading, sometimes in that order.

"An impressive-repulsive disorder. Impress, repel. An impressive impressive-repulsive disorder. Impress, repel. Impress, repel," said one of the parody psychiatrists I was taken to as a child.

•

Women's sadness filled my childhood, Helen's most of all. My mother's sadness, though chronic, was easier for me to take away. Just get her to tell a story. Her sadness came from her having been brought up an only child. That always poisonous blessing was made worse in her case by a miraculous birth. Here's a story she liked telling: "There was a time when there were no governesses. Can you imagine that? Mothers took their children with them everywhere they went. One summer Sunday afternoon, long before I was born, my mother took her daughter to Gouverneur Hospital to visit a sick friend."

"You aren't an only child?" I said.

"Just be quiet and I'll explain. . . . The little girl was bored, so, to distract her, a well-meaning nurse rolled her ball down the corridor. The French door at the end of the corridor was open, the ball rolled out, the child followed it, fell into the street and was killed. My mother lost the use of her legs and was paralyzed until I was born."

In later life, no good fortune came as a surprise to her. None satisfied her either. Not my father's wealth, or his celebrity, or his influence; not the admiration of others, or even their adoration: all was her due. She liked telling of how defiant she'd been as a girl. Once, when she was sixteen, she put makeup on in the ladies' room of a downtown department store and went with a girlfriend to the Blue Grotto restaurant on Mulberry Street where gangsters used to go. "The waiter came over and told us that the gentleman in the corner wanted to buy us a drink. I looked at him and he didn't look like a gentleman to me, so I told the waiter no thank you and the waiter said, 'Lady, no one says no to Louie Lepke.' . . . Now, if only your sister could be more like that."

•

For me at least, she was never the spirited and defiant girl of her stories. Not when male authority was present. I remember this incident, after Helen went to college.

A pair of diamond earrings is missing, I'm accused of stealing them, and I'm questioned by a New York City detective and an investigator from the insurance company. We're alone in the small downstairs dining room.

"We have ways of making you talk," the detective says to me. I am ten years old, but his threat makes me feel like Brennan of the moors.

Emboldened, I say, "Then I'll tell you that a gang forced me to do it."

"Show him your fish," the insurance cop says.

"My what?" says the city detective.

"Your fish. Your tin," the insurance cop says.

The detective shows me his gold and blue badge. "We call this our shield," he says to the insurance cop.

"We always used to call it a fish."

"The gang is the Dukes," I say to them on my way out. "Their leader is Norman Schwarzkopf." The Dukes must have come from *The Amboy Dukes*, a favorite "dirty" book of the time. Norman Schwarzkopf was a name from the radio program *Gangbusters*, which at the end gave the names of the FBI's Ten Most

Wanted. "Don't try to apprehend these dangerous criminals yourself, but call your local FBI or Colonel H. Norman Schwarzkopf of the New Jersey State Police."

Afterwards my mother asks how I liked being questioned. "Very interesting," I say. "The city cop was smarter. He was strict but fair. Where were you?" It turns out that she was upstairs questioning one of the upstairs maids.

"Did she confess?" I say.

"No, but I fired her anyway," she says. And why had she let me be questioned? "Well, you said it was interesting, didn't you?"

I say, "Yes . . ."

And she says, "Well, there you are."

Yes, well, there we were.

•

After her freshman year at Vassar, Helen was told she could decorate her own room in her own way. Flowers and birds, birds and flowers. A toile de Jouy of flowers and birds for the canopy of her four-poster bed, flowers and birds and white eyeletted lace for the skirts of her dressing table. Flowers and birds, birds and flowers. And a pale-colored carpet.

Now, I used to buy practical jokes all the time. Dribble glasses, exploding cigarettes, plaster turds, soap that makes "your victim's" hands black: the riches of the Johnson Smith (Chicago) catalogue. My one success was with this bottle that came with a shiny black metal plate. On the outside of the bottle was the word *INK*. I put them on Helen's carpet and waited until she came in. She came in, she saw it, she shrieked, I smirked. And she hit me.

A triumph. For a moment at least, I'd gotten her to come off her pose of "understanding" me (*Understanding* in her Friends Year Book was her *Saving Grace*), and I'd paid her back for going away to college and leaving me.

MY PUNIC WARS I went to Friends Seminary on Sixteenth Street and Rutherford Place, across the street from St. George's, which my father had told me was Pierpont Morgan's church. "That was Pierpont Morgan's church," I told a classmate. "Down the road [peculiar locution], on Seventeenth Street, the famous Czech composer Antonin Dvořák lived." No such information was impressive to anyone at Friends. In sixth grade there I fell in love with the second-prettiest girl in class. She was blond and lived in a townhouse on East Nineteenth Street, next to A. A. Berle. Her father was a Republican. I wrote her a letter in which I said, "Since knowing you, my feelings of friendship have blossomed into (dare I name it?) love," which I'd cribbed from a letter to Sarah Bernhardt from Victorien Sardou. She read my letter aloud to the class.

Before that happened, fortunately, I got kicked out of Friends. Why exactly, I never knew. My mother told me it was because of my "attitude." Did that mean my politics? I told myself that it did. My politics at Friends came from *Citizen Tom Paine* by Howard Fast and *An American Testament* by Joseph Freeman, as well as from *The Ballad for Americans* by Earl Robinson and John LaTouche, sung by Paul Robeson. They were Socialist politics.

"Why are you a Socialist?" said Ernie Schapiro, Meyer Schapiro's son, the smartest boy in my class.

My reasons were personal. When my father bought 19 Gramercy Park, he bought Number 20 as well and evicted the tenants, among them Norman Thomas. I became a Socialist then, in objection to my father. Ernie Schapiro turned from me in scorn, so, to win his approval, I became a Communist. I canvassed for Henry Wallace and the Progressive Party, in the presidential election of 1948, and cried in my heart for the overthrow of the U.S. Government "by violent means."

My next school was Collegiate on West Seventy-seventh Street. I went there for two years. I was doing better there than at Friends, when I was told I was going to boarding school. "Your father's idea," my mother said. "I opposed it but gave in. Even when you win with him, you lose."

The Lawrenceville School, in Lawrenceville, New Jersey, was the first place I heard, "We don't care how much money your family has." An out-and-out lie, I was sure. Only money had made them make room for me. Only sloth made me stint my revenge. Lawrenceville was also where I met my first full-blooded anti-Semites. Blond, rich, athletic, Southern boys, with beautiful manners and excellent clothes, and masters with English accents. I read Tacitus at Lawrenceville.

Modeled on Rugby, the Lawrenceville School amplified talk of good: a good game, a good fit, a good book, a good lay. The prospect of pleasure it offered was like a view from the window at home. Good form was all that mattered. To provoke them I had but to trail my coat, showing the label, of course.

There was a danger, however. Lawrenceville let us say *jigaboo*, but it also let us get beaten up. For being found in another boy's house. For wearing the wrong-colored tie. Apprised of these "punishments" in advance, the masters stayed out of the way. Once in Latin class, which our housemaster gave, after I'd been terrorized by older boys the night before, I quoted aloud from Horace in the ode about Regulus:

atqui sciebat quae sibi barbarus
tortor pararet.
[And yet he knew what the barbarian torturer
Had ready for him.]

To what effect, though? Did he so much as blink? Like all the others he couldn't be shamed by something he merely taught.

The trials of Oscar Wilde had come out in transcript the year before.

Q. Do you drink champagne yourself?
A. Yes; iced champagne is a favourite drink of mine—strongly against my doctor's orders.
Q. Never mind your doctor's orders, sir.
A. I never do.

I'd begun to take my politics from Wilde's "Decay of Lying." (My other source was André Gide.) Yet the trials were a poor source of principle. Not only because like most comic art, especially for the stage, they delighted too much in the very things they struck at and tried to reform. But also because no one I knew, at school anyhow, had read them. Nevertheless, I thought Wilde was me. Incorrigible, irresistible, foolhardy, funny and false. And I thought, yes, that is what a star is: someone important for his mistakes. And I thought, why not be a queer? No doubt at all, as Theodor Adorno declares in "The Truth about Hedda Gabler," "Retention of strangeness is the only antidote to estrangement."

I found the trials pornographic as well. First, in their setting lewdness with manners and often vivid expense, among other aspects of social class. Second, because they were mindful of taste as an urgent and complex question. And finally because the taste frequently was taste in furniture, furnishings, rooms. (Proust surely made this connection when he gave his dead mother's furniture to the male brothel he helped to set up.) Like everyone else I wept hot tears at Desdemona shrieking, "*Ah! Emilia, Emilia, addio,*" in Act IV of *Otello;* like not a few I was broken up when, towards the end of *A Streetcar Named Desire,* Blanche asks about the woman she hears is waiting in front of the house, who is the Matron, "I cannot imagine who this 'lady' could be! How is she dressed?" and Eunice replies, "Just—just a sort of a—plain-tailored outfit." But who besides me was affected by Wilde's last remark below? It occurs not long after his famous speech explaining "the Love that dare not speak its name" when Wilde was at almost his worst beset; it mentions his co-defendant who procured for him.

Q. You saw nothing peculiar or suggestive in the arrangement of Taylor's rooms?
A. I cannot say that I did. They were Bohemian. That is all.
I have seen stranger rooms.

I got kicked out of Lawrenceville: *poor marks, immoral influence;* and the next school I went to was Loomis, in Windsor, Connecticut. Here they took positions on Alger Hiss and on Ezra Pound's being given the Bollingen award. The prospect of pleasure at Loomis was bleak. The sum of it was: chapel is not compulsory here. On Sundays, when I was in my room, playing *Til Eulenspiegel,* hymns rose up to me from the chapel. I turned the volume up. Still, I heard "Pity my simplicity." I used to think that "plicity" was a detention hall for mice.

At Loomis I learned to love Robert Frost and hate Emerson. My politics there came from André Breton and the Surrealists. I lasted there for a shorter time than at Lawrenceville.

•

The stranger rooms I came to know at school were the empty dining rooms late at night after the house was asleep, always

smelling of milk and stainless steel; empty classrooms on Saturday afternoons when the rest of the school was at a football game;
the second floor of the Lawrenceville library where the French
books were and where, after being fellated, I read volume upon
volume of *Les Hommes de bonne volonté* of Jules Romains. I paid the
boys I had sex with in cash and I paid protection of a sort by
lending out the pornographic books I'd brought back with me
from Paris, where I first went with my family in 1949. These
were *Tropic of Capricorn* and *Tropic of Cancer* by Henry Miller, *My
Life and Loves* by Frank Harris (more mysterious to me in *My Life
and Loves* than the details of cunnilingus were the words "colonic
irrigation"), *The Perfumed Garden*, *Fanny Hill*, *Venus in Furs* by
Leopold von Sacher-Masoch, *Justine or the Misfortunes of Virtue* by
the Marquis de Sade and *Memoirs of a Lady of Pleasure* (with the
almost too exciting "one hand was thrust into the Bush of Venus,
while with the other she vigorously agitated the nipples of the
Queen").

For me, as doubtless for many men, a love of literature began
in masturbation and was always linked to pornography. Especially, in my case, to the works of the Marquis de Sade.

OUR BREWSTER-PACKARD-CADILLAC-ROLLS All our
cars were outlandish-looking custom-built affairs, more stately
comfortable carriage than streamlined automobile, nothing racy
or aerodynamic like Ellery Queen's Duesenberg. They weren't
machines but sumptuous small interiors that moved, implying a
not truly high regard for travel, let alone speed. "A Brewster
body on a thirty-nine Ford chassis." That sort of car. The chauffeur was always having to say; otherwise no one could know. "It
is a forty-one Packard town car." Noticeable on the rainiest night
outside of Twenty-One. Each of our cars had a pedigree, too.
Somebody prominent had had it built. This or that "Missus
Warren Wampum, a name as old as the Hudson." None was new
with us. Our chauffeur was named James and bought his uni-
forms, including black leggings, at Dornan's, I believe it was
called, where I think the maids were outfitted, too.

We were driven on Sundays in the Brewster to my grandmother's for lunch, my father's mother on Riverside Drive and
112th: up past the hulk of the *Normandie*, the Reichstag of the

rentier class. I say "we," but I mean my father and me. My sister came with us rarely, my mother never. She and my father's mother were enemies, something to do with the younger sister (Belle) having wanted to marry and my mother having taken her part. There was silence when my mother's name came up. Everyone in the Sonnenberg family was used to silences. Silence at mealtimes, clamorous with their resentment.

"I'll never," says Coriolanus, "Be such a gosling to obey instinct . . ." My father always made a show of despising his mother. He visited upon her many of the sadistic beneficences of a successful son: charge accounts, furs, an expensive apartment (far from where we lived), costly appliances. To his mother our weekly visits must have seemed as from somewhere empyrean, the car and driver downstairs, the panoply of stories about the powerful and famous. To my father these weekly visits were meant to annul his mother. "As if a man were author of himself," as is said of Coriolanus, "And knew no other kin." He inhabited a world she knew only from the gossip columns, which she read avidly. On our visits I was made to seem an heir of this world, more than I was at home. His cruelest kindness to his mother was without doubt that of getting his two sisters to give up their jobs and live with her.

These women had an intelligence as great as his. Yet he feared and belittled them. He justified his behavior by stories of how his mother had mistreated his father. "A sweet, pious man married to a shrew." He told me that his mother had been the only atheist in the village where she was born. "A strong-willed passionate woman, with strong passionate opinions." He always stressed how "passionate" she was. "Passionate and materialistic. Passionate and bitter." Why was she bitter? She had "*had*" to travel to America from Lvov when she wanted to go from Antwerp, and for five years her husband had left her alone in the Old World: that "passionate young woman with passionate appetites": and when she arrived in New York she found that life here was hard. "She never forgave my father. I've never forgiven her."

In the summer we used to be driven, in a prewar Cadillac touring car, to summer houses that, from the point of view of the city, were outside; but from that of the summer, inside. The car, too: convertible, but with four, not two, doors: never seemed really open, even with the top down.

We rented from people who'd never seen Jews up close before.
My mother and father liked making this point. Country club
people whose own kind could no longer rent as we could, it was
said, bringing a full staff. Mannerly bankers with soft-spoken
wives, good-looking dogs and Purdey guns, they had all been
ruined in the '29 crash. Ruined? They looked sounder than us.
Their state of being before must have been unimaginably intact.
We always left them our new croquet set (we brought a new one
each May). Why this exactly, I never found out. But comic
propitiation was soon my pass into adult life. At home, all that
solemn permanence, tinged with absurdity; away, an imperma-
nence which also was solemn and absurd.

MÜNCHAUSEN   In *My Life and Loves*, which I read at thirteen,
Frank Harris tells of conquering London by reciting Shakespeare
at it. Half-Irish, dubious and déclassé, ill-dressed, ill-mannered
and a runt; yet when challenged, he knew Shakespeare better
than the English. A capital way to social success. I memorized
The Ballad of Reading Gaol, only no one challenged me.
    I started to write my memoirs, also at thirteen, inspired by
Casanova. I soon saw that something was missing. It was the
experience of The Leads in Venice, where Casanova had been
imprisoned by the Holy Inquisition. Here began my lifelong
compulsion to be noticed by the police, something like Münchausen's Syndrome as described in *Jablonski's Illustrated Dictionary
of Eponymic Syndromes and Diseases:* "Typically, the affected person
presents himself to a hospital with a dramatic account of severe
illness that cannot be verified. Upon admission, he will quarrel
violently with the doctor and nurses and, occasionally, to prove
a point he may attempt self-mutilation. . . ."
    In my memoirs I tried to write about losing my virginity. That
had happened the summer before with a maid-of-all-work at a
hotel in the south of France. I'd have preferred Hazel Scott. The
great jazz pianist Hazel Scott had once danced a fox trot with me
at an Urban League Ball when I was ten. Hazel Scott! Hazel
Scott! *She'd* have known what to do. My virginity would have
slipped from me with her. And afterwards, light-hearted, *dén-
iaisé*, I'd have gone back to the Savoy and danced with the Cotton
Club girls.
    But to have had my virginity *taken:* and by the maid (her name

was Raimonde): left me feeling angry and cheated. (*N'est-ce que ça?* That's it? says Julien Sorel after his first time.) With no time to memorize the sights upstairs of Raimonde's tiny room (smelling doubtless of urine and sex and Gitanes), with no time to prepare an attitude, I left the next morning for Paris. Acting world-weary and newly wise, I spoke to my mother and Helen in a jaded, superior voice, meant to sound like Herbert Marshall's, if I spoke to them at all. From my own room at the hotel, which was called Chez Paquay, three floors below Raimonde's, I'd looked down on the terrace every night, and heard the umbrellas being shut up one by one, *plok! plok!* an epoch ending each night. An epoch had ended for me indeed. But who was there to tell?

My father was at the Plaza-Athénée with a tall, smooth-mannered White Russian named Constantin Nepo. He was married to Yvette Chauviré, a star of the Paris Ballet. He wanted my father to back him in some business deal. He smoked a silver-banded "military" pipe and wore a cavalry officer's mustache. He took me back to the Hôtel Saint-Régis in the rue Jean Goujon where I and my mother and sister were staying. He was wearing unlined leather "guardsman's" gloves. The next day he came and brought me books (*Chants de Maldoror, Ce Vice impuni: la lecture, Sentiers et routes de la poésie:* I have them still. Lautréamont, Larbaud, Éluard) and he took me to the Palais-Royal to meet Colette, lying in bed in her apartment. *Enchantée, cher jeune Américain, Costya, ta femme, ma Yvette, comment va-t-elle, ah, non, chéri* [This to me?], *pas lá, passe par ici ou nous pouvons tous profiter de tes couleurs fraîches et clins d'oeil gamins . . ."* [She was delighted to meet me, she asked after Nepo's wife, she called me *chéri*, she asked me to sit near the window so as better to enjoy my complexion and the play of my eyes.] I was a fat unpleasant boy, very far from the cherub Colette addressed, more Falstaff (at thirteen!) than page to the Duke of Norfolk. And I was to go from *this* back to prep school? Nepo showed me where Cocteau was living, on the other side of the Palais-Royale, and then took me to the Opéra to see his wife dance her famous Dying Swan.

"Well, what do you make of Nepo?" my father said.

"A con man, a cheat, a phony. And," I said, "he is a pansy."

This was a lie, with respect both to my feelings and to what I knew. But keeping a secret (I mean the secret of my loss of virginity) made me irritable, and its discharge resulted in my betrayal of Nepo, conspicuous, bystanding, beautiful, kind. The burden discharged, I felt reconciled to prep school and being fat. I was later to find that a morbid reflex like this afflicts many at low levels in large organizations.

Like many boys of thirteen I knew that if you dialed a certain number in New York and said the words *Amber Gus*, you could get to go to bed with the woman who answered.

I owed money at thirteen to Brooks Brothers for shirts and ties and to the Liberty Music Shop for records of classical music. The bills came to my father. "I care nothing about money, save as a lubricant," he wrote to me at school. "My capacity to earn is only a compensation for the early chagrin that I experienced for being without it. Whatever measure of it I have is at the disposal of my family. Yet I feel you have a lackadaisical casualness about you. That you are not concerned with how it comes upon you from the source. That you engage in middle-age largesse. You send presents and scatter your money about. . . . Your bills amount to almost seven hundred dollars. I will not mention your school fees. But I would like you to do a little stocktaking of your own. Do not confuse my circumstances with those of the parents of other boys at Lawrenceville. . . . I am today paying on your behalf three hundred dollars to Brooks Brothers and one hundred dollars to the Holliday Bookshop. How the other bills are paid I leave to you. . . ."

At fifteen I read Ezra Pound's *The Spirit of Romance*. There I read of the invention of Love, in the thirteenth century, by the Troubadour poets of Provence, and I learned that while Men in Love were pure of heart, the Beloved was always cruel, remote, capricious and faithless.

I knew from my reading that Love was won only after an Ordeal. Still, like many boys of fifteen, I believed that an infallible way to get someone into bed was to write *Fuck Me* with your finger on her bedspread.

But I got Noémi to go to bed with me in Provincetown that summer by telling her I was an associate editor of *Partisan Review*. Nothing I'd read quite prepared me for the erotic power of lying. Noémi was a graduate student at Radcliffe; she lived on Linnaean Street in Cambridge. She had a little boy whose father had committed suicide the year before. I told her I was a teacher at the prep school where I was a junior and I told the school that I wanted to go to weekend lectures on Pragmatism at Harvard given by Ralph Barton Perry. One Saturday while she was making dinner I read Noémi's journal. Most of it was in French, but there was this in English: "Ray last night. I had fourteen orgasms." Fourteen! Our talk over dinner that night was strained, I made many cryptic and ironical remarks. Next week Noémi wrote me that she had jaundice. I went to Cambridge anyway and promised to visit her in the hospital. I mentioned the jaundice to the friend of my father's with whom I was staying. He said, "I saw men with jaundice during the war when I was a brigadier general. Their testicles swelled up like balloons." I didn't go to the hospital. I saw Noémi no more after that.

I never bragged of Noémi to anyone at school. Here's why: after meeting her I lost weight rapidly. Almost one hundred pounds in less than a year, in one of those glandular inundations that sweep over the innocent adolescent boy and leave him gasping and happy. Still, one time with Noémi, I'd said, "Let's do this," and she'd said, "No, no, you're too fat," and fat being bound up like that with sex, I was too embarrassed to want to boast.

I did give up sex with boys. I'd fallen in love at Loomis with a French boy named Yves. He had stringy red hair and weak blue eyes. A mane of blond hairs ran down his spine and ended (I swear this is true) in a little tail, a small anal flap. He was younger than I, but his coldness to me was like a senior's. Yves had grown up in Paris. It would have meant nothing to him that I'd met Colette. My Henry Miller and Frank Harris, even my *Philosophie dans le boudoir*, would have meant nothing to him. My love was chilled by the value I placed on his ego. I felt I couldn't lie to boys. I could lie to women because they lied to men.

CHERUBINO, CHÉRI, QUINQUIN

> Si l'Amour porte des ailes,
> N'est-ce pas pour voltiger?
> [Why has Cupid been given wings,
> If not to fly?]

> Beaumarchais, *Le Mariage de Figaro*

When I was sixteen, and it became clear that I wasn't going to graduate from Loomis, Helen came and got me. She'd persuaded my parents to agree that if I went to a psychoanalyst I could drop out of school and live at home. At that stage even analysis looked good, better than school anyway, and I blessed Helen then (and do to this day) for intervening like that. To top it off she gave me a dog, an Airedale I named Roderic (why, I forget). Roderic disliked my father and lifted his leg on the furniture in the library.

At seventeen I read *Le Rouge et le Noir* and Stendahl's *Life of Rossini*. I began to want a Rossini-like life: one success after another, which like Rossini I could give up abruptly, at thirty or thereabouts, so as to devote myself to cooking and being depressed.

I kept trying to pick up women at concerts and in museums, in espresso houses and bookstores. Jane White, a friend of my parents, was painting my portrait. Stendahl said to try every time you are alone with a woman and you will be successful three times out of five. I persisted with Jane (who called me *Chéri*) until finally, to get rid of me, she introduced me to Posie.

Posie (not her real name) was the widow of a concert pianist, killed (not yet forty) in a plane crash in the South Pacific the summer before. She had two small children and lived with them and a baby grand, in an apartment on Ninety-first and Madison. Posie was twenty-seven. She had very white skin and very red hair and looked (I was reading *Swann's Way*) like Botticelli's Jethro's daughter, in the Sistine Chapel, to whom Swann likens Odette de Crécy.

Our first night we went to a reading of *Strange Interlude* at the New School and after to dinner at Lüchow's, where I signed the check like my father, and after that to the Oak Room at the Plaza, where I again signed the check, and after that we drove through Central Park in a horsedrawn carriage and I told the driver to drop us off at Madison Avenue and Ninety-first Street, and it had been thrilling to get the driver to do something like that a little out of the ordinary and then look at me with wonder, confident of his tip.

A day or two later, Posie and I went riding in Central Park. Posie didn't ride well; her seat was bad and her elbows flapped. I didn't care; we were lovers, and I was in love. The fruit trees were in blossom. Petals fell on us as we rode. I was terrified that she might fall off or that her horse might run away and I wouldn't know what to do.

This was my first real love affair. It clashed with 19 Gramercy Park, but it was still keyed to the house, showing how (in the harsh but moving phrase of one of the Frankfurt School) in a "conceptual hierarchy which relentlessly demands responsibility on its terms, only irresponsibility can call that hierarchy by its real name." I got into an actual physical fight with a butler who'd been instructed by my father not to let me go out; I stole expensive objets d'art from the house to give to Posie; and I began ensnaring my parents by going to stores *en client sérieux* to buy presents for her, for Posie (my second widow!), knowing perfectly well I couldn't pay for them.

•

Here's a typical dinner party at Gramercy Park at about this time. Nominally it is for Sir John and Lady M—— (Sir John is head of the Fitzwilliam or the Wallace or the Tate). The guests, in formal attire, gather in the "William and Mary Room." There are the Adam mantle, a portrait by Tintoretto (a present from Robert Lehman), a Giacometti sculpture (a present from Joe Hirshhorn), drawings by Goya and Van Gogh, Queen Anne tables and Charles the First mirrors, the whole room stiff with wealth. Dinner is served, says Mears to my mother who is a little high. All descend to the dining room. Lighted candles are everywhere. Georgian silver in glass-fronted cases; and, on the wall opposite, a portrait of a young girl by Greuze. The china, the crystal, the silver: everything scintillates.

My father sits at the head; to his right, Lady M——; to his left, Jane Cooke (Mrs. Alistair Cooke); then (going clockwise) Sam Newhouse, a client; then the actress Irene Worth; then Jay Rousuck (of Wildenstein & Co., the art dealers); then my mother. To her left are Sir John M——, Edna Ferber, T. H. (Teddy) White, the actress Cathleen Nesbitt (who, I'm constantly being reminded, was the last fiancée of Rupert Brooke), then me, then Mrs. Newhouse, then Alistair Cooke (*always* Alistair Cooke).

The dinner is served on the right side by Mears and on the left by the second butler. A serving maid follows the butlers with the vegetables. Finally, dessert in what seems to be an elaborate glass bowl. "Break the bowl," whispers Mears to Lady M—— who naturally looks startled. "Break it!" Mears says, and Lady M—— does. The bowl is made of spun sugar. Everyone titters. After coffee, cigars, and Mears going round murmuring, "Brandy, Benedictine, liqueur," we go upstairs to the Red Room. Others arrive. More talk. More drinks. And then we all watch a movie. (Usually here's where my father cuts out. He goes to his library and reads, leaving his guests to find their ways out. Staying to the end upstairs, my mother sings show songs with Abe Burrows or Frank Loesser before going, laughing and angry, to bed.)

The satisfaction of such an evening must have been great for my father. For my mother it was nil. For me it consisted entirely in sitting next to Jane Cooke in the dark, on one of the big "hallporter" chairs, holding hands with her during the movie while she called me *Chéri*.

"YOU KNOW HOW TO HANDLE SERVANTS" Patronage formed a very large part of my parents' lives. They struggled to strike the exact right note in nothing else so much. "You know how to handle servants," an accolade of theirs, resounded in my love of hotels, restaurants and cafés. Which is why I later mistook retail debt for a kind of affection, I think. Judging from Restoration plays, as well as from George Meredith's *The Ordeal of Richard Feverel*, not to speak of the lives of Shelley and Baudelaire, I had the old inclination of sons of the upper-middle class to forge my habits of spending together with my erotic life into a compulsion upon my parents. A number of meanings of *folly* and *dissipation* are here.

Folly for me began with clothes. I thrilled to my first handmade suit as much as to my new love affair. Both occurred at about the same age. At the next-to-last fitting I felt such content, I had to make an excuse. Like many at this precise juncture, I said to the tailor, "I've just had lunch." To which he replied, "We hope you will again, sir." The right note! And struck by a tailor kneeling to fix my cuffs! How it chimed with the insolent deference that I was used to at home!

Dissipation began with confusion. How could a Princess like Posie have chosen a Frog like me? How was I supposed to behave? Posie played me her husband's records, introduced me to her husband's friends ("Ben is a poet"), and gave me her husband's silk shirts to wear, which I did, though they were too small for me. I began to affect the mannerisms of a concert pianist. I said, "This is important, no?" I spoke of *key signatures* and *ornamentation* and *melismas.* I wore my fingernails short. At recitals I asked to be seated "on the keyboard side," and during intermission I pretended to be playing on an imaginary keyboard.

I bathed Posie's children and read to them, like Julien Sorel in *Le Rouge et le Noir* with the children of Sophie de Rênal. I tried making her family my own. Yet in love though I was, I felt detached, the same as at 19 Gramercy Park: neither a stranger nor quite at home: misshapen by a peculiar burden of spirit, I think. I kept things from being surprising by that same sort of pride which at seventeen makes Julien Sorel pretend he is "accustomed to the subjugation of women." *Orgueil bizarre:* not propitious in love. (*N'est-ce que ça?* That's it?) I also tried to impersonate Stendahl at forty-six, the age he began writing *Le Rouge et le Noir,* by acting as if fully conscious of the qualities I was spoiling. I was excited, I was proud: and happy, unspeakably happy; but I stifled my feelings by reference to my reading: *orgueil bizarre* of the autodidact.

Alfred de Musset, in a striking paragraph in *La Confession d'un enfant du siècle,* compares his state of mind at about this age to a room of the 1820s where, he says, vast eclecticism prevails; where all purposes, periods, nations and tastes are assembled pell-mell; which Musset says feels like the end of the world. So much jumbled up, in a fashion both costly and without precedent, *"en sorte que nous ne vivons que de débris, comme si la fin du monde était proche"* [so that we live only on débris, as if the end of the world were near]. This passage reflects a little of my own special burden of spirit: feeling I always had to appraise, to appraise and to be not unworthy of *being* appraised, and meanwhile the end of the world was at hand.

Called on to repent, I responded, *More clothes! more gifts! more debt!*

MY PSYCHOANALYSIS   There were two eminent psychoanalysts in my parents' circle. One was Sandor Rado, a short, bald, priapic Hungarian. His specialty was drug addiction, which he called *pharmacothymia*. I used to see Rado on Ballston Beach in Truro, in the summers, on Cape Cod. He'd be talking to some young beauty and suddenly there'd be a scream. "Doctor *Rado!*" The young beauty was on her feet; Rado, embarrassed not at all, looked my way and smiled. One summer Rado told me: "Anti-Zemitism: strangely attractive to all men of genius, in Europe then. Wagner, Nietzsche, even Heine and Marx who were Jewish themselves. A puzzle, no? I half figured out why." A young woman walked by, so I never heard more.

The other psychoanalyst was Gregory Zilboorg. I used to see him in Twenty-One: a fat, white-mustachioed Russian. A lot of *New Yorker* writers went to him, yet his English was poor. His translation of Leonid Andreiev's play, *He Who Gets Slapped*, was in print for years. At the end of Act One was this stage direction: *Comes now the pause.*

My own psychoanalyst was Marion Kenworthy. She'd been treating my sister for years. Marion *Edwina* Kenworthy. A tall, handsome, patrician woman of the Emerson-Alcott type. She often said of something that "it didn't spring full-born like Athena from the head of Zeus, you know." Was that a clue to her? Edwin, her father, for whom she was named, was Zeus to her Athena, perhaps: as with Edith Hamilton and her father? I mentioned that to her once; she smiled. She had blue eyes, and mostly she wore blue. A photograph of her own analyst (Adolf Meyer, I think) stood on a bookshelf in the dark behind her consulting room door: a glowering, bespectacled man. I knew that among her patients had been the multimillionaire newspaperman Eugene Meyer, her neighbor in Bedford, New York. "I think he may have helped her financially," my father said. She lived in a large apartment at 1035 Fifth Avenue; in the country she lived with a woman who raised Dandie Dinmont terriers. "Your mother thinks she's a lesbian." What did I care? To me the important thing was, she let me bring my dog. "He goes everywhere with me," I used to say.

Practically speaking, my psychoanalysis was an instant success. Marion got my father to allow me forty dollars a week.

Theoretically speaking, psychoanalysis was a disappointment. I wrote in my notebook: "While Freud's aphorisms are superior to his system, they are nevertheless inferior to those of Schopenhauer, Novalis and Nietzsche, not to mention Pascal."

And therapeutically speaking, analysis was redundant. I'd no sooner begun with Marion than I met Posie. Except for my hatred of my father, then, and of everything he stood for, my life's problems were at an end.

However, so as not to antagonize my parents, who could still have sent me back to school and cut off my allowance, I did my best to appear not to be wasting Marion's time. I read Ferenczi, Jung, and Abraham; I read Fenichel, and Hartmann, Lewin and Kris; I read every last volume of the Standard Edition of Freud. I read Ernest Jones's biography; and I subscribed to the *International Journal of Psychoanalysis* and to *Psychoanalytic Quarterly*. I read the novel *Gradiva* by the Danish Johannes Vilhelm Jensen because it figured in an essay by Freud. For the same reason I read many Dramas of Fate, such as *König Ottokars Glück und Ende* by the Austrian Franz Grillparzer (whose work Freud misrepresented). And I prepared a refutation of Freud's famous essay on Oedipus, the one beginning "The Oedipus Rex is a tragedy of fate." A breathtaking critique. Like my criticism of the preface to *An Interpretation of Dreams*, where Freud refers to the death of a father (*a* father!) as the single most important event in the psychic life of a man. I don't recall much of what I wrote, except the conclusion: "If so, then silence must follow."

I often began my sessions by saying, more or less, "As Ernst Kris says in his *Psychoanalytic Explorations in Art*— . . ." I was hoping to *present* a case as interesting as the ones in Freud: The Wolf Man, Little Hans, A Child Is Being Beaten, and such. I tried to get Marion to talk with me about ideas. Or about the books on her shelves. Or at least about Lord Byron (in her waiting room was *The Last Attachment* by Iris Origo, about Byron and the Countess Guiccioli). But she never spoke to me about books and the most she ever said to me about ideas was that she was going to vote for Eisenhower in 1956, because of "the deep depressive lines in Adlai Stevenson's face." By the time we got to talking about me and my family, I'd decided that psychoanalysis was a fraud, or if not a fraud, then another despotism to be resisted. Still, what fun to talk with a woman about sex with another woman the night before. "The second time sometimes is painful. And the third and fourth times— . . ."

Marion saw me five days a week for almost four years from when I was sixteen. For my twentieth birthday, as a sign that we were near the end, she gave me the *Complete Piano Works of Mozart* played by Walter Gieseking (a six-record set) and I gave her *Instincts of the Herd in Peace and War* by Wilfred Trotter, being sure to tell her that Trotter was the author of the best one-line medical joke I knew: "Mister Anaesthetist, if the patient can stay awake, I'm sure you can, too."

•

My analysis may well have been a triumph from my point of view: I'd prevailed in an uneven contest through mischief, laughter and lies. But what of my psychoanalysis from Marion's point of view? Could she have seen it as other than an unqualified failure? My question comes from two acts of bad faith.

The first act was this. At the beginning Marion said that she wasn't going to take money from my father for my treatment, "because the question of money and your father is at the root of things." Now, in the 1950s psychoanalysis cost fifty dollars an hour; my total time would have come to about fifty thousand dollars. Marion was telling me she was making a financial sacrifice in my interest. But what she failed to mention is that, during the time she was treating me, my father was raising a huge sum for the New York School of Social Work, to which she was attached. This arrangement ended when my analysis did. I call that bad faith. Money truly was an abundant source of trouble between my father and me; but *secrecy* about money was what was at "the root." At "the root" of trouble with others was the question of disinterest.

*A BLURRED SAGACITY** A second act of bad faith had to do with my sister and me.

When I was twelve and Helen was twenty-two, she fell in love with a tall, dark-haired man whom she'd met at the Boca Raton Club Hotel during my Christmas vacation. He'd been working as a Fred Astaire Dancing School teacher. Our mother encouraged their romance, at the beginning at least. "It'll help bring you out," she told Helen. "You *need* sparkle, romance, life."

* From "Eros Turannos," by E. A. Robinson.

To me she said, "Just between you and me, I prefer the Aronson boy. . . . You don't think she'll *marry* this one?"

"Let be," I said; it was her sort of phrase. "Remember when you were her age." And the Aronson boy? Your standard-issue, check-chasing, ambitious, greedy, vain, good-looking, deceitful, dark, charming, glossy-haired, lecherous Harvard grad who played tennis and gin well enough to lose. (He later married the heiress to a corner tobacco store fortune.) Helen used to waver between that type, who frightened her (rightly, I think), and boys of whom our father would say, *Do you think he's a pansy?* and of whom our mother would answer, *I don't think he's one thing or another.*

"I don't give a damn who she sleeps with," said our father on one of our walks: one man of the world to another. "She's had a good education. She doesn't *have to* marry him. . . ." We stopped at Ratner's, as usual, for more talk man-to-man. "She's got a good head on her shoulders. Let her sleep with whoever she wants." I was shocked to be thinking of Helen like that. Well, maybe with a musician (classical), or an archaeologist, or a sportsman. . . .

And then, when I was seventeen and Helen was twenty-seven, she announced that she *would* marry him, come what may. Suddenly everything changed. From our mother, vituperation. From our father, bribery of many sorts. But Helen's determination (loyally applauded by me) was firm, which caused yet another sudden change. Our mother began to speak warmly of her future son-in-law; our father went from acting urbane to looking stricken. Once natty, now with a spot on his tie, he began to walk with a limp. He staggered, he stammered: at home anyway. Speaking up for my sister was now not a duty but a joy. Each loyal word I uttered made my father writhe.

Helen's wedding was, at the very least, a crucial event in my life, presenting paths into my heart which no paltry guile of mine could have blocked. I was racked with anger, fear and shame. No avenging relation in Verdi felt more passion than I. Yet from Marion what did I get? A principle: she couldn't talk with me about another patient.

Not talk with me about Helen? To insist instead on formulas? Why such an obdurate scruple? I understood that I couldn't *progress* without accepting restrictions. I understood that submission had to come before freedom did. But the freedom being offered by psychoanalysis was that of preferring social goals to my own selfish, sexual ones, and my naïve revulsion from both kinds of goal was great.

ART

PANDAR'S ORCHARD My father bought art and bought art and bought art. He and my mother appeared most at one placing this "amusing scrap" or shifting that "little piece."

Interior decoration was also the source of their most bitter fights. "I no longer know where to go in the house": I can hear my mother saying that since at least 1945. That was when my father bought 19 Gramercy Park, which before they had only rented, and the rooms they had lived in as tenants began their transfiguration. Here's how it worked: my father introduced a small, exquisite, expensive object: a Tanagra figure, a Queen Anne tea stand: and the rest of the room, with its assortment of furniture from Allen Street, lovingly collected, and friends' prints and paintings and photos, started to look shabby. The change began. "Museum quality" furniture was suddenly everywhere, fine drawings and oils appeared on the walls, fine bindings were on the shelves. Room by room and floor by floor, till the whole was a little abridgment of the suites, galleries and apartments in the very grand English houses my father liked to visit.

And where so much of the furniture had come from originally. One result was that, in the end (The end? Would the end ever come?), the furniture looked right, the servants looked right, the silver and plates and pictures looked right. But did I? Did my mother and father?

My mother resisted, finding nothing but expense and extravagance in the rooms. "I don't belong here," she used to say.

"Your mother belongs in Sunnyside, Queens," my father used to say, "in a garden apartment with a man who comes home every evening. I moved uptown in my life, so to speak, your mother's still on Grand Street."

Not only did art dealers minister to this often troubled household, they had also always noticed me as at least an important object. I repaid the favor, trying to be as much like them as I could. I copied their accents, wore tweed caps and smoked *Le Khédive* cigarettes. Could such a life be mine? "And to think," I might say, in the late afternoons, over the licentious drawings of Constantin Guys, the lubricious engravings of Félicien Rops, to some young woman bemused by my ritual delay, "there are men who'd show a young girl *this* . . . and *this*. . . ." Only eighteen and already big with brokers, agents and props! (Or, only eighteen and still posing! Significant both of having grown up with ceremony and servants, and of a sadism that can be truly practiced only by liars.)

Choosing works of art to make girls has of course a number of meanings. One is that connoisseurship is an exemplary bourgeois fault. And so it naturally was with me, as also with Shakespeare's Troilus, whose *I am giddy* soliloquy is a typical false position of strength taken by privilege in its fight with even normal desire:

> . . . and I do fear besides
> That I shall lose distinction in my joys.

Walter Benjamin, brought up in town like me in a house with many servants, wrote in "A Berlin Chronicle" that "the economic basis on which the finances of my parents rested was surrounded, long past my childhood and adolescence, by deepest secrecy." This may be the rule in rich parvenu homes, whether Jewish or not. It certainly was in mine. Secrecy lay at the very core of my father's power at home. In addition, mystification was a genuine part of his work. He justified earning money by incantatory allusions to a fabulous boyhood (it seemed so to me) with actual deprivations. "I grew up," he proclaimed, "an immigrant boy, in a tenement house on the Lower East Side. The plumbing was out in the hall."

But in fact justification was called for by no one but him. He pointed thereby to a pre-bourgeois past that, to quote Adorno, "survives in the shame felt at being paid for personal services and favors." The pre-bourgeois world, involving pogroms with dreams of consoling wealth, though frankly a legend, was used nonetheless to explain why he'd had to earn money in amounts as large as *they* would allow for as long as *they* would allow it. That world for us was Brest-Litovsk, my father's place of birth, a city that was historically now Polish, now Russian, now both.

The shame had a meaning besides. His business was public relations. Our house was a blush for this fact. Not only in looking established, while public relations was deemed "fly-by-night," as he himself often remarked. But in being so brazenly stagey. That argued no real difference between the public and the private. Indeed, when my father was showing off, there *was* nowhere private at home. What things had cost was a part of his spiel as he took strangers through the house. No one corner was different from the rest of the house in taste. The "style of the whole" was in cupboards and drawers as well as in every room.

Staginess made an embarrassment of the truthful and ideal. I reacted the more against sound common sense. All was a shibboleth. "You'll have to earn your own living some day." What sort of fool did he think I was? Everything there told me that wasn't so. On this point at least, I'm inclined to believe, the house was no less a frustration to him than a riddle to me.

•

It is said that for many Americans politics starts in brand-name loyalty. Romance and disillusion surely began there for me. My father's corporate clients seemed limitless in their power. Their power to make my father jump, which of course he resented, delighted me. But the actual boring embodiments of these glamorous brands: Philip Morris, Pan Am, Pepsodent, Sperry-Rand: they were such contemptible "little" men. My father didn't like himself for being a tool of theirs. His self-contempt was disturbing. As William Blake says: "As water to the fish, as air to the bird, so is contempt to the contemptible."

His real work was in proving that he was above the services his clients paid him for; that he was himself the purchaser of services richer than they could devise. He did this through numerous parties, sometimes as many as five a week; and through his ceaseless collecting and placing of *objects* and *things*. He was both a success in the usual sense and the adept at home of something quite strange.

In the *New Yorker* profile, Geoffrey Hellman wrote, "The people who talk about him generally ignore his professional activities, which are somewhat arcane, and concentrate on his house and clothes. . . ." Yet really the house and clothes were arcane. They more than enveloped and more than declared. With the profile, a Saul Steinberg drawing showed a short, rotund man with a walrus mustache in a four-button suit and a bowler. He stands daintily in a room of his house. And crowded though the scene is with things: "oriental" tables and English chairs, candelabra and bric-a-brac: each moves with the other and all move with him. Excess, eccentricity and expense resulted with him in a look that was, wherever he stood, for most of my life, quasi-comic and quasi-holy: a look of jocose ministration to rare goods, rare finds, rare arrangements.

WHY I CLEARED OUT, ALMOST My father used to make a show of "staying clear" of my girlfriends. But once he took one of them, Posie, to lunch. At The Colony. It was a flop. He must have wanted to bribe her. "She already *knows* you're rich": that to me. "*You* know I'm rich," he told her. As she was a widow, he may have thought being mundane was all right.

They were seated at once. That was also a sign that subterfuge wasn't the plan. Not about money. Not there, anyhow: at the *"Rendezvous de l'Élite."*

My father moved in that nimble way common to short public men. "Greetings!" His friends were everywhere. Friends? His vast clientèle. Seated at his usual table, the first banquette in the bar, he will have said: "Anita Loos. *You* know who she is. . . ." I used to love how he made those he knew fabulous, even the famous.

One eye of his fixed you, the other eye roamed. His talk was half confidential. The bombastic other half, the roaming half, prevailed, helping to annul the distinction between lying and telling the truth.

Money talks: so I doubt if he needed to ask, "How much do you want?" I also doubt whether he came out and said, "I love my son. Do you?" Soon, though, the air was heavy with terms. They quickened too much or were still. "On the matter of money," he will have said, "I care nothing about it. It is a lubricant. . . . Now my son is on an allowance. Yet he sends presents and scatters his money about as if it came from a bottomless vessel. Which I suppose I am, in a way. Bottomless, vast. Yes, I am vast. The rascal knows I can always be blackmailed, and I know he can be bribed. Now you have only to look at me to see that I am not a man who does things on a shoestring. . . . Dessert? . . .

"My son and I, we have never been close. Perhaps it's because I am perched high up on some pyramid. I'm told that I awe people. Maybe that's why my son is afraid to take me into his confidence. . . ."

By the time I arrived ("with the coffee": that was our jaunty plan), Posie looked angry, frightened and sick. My god! was it just like a meal at home? Didn't being out matter a bit?

He waved for and scribbled his name on the check. "Now, children, I've got to work." He shoved back the table and left. This last too palpable insult showed how bitter and baffled he was. Yet again I'd conspired with a woman to make him out to be crass. A bully, when all the while really he was a Talleyrand, a Disraeli!

"Am I angry?" he said to me later. "Bitter?" We were sitting in his library, not quite face-to-face. On his dressing-gown collar, as in the lapel of every coat and jacket he owned, was his ribbon of the *Légion d'Honneur* (of which he liked saying the chic was in not having accepted a higher grade). As a rule he read while he talked to me. "Not at all." I had time to stare. Facing Biography, I always made anagrams of the same titles. Emma Goldman, *My Life:* FLY ME IN MADAM GOLEM; *Byron in Italy:* ONLY A TINY RIB . . . Sometimes he would ask me to read a passage he'd marked in a book. *I sighed like a lover and obeyed like a son*, from Gibbon's *Autobiography*. Once he tossed me a packet of papers. "Read this." It was his will. I remember only that it provided equally for my sister and me.

Then there it was: the last straw (almost). His last phrase to me was the voice of the place: emollient, repellent, a lie. "Not angry at all, *my dear boy*."

*"BE NOT TOO MUCH DISCOURAGED . . ."** In our ten or so months together, Posie told me that she had not come. Not once? Not ever.

Not with the famous playwright dying of cancer in his room at

---

* Coleridge: "Be not too much discouraged if any virtue should be mixed in your consciousness with affectation and imperfect sincerity, and some vanity—*disapprove* of this—and continue the practice, and the good feeling even thus mixed—*it will gradually purify itself*." (*Notebooks*, Volume 2, ed. Kathleen Coburn)

the Mayflower Hotel? (My father had known him.) Not with the Italian whose pipe I'd found on the bathtub while bathing her children? Not ever. And she went on. Not with G. in his studio on Twenty-third Street, not with S. at the Hotel Albert. Not with A.— . . . Not even with her dead husband? Not ever! And not even, with me, when— ? "I *lied!*"

She was crying. Lying naked on her bed, she kept lighting cigarettes and getting them wet. I kept taking the wet cigarettes away. Her white skin looked whiter than ever, her red hair more red. So this was the end? She was in pain; what was I going to do? Where was I going to go?

First of all I noted my easy accommodation of sexual jealousy. My pain and humiliation were great; I'd been exploited, used by her as a baby-sitter while she went out with other men; she'd paid me off with sex. I was brokenhearted. Yet there I was listing her lovers with her and noticing (*noticing!*) how my urbanity was making room for "understanding." I was proud of my complaisance.

Leaving for the last time, I surveyed the apartment I'd "owned," the life I'd hoped would be mine. Not two months before I'd said to her, "Where are we going next summer?" And she'd answered scornfully, Next summer! You *do* tend to hang your hat. Now holding my hat (a Cavanaugh) over the wound in my heart, I made to go, planning vaguely to return years later and take my revenge, as at the end of *Le Rouge et le Noir* Julien Sorel comes back and murders Sophie de Rênal. I'd been in love with her? With *her?* It was incredible. I'd wanted a place in *her* bourgeois life, among the tacky furniture and Museum of Modern Art reproductions? Incredible.

Now, what *was* I to do without her? Where *was* I to go?

To Italy; there to be myself: dark, doomed, fatal, stricken, bereft. The soprano Eleanor Steber once shrieked as I'd walked into the restaurant L'Aiglon with Posie on my arm, "Why, he looks just like Chopin!" I didn't look like Chopin; had never been slender and slight of form (*mince*, as the French say). All the same, in Italy, Chopin, along with Byron, Goethe, Musset: the whole of the nineteenth century: would show me how to behave. Julien and Fabrice, Lucien Leuwen and Lucien de Rubempré; Adolphe, Frédéric, Werther, Harold, Pechorin. . . . The men all played by Gérard Philipe, their women by Arletty. (And waiting for me below stairs: lubricious Simone Simon and Simone Signoret.)

I sailed for Naples one morning in March on the *Andrea Doria* with my best friend, Henry. Henry had been one of Posie's husband's hangers-on. He was more musical than I, and he took up the instruction in taste which Posie had begun. Thanks to Henry, I came to know of the conductors Erich Kleiber and Clemens Krauss; thanks to Henry, I met Glenn Gould. Henry worked in Washington for the United Press, a specialist in Latin American affairs. (He'd been brought up in Buenos Aires.) He looked like a D.P., yet his success with women was great. Phthisical, eyes close together: how did he do it? By the time we reached Italy Henry had scored I don't know how many times; while I'd had to pretend I was Joseph, the world was Potiphar's wife, and that far from being overlooked, I was in fact spurning numberless bids to knock at women's stateroom doors.

In Rome I wanted to be alone in the Sistine Chapel with the Botticelli fresco of Jethro's daughter, so cruelly like Posie. (Ah, Swann! ah, Odette!) In Florence I often was alone with the frescoes by Masaccio and Filippino Lippi in the Santa Maria del Carmine. There is where Berenson tells us that "tactile values" began. And there is where I saw myself in the naked young prince being brought back to life by Saint Peter in the Lippi fresco: so long dead, so little corrupted. Yes, yes, that was me. Posie wrote to say that she was going to marry. My consolation now was in Boccaccio's *Nastagio degli amanti:* Nastagio returning home and dismembering his beloved's suitors. A photograph of me in Florence shows a smiling, well-nourished young man in front of a poster for the Maggio Musicale. I am wearing a seersucker jacket from Chipp and a Brooks Brothers shirt with an open button-down collar. My pose is that of F. Scott Fitzgerald on the cover of *This Side of Paradise*. Nothing sad, nothing stricken, nothing doomed. Not minatory even, except that the poster is for *Otello*. So long dead, so little corrupted? The person taking the picture: a young woman met backstage at the Maggio, where she was singing in the chorus.

In Paris I started seducing Henry's girlfriends away, often if possible under his nose. The first of these was an American girl named Janine. She was an opera singer. I took her to St. Jean-de-Luz. Here's the moment I knew I wasn't in love with Janine. We'd gone to rent motorbikes in St. Jean-de-Luz and she fell off the bike. As I watched her fall off, indifferent to whether she'd hurt herself, I thought only of Posie, remembering how the petals fell on us on our first ride.

Back in Paris I heard from a friend of my father's that no one is truly a man until his heart has been broken three times. So I was one-third there? Heartbreak, however: how hard to leave off. Its attitudes so handy, its poems and songs so profuse. And women, always so interested in the ghost of the woman before. Back home, I dated Posie's sister, I slept several times with Posie's best friend (with Janine's best friend, too). I needed money for my new career of dissoluteness and heartbreak. But when I asked my father, I was reminded of my having to earn my own living. Otherwise his response was as to a seven-year-old. "Look around you, dear boy, all this is yours. Now, if it were an emergency, if some day you get a girl in trouble . . ."

And I'd look around at the treasure stored, for me, "dear boy," against the Event, feeling pleasantly like a seven-year-old, appeased by that "some day": the gorgeous Event bringing with it unlimited wealth!

Nil mihi das vivus: dicis post fata daturum.
Si non es stultus, scis, Maro, quid cupiam.

[You give me nothing now. "Ah, yes,"
You say, "but you're one of my heirs."
Unless you're stupid, you can guess
How hopefully I say my prayers.]*

A cable announcing "TESTS POSITIVE" arrived from Janine one afternoon, addressed to Ben Sonnenberg, meaning me but opened by him ("That hated junior," said Henry James). She asked for $600. I got the money finally, but looking around, "dear boy" no longer saw a treasure hoarded for him. He saw a collection which no event, no convulsion of his, would disturb.

* Martial, *Epigrams*, XI, 67. Translated by James Michie.

POLONAISE The next girl I took from Henry was Nina, a principal dancer with the Ballet Russe de Monte Carlo in New York. She was creating the Unicorn in the Rosen-Chailly-Cocteau ballet *La Dame à la Licorne*. Henry told me that he was in love with her. She clearly wasn't in love with him. Think of a revolving door: Henry goes in with Nina, I go in alone; next I come out with Nina and Henry comes out alone.

Of course Nina was far from being a girl. She'd seen the destruction of Warsaw; married an American officer to escape from Poland after the war; been the lover of Sergei Denham, the General Manager of the Ballet Russe. And yet she fell in love with me. "*Mordecseska*, I created the Unicorn for you." I was eighteen and I had a Mistress who was a Prima Ballerina. Eighteen! At eighteen, was Baudelaire as far along as I?

So I had to earn my own living? I would be Nina's agent, an impresario. I'd lunch at the Russian Tea Room with Sol Hurok every day. Nina agreed, her paycheck was sent to me, and I paid myself 20 percent. I went to Battaglia and bought a silk raincoat, black and white, which I wore like a cape. I swaggered backstage at theaters in Toronto, Atlanta, Cleveland, Detroit. Alicia Alonso knew who I was, and I was on first-name terms with Igor Yousekevich and Fredric Franklin.

I read long passages from Théophile Gautier to my mother and father, and, in a Russian accent, talked to them about Fokine and Bakst, Benois and Karsavina. Without compromising an ignorance as self-satisfied as it was ill-disguised, in two or three weeks I passed from being something less than a fan to being a master of at least the jargon of Nina's art, a role with which I was content.

"Can you imagine, there are some people who don't even know the names of Grisi, Taglioni, Cerito and Grahn?"

"Incredible," said my mother.

"Incredible," my father said.

But when I took Nina to meet them, I was not content. Impeccably well-mannered, beautiful, noble and merry, Nina looked a part of their world, sitting there with them, so far as the setting suggested, in its assembly of rich woods, brass accents and costly fabrics, a vanished Old World of culture, ceremony and class. She looked more a part of their world than mine, and afterwards I grew annoyed at how prompt her sadness always was, excessive, so much more than personal. The soup was cold? Nina's eyes filled with tears. I was late? Her upper lip trembled. "You hate me because I am polish."

"You are Polish, not polish."

So what if her mother had died in Auschwitz? So what if Nina had barely escaped? Didn't I have sad stories of my own?

I saw that, in time, with Nina, I would come to enjoy looking like a man living off the earnings of an older woman. Sallow, jealous and furtive, I'd order white-on-white shirts from Lew Magram ("Shirt-maker to the Stars"). I'd have a gold bracelet and wear a pencil mustache. And so I broke off with Nina when Henry introduced me to Artemisia.

"I think I'm in love with Artemisia," Henry said to me, and then he left me alone with her at a table in the Oak Room at the Plaza. Incredible! I thought. Artemisia was also a dancer, the only white member of the Katherine Dunham troupe. Being Italian (well, *half*-Italian) she allowed for my tragic (well, *semi*-tragic) airs and attitudes.

In the next month or so, Artemisia saw a great deal of me. She saw a little of Henry, as well. He lived in Washington, I in New York, and Artemisia's mother (she stayed with her mother sometimes) lived in Philadelphia. I don't know what Artemisia told Henry; me she told of Umberto Saba, Giuseppe Ungaretti, Eugenio Montale and Salvatore Quasimodo. Then she dropped us both, for a businessman who lived in Puerto Rico. So I wouldn't feel bad, she set me up with her best friend in New York. "You'll break a tooth on Sabina," she said.

ADOPTED CHILDREN My parents were always adopting young men: "gentlemen" of the penniless, weak, indecisive kind. These in my parents' view composed a significant part of any year at any Ivy League school, to none of which I was going. Their role in our household was to reproach me. I consoled myself for the effortless way these youths seemed to harvest esteem by exalting the virtue of rudeness and exaggerating whatever it was that made them hate and fear me. For instance, I was brilliant. I quoted Baudelaire and Oscar Wilde. I quoted *Pelham* by Bulwer-Lytton: *You look very much like a magpie.* The trouble with such stratagems is, I was appealing for judgment from rivals I knew to have none.

Thus ambiguousness, and not brilliance, became my stock in trade. I brought it to bear at Sabina's house, where Artemisia was "like a daughter." Sabina's parents, Hans and Kate Dreier, soon adopted me. I showed a "filial" interest in the Dreier Gallery, run from their apartment on Park Avenue. My ambiguousness let me pretend that the Dreiers loved me because they discerned that behind my mask of foppish, saturnine indifference was a practically Russian profuseness of pure and noble feeling, as well as a Shelley-like loathing of property and wealth.

IDEAL

*"I SEE A WOMAN MAY BE MADE A FOOL . . ." • YOUTH MEANS
RETRIBUTION • SPLENDORS AND MISERIES • THE IMPORTANCE OF
KNOWING UNIMPORTANT PEOPLE*

*"I SEE A WOMAN MAY BE MADE A FOOL . . ."** There
was a Rembrandt drawing of a lion above Sabina's bed. When
Artemisia slept there, the lion looked down on *Rose White and
Briar Rose Slumbering,* or some such scene by Burne-Jones. By day
the Rembrandt lion beheld Sabina and Artemisia getting dressed
and undressed (sometimes with me in the room). They sang
Schumann duets and smelled of Doblis. Now and then they're
convulsed by certain words only they understood: *Baldwin!* . . .
Pur-ple Heart! . . . Now and then, through the smoke of my
cigarette (in a wooden holder from Dunhill), I'd see their nipples
and pubic hair, the air warm from the minor labors of young
women wearing perfume.

Sabina's room was filled with books. Something in their arrangement told me that she was lonely and proud. I thought,
lonely like me. And, I thought, if we become lovers, as Artemisia
wants, Sabina's pride will help keep me from being a failure. . . .
Sabina was good-looking, with a wonderful figure, lots of blond
hair (like her lion) and very small hands and feet.

I was transferred from Artemisia to Sabina easily, as if she and
Artemisia were doing a thing they'd done often before. First we
went out as a threesome; then Sabina and I were going to see
Artemisia in, I remember, *The Apollo of Bellac;* then Sabina and I
were going to operas and concerts and plays by ourselves. Soon
I was smiling. Sabina was *all* smiles. Artemisia was smiling, too.

Sabina was six years older than I, better schooled, better read,
better traveled: she would teach me everything. Sabina was *fierce*
(a word with her: *fierce*), and her anger, having authority, drew
others near; whereas my bad manners just put people off.
Sabina was an Enigma, I was a "problem." Sabina was discon-

---

* "I see a woman may be made a fool/ If she had not a spirit to resist." *The Taming of
the Shrew,* III, ii.

solate, I was "sullen." She looked like a Lady in Tennyson: immured, enchancelled, enisled. *Rouse me!* her eyes said. Her lips said, *Fuck off!* Pretentious to others, Sabina was adorable to me.

I wanted to write stories about New York like those by James Joyce about Dublin. I wrote one about an out-of-work governess, Johanna Kibbe. One winter evening she goes into a *Konditorei* on Third Avenue near Eighty-sixth Street. Waiting her turn, she meets another governess. "Why, Johanna Kibbe!" "Why, Maria Bench!" They haven't seen each other for years and they sit down and have coffee. Maria Bench tells her a story from the *Daily Mirror* that day. A man commits suicide in an Automat by sprinkling cyanide on his piece of pie and eating it and then an old woman is found dead of cyanide on the street not two blocks away. The old woman was a scavenger who haunted the Automat balcony. When she saw someone leave she ran down and ate the food that was left. Maria Bench, who has worked for the same Jewish family for years, asks about the family Kibbe is working for, and Kibbe lies. They say good-bye and Kibbe goes to the Automat for dinner. Crossing Eighty-sixth street, she feels envious of Maria, whom she had always despised. After her dinner she starts to list the many city playgrounds she has been to over the years: "all the mean enclosures of the city." (The story was called "A Small Enclosure.") The loneliness of her life is about to overwhelm her. She is watching a man who is eating alone at the table next to her. When he gets up she sees that he hasn't finished his pie. She reaches out and grabs it. The last line of the story was, "It burst jubilantly through her fingers."

Sabina was writing a story about a retired diplomat who lived alone in the Camargue. The story involved the legend of the two Marys: Mary, Mother of Christ, and Mary Magdalene, who came, after the Crucifixion, "with their dark servant Sarah," to the coast of France (to Les Stes Maries). Sabina wrote the beginning over and over again. I never learned how the story went on. She was also writing an essay about Remy de Gourmont, the author of *Letters to the Amazon* and *The Physiology of Love.* On her shelves were the many yellow-backed volumes of his *Promenades littéraires* and *Promenades philosophiques.*

Our summers together were filled with books and music and cooking and long drives. Strauss's *Ariadne auf Naxos* and Wolf's

Spanish and Italian songbooks were our favorite music. We read
La Chute by Albert Camus, *Zazie dans le métro* by Raymond Que-
neau, *L'Histoire d'O* by "Pauline Réage" and *Anti-Dühring* by
Friedrich Engels.

I liked our both being writers and I liked Sabina being
"blocked." I liked it that our reactions were the same to music
and books and people, that our locutions were often the same and
that we twirled our hair the same way as we spoke. I liked it that,
although we were lovers for more than two years, we had almost
no jealous scenes.

I did not like it that we both lived with our parents. I did not
like it that her menstrual periods were so painful that for half of
each month her breasts were swollen and I couldn't touch them.
I did not like it that often there was a question about whether
we'd sleep together that night. And I did not like it that while
Sabina had a job, in publishing, I could find nothing "gainful" to
do. Surely that would change if we lived together? We never
managed to, alas, except in the summers in the country, in St.
James and Cutchogue, Long Island, where there were no jobs
worth having.

Of course, to imply that I never was jealous isn't strictly true.
My jealousy was (how should I put this?) *thinned* by my latent
sense of Sabina's bisexuality: when together with Artemisia, the
picture was half *Gabrielle d'Estrée et sa soeur Jacqueline* (School of
Fontainebleau, in the Louvre), half Egon Schiele in some imagined stage design for Wedekind's *Lulu* plays.

After our second summer, my father said to me, "Are you
being fair to Sabina?" Meaning was I keeping her from meeting
someone more suitable? I didn't know if I wanted to marry, but
I was in love with Sabina and she was in love with me. I wanted
to live with Sabina, and now and then we looked at apartments
to rent.

YOUTH MEANS RETRIBUTION*   Hans Dreier, Sabina's father, was a dealer in Old Master paintings. He'd been a magis-
trate once in Berlin, but his real love was music, not the law, and
he played the violin. He'd left Berlin with his family in 1935.

* From *The Master Builder* by Ibsen.

Like Adorno and Benjamin, he may have thought the Nazis would just disappear. Like them, he showed a measure of blindness and unhaste. First he settled in Holland. . . . He was a loyal German citizen, had served in the War, the Great War, and had a medal to prove it. How Jewish *was* he anyway? One-eighth? Maybe not even that. Sadly, he gave up hope of returning to Berlin. But after nineteen years in New York, he still had the air not of being a Jew but of somehow counting as one.

Another of his airs Hans had not had in Berlin, I was sure. Self-made man. Wasn't that New York? And with it, the lures thrown incessantly to atonement, to expiation? I used to rise to them, teasing his obsession with death. Well, not with death exactly. When he and his pals got together, the talk was all about funerals. How each would go off in some not large church: San Miniato, the Sainte Chapelle . . . *A timor mortis*, already benign, made more soft by art. Mosse, the psychoanalyst: *I want the Berlioz Requiem with Ernest Ansermet*. Thielman, who's married an Endicott and had "the wherewithal now" to collect: *Busch and the Mozart C-minor Mass*. Arens, the art restorer: *The Verdi, naturally*. Then Hans would say: *Who with?* And Arens: *Toscanini*. Then Hans would say: *Too late!* "Too late?" *Yes! I already got him! Ha! Ha!* Everyone would laugh.

They would then look at me with a sort of chagrin. That made me feel important. Part Eros, part Nemesis, part Frog Prince: they feared me? A never-before conscious power began to crystallize. At other times I felt spellbound by my own duplicity. That is the faculty that made me apt for the art dealers' favorite pastime, the shaping of vignettes. They told tales to me and each other about Erich Maria Remarque and Paulette Goddard: the German novelist and his wife collected Old Master drawings: and I told them stories about Stefan George and Hugo von Hofmannsthal. How did I know such stories? They professed amazement at my precocity.

Yes, and over all the bewitchment of a faith in predestination! Why not? A function of being in love (Artemisia first, then Sabina), that faith was fostered by furniture, too; by artworks evoking the great and the dead, and by decorum evocative of the great dead premodern world. Predestination: a faith with hymns by Schubert, Schumann and Wolf whose songs were sung by

Sabina's mother, who had studied with Lotte Lehmann, and by
Sabina herself. Predestination enabled skills that from childhood
I knew very well how to prize: cajoling women and outsmarting
men, lying and domineering through taste in clothes and art.

Art dealing had a high standing in the fifties in New York,
unclouded as yet by the postwar swarm of customers' men and
crooks. It was almost a learned profession; not quite a profession,
in fact. Some had the added glamour of being refugees. Refugees,
but stamped nowhere by fear, sudden flight, conscience or peril
or pain. They were defying Hitler by prospering in New York,
by relishing America to a sometimes silly degree. They were
always pledging allegiance to Toscanini and Thomas Mann.
Their merest inclinations were now the feats of a strenuous politics. Riches here, fatality there . . . Each was a Jew who understood art. Each was, as well, in his overseas home, under
perpetual sentence of death, like Paul Henreid in *Casablanca*.

How pervasive the glamour of those who are like our parents
but better at it! These Jews owned art but without the fuss of 19
Gramercy Park. They dealt, to be sure; only art dealing showed
how little they were in thrall. The glamour spread to their daughters, their dogs, through their homes to their "little collections" of
kitsch, to their lengthy meals. . . . To all but their clothes: Alice
Schweitzer and Sulka and Knize. The women's hems always a
fraction too long, the men's suit jackets too short. Still, in this
New World city, where both sexes dressed with unflagging regard for Europe (especially then), even these tiny symbols of
difference were powerful charms, seeming meant to evoke the
historical Jew. Yes, and at no small expense.

What appealed to me most? I never could decide. To be like
them in their art-dealing work? To be like them as ideal victims
of an ideal villainy? Or to be like them in their apartments, where
property and pleasure were so indissolubly linked? Besides, they
had glamour as cultured Jews who nevertheless were adepts at
imprecation and doom: most of all about music. If Sterba liked
Schnabel while Mosse liked Kempff, then in the one's eyes the
other was not only incurably stupid but unforgivably rude. And
about *music!* A subject unknown to my parents. The same with
composers: on into the twentieth century, on back to before
Buxtehude. I was certain no German or Austrian Jew could utter

a word on the subject without thereby causing mortal offense to some other German or Austrian Jew.

Their absolutism was an effect of a then-worldwide shriveling up of judgment into a worship of "the barbarism of perfection" (the phrase is in Adorno's *Minima Moralia*). That, and the anguished domination that émigrés and exiles seek in whatever city they stop. Still, for me, a Collectors' Child, for whom the wall was as much as the work, the donor as much as the artist, their absolutism translated from musical into general terms, becoming, first and foremost, a foil for the lax cupidity with which I appreciated painting (or watched it appreciate). And second, a very great comfort. For here were severe intellectual men (dogmatic and expert at least) to whom location, provenance and cash value were important. To please them, however demanding they were, I needed only to cultivate my own innate talents and tastes. By contrast, at home the formation of these led invariably to resentment and fights.

To be a Benjamin to the Dreiers, what did I not do? I read German, studied lieder. . . . Their household was filled with women: I was gallant and flirted with them. Sisters-in-law and others like aunts, even *petites amies*. I wooed them by being mischievous, tender and sincere. Not for the first time, I liked finding out that whereas with men I was usually tongue-tied and apathetic, with women I felt happy and free. This busied me so, I could scarcely have seen with what pain they perceived, men and women alike, living in a foreign land (New York City a foreign land!), the shrinking of propriety, by force of displacement, through no fault of theirs, into a sometimes convenient but mostly detested *vie de bohème*. I was also blind to why they were mad to be not Jewish but German.

One thing I did see, however. Art dealing wasn't for me. It offered sex, condescension, contempt (frequently all three at once), commercial excitement and civilized calm; but its inventories and ledgers! details and dates and chores! . . . It was finally perhaps too much a case of "supplying a productive apparatus without changing it." Or being (in other than the fastidious words of Walter Benjamin) too much like hard work.

SPLENDORS AND MISERIES   After two years, encouraged by Marion, I took the great risk of separating from Sabina. I prom-

ised her I'd find us a house overlooking the Mediterranean where
she'd have a workroom and I'd have one, too. One of my father's
clients was American Export Lines. He got me the "owner's
cabin" on a tramp steamer for Lisbon, and in 1957, in early
spring, I embarked with my car and several boxes of books. I
wore a long-skirted raincoat and carried an ashplant as I thought
became an exile.

In Lisbon I met a collector of art, Carlos Cudell-Goetz. Hans
Dreier had given me his name. He lived in a small apartment
with his enormous collection. Paintings, sculpture, pottery;
North German painting and icons from Crete, Gothic wood carvings, Catalan frescoes and Japanese woodblock prints. Paintings
and sculpture were everywhere. Chinese, Coptic and pre-
Columbian art. On the ceilings, the backs of the doors. He had
an Egyptian sarcophagus and a totem pole. He told me that he
collected only what he could restore.

While I was there a small neat man let himself in without
knocking. "Benslimon, Oswaldo." He made a short bow.

"My best friend," said Cudell-Goetz. Senhor Benslimon wore
a loose gold bracelet on his left wrist, and I noticed that Cudell-
Goetz had on two expensive gold wrist watches. They took me to
a nightclub to hear the fado singer Amalia Rodriguez, with whom
Cudell-Goetz appeared to be on intimate terms. Senhor Benslimon put his hand on my thigh. He told me he ran a parador,
under license from the government, and asked me if I'd make a
delivery for him on my way south. A package that Senhor Cudell-
Goetz would give me in a day or two. "Glad to," I said. "What's
in it?"

"Cigarette lighters," he said. "You need a license to own a
lighter in Portugal. Can you believe that?"

"What a barbarity," I said.

The package wasn't large. I delivered it. Senhor Benslimon
showed me his own collection. He said it was "a *sentimental* collection." Meerschaum pipes, fans, mantillas, parasols, cigarette
cases, razors . . . Best of all, in expensive wood frames, hinged to
the wall, in an upstairs room, a vast array of cigar bands with
portraits on them of the rulers of Europe, Africa, South America
and Asia, many long deposed: King Carol, King Zog, Czar Nicholas II, Kaisers Wilhelm I and II, Otto von Bismarck, King
George V, King Chulalongkorn (of Siam), King Manuel II, King

Alfonse XIII, and Sgt. Fulgeneio Batista. Senhor Benslimon made a pass at me there, as I knew he would. I said no: politely, I hope: and drove south, never again to see so impressive a private cigar-band collection.*

I found a small farm east of Málaga, Granja Amos, and moved in. First, though, I spent a month in Madrid. One morning, after the Prado, I picked up a lonely young English girl. "Where shall I take you?" I asked her. Her eyes said, Take me wherever you want. I took her instead to the church of San Antonio de la Florida, to see the Goya decorations there.

I also met a young woman at a horse show one day. We went riding a couple of times. Her seat was faultless, her hands were just right. She lived with her diplomat parents in the calle Serrano. I took her to the Instituto Valencia y Don Juan to see the Hispano-Moresque pottery, and otherwise spoiled my chances with her by telling her of Sabina.

Another morning, after the Prado, I ran into the violinist Alexander Schneider. Who was it Posie was fucking at the Hotel Albert? he said. I said, Why, Sasha, I thought it was you: feeling both retroactive jealousy and pride in my urbanity. I told him I was going to Salzburg to see Glenn Gould. Does Glenn sleep with women? Does Glenn sleep with men? Sasha told me of an older woman in Toronto who he said was Glenn's patron. I kept trying to walk arm in arm with him which I thought was continental. Every few steps he would stop and stand away until finally I got the message.

At Granja Amos I grew a beard. Waiting for Sabina, I looked at the Mediterranean in the evening and said, *Alas, so all things now do hold their peace. . . . The sea is calm, the waves work less and less. . . .*

I wasn't calm. I was restless and lonely. I worked at my writing less and less. I missed Sabina. Jealousy came in astonishing fits. I had never been so jealous before. I had looked forward to an ideal life with Sabina: good books, good talk, good faith, good sex. Now even her letters, with their amusing reports of bland and blameless activities, made me jealous. I studied them for

---

* A still greater cigar-band collection is in the Mares Museum in Barcelona. There used to be outdoor cigar-band bazaars each Sunday in the Plaza Mayor in Madrid.

evidence of lust and riot underneath. I kept remembering a photograph of her that hung in her bathroom in New York. She was naked on a beach. Only her lower torso showed. A mollusk shell was on her stomach. Her legs were a little apart. The photographer had been her lover. What if *he* turned up in New York?

> A thousand fantasies
> Begin to throng into my memory
> Of calling shapes, and beckoning shadows dire,
> And airy tongues . . .

Sabina was coming in September. And it was only May.

I went to Morocco. In Moslem countries, Freud tells us, in "Certain Neurotic Mechanisms in Jealousy, Homosexuality and Paranoia," men look on one another as potential objects of affection and not as rivals for the love of a woman. In Tangiers I tried to act jaded, like Michel in Gide's *L'Immoraliste*. I saw a male brothel. A teacher of mine from prep school went in and I told myself there was syphilis there, so I didn't go in myself. In Fez I was excited to find that, with my beard and speaking French, I wasn't noticed. Invisibility! Dream of my life! But invisible as I was (open as I was), and I *was*, no adventure followed. No kif, no oboes, no tambourines, no Arab boy dancing naked in the *hammam*. Nothing I did brought me near to the thrills I knew were out there.

I flew to Salzburg to join Glenn Gould. I wanted to talk about music with Glenn, he wanted to talk about literature. I told him how thrilled I was to be among German-speaking people, to be where all music tended to either Strauss or Mahler. I told him how thrilled I had been to see, when I went to hear Fischer-Dieskau sing the Brahms Magelone Lieder the night before, the same serious, prosperous audience I was used to seeing in New York. Most music-lovers I knew in New York refused to visit Austria, most musicians I knew wouldn't play there. "When people ask me if I'm Jewish," Glenn said, "I always tell them that I was Jewish during the war." And when they ask you if you're queer? Glenn said, "I always quote Horowitz, that there are three kinds of pianists: homosexual pianists, Jewish pianists, and bad pianists. And I add, pianists who play better than Horowitz."

I gave Glenn a story of mine and after he read it, he said something odd. The story had to do with an elevator operator in an apartment building. His father is a retired policeman. The elevator operator has fits of rage which he appeases by borrowing money. Every day after work he meets a loan shark named Malloy in a bar on Third Avenue. One day he learns that the loan shark has been murdered. His debts are canceled. But he can't remember where he was at the time of the crime. Did he murder Malloy? So he goes up to a friend of Malloy's in the bar and borrows money from him.

Glenn said, "If someone can write beautifully, why would he choose a subject like this?" I thought that was odd. Then he told me his favorite writers were W. H. Hudson, R. B. Cunninghame-Graham and John Cowper Powys; and I thought that that was still odder.

Here's a story of mine that Glenn did like. I told him of seeing Artur Rubinstein in a record store in Paris. He was buying a recording by Dinu Lipatti or William Kapell. He smiled at me and said, mock self-deprecation, "I have so much to learn." Some months later I saw Rubinstein getting his hair cut at the St. Regis barbershop in New York. After his shampoo, his hair hung down from his bald head, and he looked like the homely old man he was. Then he took a comb from the barber and teased his hair up until he looked like Artur Rubinstein. "Ah, Maestro," said the barber as Rubinstein handed back the comb, "I have so much to learn."

Glenn and I agreed that later that summer he should come to Granja Amos. This never happened, and soon after our friendship evaporated. I'd been too heated; that was why. I was always closing with men at that age and then drawing back abruptly. In my notebook I find from about this time the following quotation from Joyce; it's from his story "A Painful Case": "Love between man and man is impossible because there must not be sexual intercourse and friendship between man and woman is impossible because there must be sexual intercourse."

•

Back in Málaga I waited for Sabina and read Henry Charles Lea's *History of the Inquisition of the Middle Ages*. in 1212 Raimond

de Toulouse, the brave courtier and poet, wrote to a lady in
Barcelona that he was coming for her sake to raise the siege of her
city and rid her land of the foreign invader. The letter was in-
tercepted by Simon de Montfort. He was the brutal Norman
who commanded the forces sent by Innocent III to wipe out the
Albigensians. He said, "God help me as much as I little fear one
who comes for the sake of a woman to undo the work of God!"
Alas, I thought, no one brutal will ever say something like that
about me.

Sabina arrived and we drove from Málaga to San Sebastian
and Barcelona and to the Camargue. I was happy and excited and
forgot my jealousy. Next we drove to Tours and through the
Loire Valley to Paris. Most of the places we drove to Sabina had
been to before, but not Amboise. In Amboise I picked a fight.
She was driving and I said turn right and she drove on, or I said
drive on and she turned right. I tore the keys from the ignition
and threw them out of the window. Why don't you listen to me!
Why must I always do what *you* say! Why did you leave me
alone! I got out and picked up the keys from the road. I was
crying. I gave them back. I'm sorry, I said.

In Paris we checked into the France et Choiseul, where I'd
been told Alfred de Musset had once stayed with George Sand.
Sabina showed me the place de Furstenberg. She had been lonely
in Paris when she lived there some years before. If ever I think of
the loneliness of a young woman alone in Paris, I see the place de
Furstenberg. I bought Sabina scarves and soap. I took her to buy
gloves. The *gantier* said that he'd never seen such small hands on
a grown woman before. I met her friends at the cafés where she
used to hang out. Le Tournon, Le Flore. I met the photographer.
He was older than I expected, and not so droll. *Drôle* was their
word. Sabina spoke rapidly with her friends. Idiomatically, I
suppose. She said, *"Et elle était endimanchée: même les dimanches."*
[She dressed in her Sunday best, even on Sunday.] And everyone
laughed. She took me to the old Romanesque church, St. Julien-
le-pauvre. She took me to see a Gothic wood carving of the
Magdalene at the Musée de Cluny. "They tell me she looks like
me," she said. *They* tell her? Did she take me for a fool? All the
same, from then on she looked different to me, especially when
angry, or sad.

We drove from Paris by way of Arles to Florence where her parents were. It was exciting to be there openly with Sabina. We visited an old German woman who lived in a tower called Torre del Diablo. She had been the mistress of Ferruccio Busoni and she showed us some of his manuscript scores.

I drove from Florence to Vienna where my father was staying at the Sacher. He told me again I would soon have to earn my own living. "You're depleting your trust fund," he said. "You must find a way to *increment* your income." Sometimes he said, "You must find a way to *implement* your income." We looked at drawings at the Albertina and went to the opera to see *Fidelio*. I told him that young German couples went to *Fidelio* when they got engaged. I could not bring myself to tell him that I wanted to marry Sabina. He would have said something about young men married to older women, about how they castrate them. He would have repeated, "Are you being fair to her?"

"How do you feel in Vienna?" I asked. My father and mother had often said they could never go to Germany or Austria. He was there because I'd insisted.

"I feel like Schnitzler's Anatol," he said. "I know the ropes." His allusion was to the Max and Anatol stories of Arthur Schnitzler. Naïve Max, and Anatol, man of the world. And he said, "For the first time in history being Jewish is chic."

"Which makes it more dangerous surely?"

"*Not* if you know the ropes."

"Very droll," I said.

From Vienna I drove to Munich where Sabina was. We decided to get married in December in Germany. I gave her a wooden ring that I'd bought from a jeweler in London who'd told me it was Turkish. She went back to New York to tell her parents. Her best friend, LeAnne, found me a room in Kaulbachstrasse, in Schwabing. Waiting for Sabina, I walked around Munich and looked at where, in Prinzregentenstrasse, Hitler had lived with his young niece Geli Raubel, and where, after Geli Raubel committed suicide, Hitler became a vegetarian.

One afternoon there were police outside the Alte Pinotek. A young man had destroyed a masterpiece in the museum, someone said. More police brought the young man out. The masterpiece was *The Descent of the Damned into Hell* by Rubens. I went

into the museum and looked at where the young man had thrown
acid on the painting. It was hard to see where, the painting is
huge. It was also hard to see why. Many lewder paintings hung
nearby. Some depicted more sacred scenes. The Rubens isn't
lewd at all. My notion of desecration came from two stories:
Mann's *"Gladius Dei"* and "Erostrate" by Jean-Paul Sartre; that is,
from Savanorola and from the figure in antiquity who burned
down the temple of Diana at Ephesus so as to be remembered for
all time.

Sabina came back and we drove to Obersdorf to tell her godmother of our "betrothal." She played a yodel record for us and
we all drank a toast. There was a photograph on the bookcase of
a young man in a *Luftwaffe* uniform. It was her godmother's
son-in-law, shot down over London and killed. He had been the
son of Franz von Papen, one of Hitler's ministers. Her godmother was petty nobility.

We drove back to Munich. It was night. There was fog. How
very far I had come. Yodel records, the photograph of someone
in a *Luftwaffe* uniform . . . The trees on the road came up out of
the fog. A big car passed us. The trees kept coming up fast. Then
brilliant crystals lay on the road. The big car was smashed. A
cyclist was lying on the road.

Before we got to Munich I told Sabina I wanted to wait. I tried
to explain. I said, You see. But already Sabina was pushing the
wooden ring into my hand.

*THE IMPORTANCE OF KNOWING UNIMPORTANT PEO-
PLE.* The Duchess of Windsor said to the Duke, "David, go
back and see to the dogs." We were in the casino at Biarritz. The

NOTE: *Not her real name.* Sabina read these pages and demanded that her name be
changed. I asked her what name she wanted. She didn't reply, so I chose Sabina
(pronounced Sa-BEENA), Sabina (pronounced Sa-BYNA) having been the prettiest
girl in my sixth-grade class. I thought of adding NHRN to every mention of Sabina,
but that would have been vengeful. Artemisia and LeAnne are NRNs, neither of
course is Hans Dreier.

It's curious how if you change someone's name in a memoir like this, you feel
you have the license to invent a past and future for them; to invent new circumstances, too: children and dogs and vices and tastes, they stop at the Bristol instead
of the Ritz, they drive Aston-Martins not Delahayes. . . . Notwithstanding which,
I've been as truthful as memory, tact and record permit.

Duchess of Windsor said to me, "David's jackets are made in London, but his trousers are made in New York. We call it *pants across the sea.*"

"That's her one joke," said my father later. "*His* one joke is the Duchess."

My father and I were staying at the Palace Hotel in Biarritz with Robert Lehman and his wife. My father had once famously said, of a famous advertising man, "Before I knew Albert Lasker, I was always seen with a beautiful girl. After I knew Albert Lasker, I was always seen with Albert Lasker." So it was with him and Bobby. He got credit from his intimacy with the owner of a great private bank, Bobby got to know interesting people.

Bobby owned a famous brass aquamanile, *Aristotle and Phyllis,* the philosopher being ridden like a horse by his termagant wife. Bobby's own marriage was like that. His wife was always getting drunk and making terrible scenes. She stayed out late, she screwed around. Bobby hired detectives. He threatened divorce, she threatened scandal. My father was always calming them down, showing a wealth of vizier skills.

Bobby was richer than my father. His collection was far greater: greater than any my father could aspire to. A great collection of paintings, a great collection of drawings, a great collection of whatever Bobby wanted to collect. To make the reflection that much of it had been inherited was mollifying to my father, as was the still more recurrent theme that, for all his wealth and education, Bobby didn't know how to enjoy life and didn't know how to "manage" his wife.

The importance of being seen with only important people was also a favorite theme of his. His notion of who these were was not fixed. Certain names came up all the time. Paul Mellon was one. Isaiah Berlin was another. "I know the difference between Irving Berlin and Isaiah Berlin, and I know them both," he once said in an interview. One meaning of this may be in a story he liked to tell. During the war Isaiah Berlin was at the British Embassy in Washington. He sent regular reports back to London; these were signed I. Berlin. Churchill read them, was impressed, and hearing that Berlin was in town had him invited to 10 Downing Street for lunch. Irving Berlin duly arrived and was seated next to Churchill who asked him questions about things in America.

"How is President Roosevelt?" To which Irving Berlin replied truthfully, "Fine, the last time I saw him." His other replies were less satisfactory, and Churchill grew irritable. "How do you envisage Europe after the war?" he asked. Berlin rose to his feet and said, "As long as I live I shall remember that Prime Minister Churchill asked my opinion of life in Europe after the war." Churchill's mutterings grew louder, in spite of attempts to whisper the truth to him. "The man's a fool." Finally Irving Berlin left and Churchill realized the confusion. He burst out laughing; and when the Cabinet convened that evening he told them all the story.

But it seemed to me that if important people wanted to know my father, it was for one reason only: because he made them or their causes famous, because of his trade. So I would have only obscure friends, and I wanted no trade. I wrote in my notebook, *A life of merited obscurity is the only life worth living.* "Come and see where I live in Málaga," I said to him in Biarritz. No one important lived in Málaga.

"You rascal, I accept gladly," my father said, making my invitation sound more like a challenge, a dare.

•

The summer after I broke up with Sabina I started an obscure love affair in Málaga with someone unimportant. For long spells that summer I was alone, thinking only about my art: about my art and getting laid: about my art and getting laid and becoming the lover of a great actress like Edwige Feuillère.

One day I went into the Italcable office. I was carrying a record. The cable clerk, a girl in her late twenties, a little overweight, told me she was studying singing. Her name was Pilár. Or Linda. After she got off work we went to a café and a day or two later I took her out for lunch. Pilár (or Linda) told me that her favorite composers were Granados, Falla and Berlioz; and after lunch we went into the woods on the hill where the Moorish castle is. There she sang for me the Berlioz song "*La Captive*" (words by Victor Hugo). She sang very badly, it seemed to me. "Let me pay for your singing lessons," I said. Her eyes filled with tears. *Io cangiero tua sorte, I'll change your fate*, as Don Giovanni sings to Zerlina.

I took her to the Pez Espada Hotel in Torremolinos. I saw her once or twice again, each time at a different hotel, each time (I now realize) attended by excruciating shame for her. Her subsequent pain and humiliation I can but imagine, for I dropped her. In another way, though, I went on with her intensely. I imagined meeting her parents and brother, who was doing his military service in Salamanca, or who had been killed while doing his military service, I didn't know just how. I imagined walking out with her in the evenings, holding hands like *novia y novio*. I imagined our looking at a house in a suburb of Málaga. There I imagined telling her I'd set her up, get her a maid and a piano and give her an allowance.

I remember reading, perhaps in Unamuno, that Spanish men tend to enact three myths: the first is El Cid, the second is Don Juan and the third is Don Quixote. Here was I, after only a year in Spain, corrupting and seducing a young woman, with easy-going passion and casual villainy, and abandoning her like Don Juan, and dreaming about it all afterwards, like Don Quixote. I wrote a story, in intimation of either Galdós (*Tristana*) or Machado de Assis (*Dom Casmurro*) or Pirandello. In my story the hero dreams of setting up house with a young woman like Pilár (or Linda) and at the end of the story he is killed by the young woman's brother who, in the story, is both imaginary and dead.

•

Granja Amos, the farm I rented for 3,500 pesetas a month, belonged to Isabél de Oyarsábal. It was left to her by her husband, an engineer who had worked in Cuba. Their daughter, Inés, was about my age. Her half-sister, Mári, called "La Mora" for her dark eyes, was about sixteen. Mári's father, Bernardo, worked the farm. The crops were a few scant kilos a year of olives, almonds and figs. They had a burro, a mule and a dog, a goat and some chickens. The farm was poor. Its main feature was that from the terrace, a meter above the main road between Málaga and Alméria, the view of the Mediterranean was 180 degrees. Isabél de Oyarsábal was poor and short and ugly. Except for being illiterate, she'd remind my father of his mother.

The main road from Málaga to Granja Amos was potholes, truck traffic, chickens and goats. It ran through six or seven tiny

towns, each one poorer than the one before. A cement plant on
the way sent up a cloud of silver dust. To drive the road with my
father was to travel the "highway" from Brest-Litovsk into a
poor, superstitious past, where, from a cellar window, in a room
packed with frightened Jews, my terrified four-year-old father
watched the hooves of the horses of the police up on the wooden
sidewalk.

To be sure, I say, Granja Amos is poor. But what a view! I
love a fine view, he agrees. A country place needs a fine view, he
adds. And look, I say, a rosemary bush. A *rosemary* bush? he
says. You don't say, I don't think I've ever seen one. Isabél
doesn't remind him of his mother, but he couldn't be more depressed if she did. And are you sure you can *drink* this water? he
says. He cheers up when he sees my shaving brushes ("Pure
Badger"), my books, my colorful tins of tea from Jackson's of
Piccadilly.

At lunch he asks about my writing. What will I do if in a few
years I find I have no talent? "I'll marry a woman with money,"
I say.

"And if you ever write your life story," he says, "you can call
it *Women Have Been Kind*."

I was stung. I'd given him *Women Have Been Kind*, the memoirs
of Lou Tellegen, a lover of Bernhardt's, as a joke.

After lunch I took him to Nerja and made sure he saw every
last one of the prehistoric paintings in the dull humid caves.
Afterwards he was exhausted. Dropping him off at the Hotel
Miramár in Málaga I promised him that that night I'd take him to
the best restaurant in town.

•

How poor exactly had my father been? Dirt poor? So poor he
didn't know where his next meal was coming from? I resented his
stories of being poor. Myths of the despotism: poverty, Poland,
pogroms: meant to make me feel unworthy. Still, I did like the
one that ended, "I want it inscribed on my gravestone that poor
as I sometimes was I never once took a nickel from Joseph
Kennedy or Howard Hughes." He had been poor enough to be
proud.

Many children of once-poor parents punish them with their

pride. Unable to be truly poor, we still live proudly in walk-ups, take no money for extras, and make do with only our trust funds. *Better yourselves!* say our parents. Our cry is *Downgrade!**

•

The best restaurant in Málaga was empty. All was ready, but there were no diners. It was empty of all but the waiters' impeccable courtesy. Nothing we wanted on the menu was ready in the kitchen. We had to make do with omelettes and *jamón serrano* and cheese. Our conversation faltered. Once again, anger and boredom and disappointment loomed. Then behind us a noisy party of English-speaking people came in.

"Ben! What the *fuck* are *you* doing here?"

An important voice! It was Orson Welles.

---

* A consequence of this was that for a long time I found that only the seedy was sexy. In Paris I lunched at the Grand Véfour (three stars) but repaired afterwards to the Hôtel de Beaujolais which lacked the amenities of a kennel. In London likewise: luncheon at Claridge's, afterwards the decrepit Russell Hotel in faraway Russell Square.

SPLEEN

RADIOS · *CONTINENTAL ARMS*
MY BAVARIA · *ERNESTA*
ENFANT PERDU

RADIOS   I was hired to work for the CIA by a Captain Merle
Dankbloom in Munich. 1958. That winter, Hungarian refugees
still walked in the Englischer-garten. Serious, handsome, whole
families: their children at their blithest looked worried and
nicotine-stained. The Hungarian Revolution of 1956 was the first
political event of which I felt wholly conscious. It was also the
first where I saw the effects of American foreign policy.

One afternoon I passed a shape, large, active and white, in the
bushes. It made a funny noise. My mind was on Sabina's best
friend. LeAnne lived across the Isar. Mostly we met at LeAnne's
house before her small son got home. However, on that day we
were to meet in Schwabing at my pension.

"*Frau* Göhmann, a lady is coming for tea."

"Very well, *Herr;* I'll change the sheets."

Munich, Germany, Europe: all so well made for adultery.

A man in the park crossed my path. Casually. He crossed my
path again. He held a lady's bag up against the short pinkish
topcoat he wore. So I'd recognize him when I saw him again?
How very soon that would be! At the Cuvilliés-theater, then at
the Haus der Kunst; at the long delayed German opening of
Chaplin's *The Great Dictator* . . . Who was he? Who was he? And
where did he sleep?

In that topcoat (known as a "British warm"), in ski clothes, in
evening dress . . . So that when at last we were introduced
("Merle Dankbloom, Ben Sonnenberg"), at a party in Bogen-
Hausen for refugee relief, I knew all about his wardrobe and he
knew all about mine.

And that shape in the bushes taking a leak? "Oh, that !" Coarse
laugh from an epicene throat. "My Voice of America girlfriend!"

Another true American voice (Midwestern academic) was that
of our host. He ran the Institut für Zeitgeschichte and *occupied* a
large rented house. (I stress "occupied.") Practically every-

one else there worked for one of the radios. VOA or RFE (Voice of America, Radio Free Europe); Radio Liberation (now Radio Liberty). That night our host seemed to be saying, *For once we're acting well.*

For once and *at last.* For acting on behalf of the U.S. government, all the American radios had at least nursed the revolution. And then? . . . The revolution had taken place, America had held back. Many at the radios took the blame on themselves for the revolution having failed. Truly, they blamed themselves. Now, then, how good to be giving aid, to be individuals; to counter the local atmosphere of savage frustration and guilt; to be free of such vengeful passions as their cynical bosses had had to exploit; not to be numb, to be humane; above all, to clothe those they couldn't have spared. . . . They gave voluptuously. Coming round to collect, our hostess would say, "It doesn't count till it hurts." She too worked for the Institut.

Each such house had a "den." There, in spiffy shoes, Merle Dankbloom made his pitch.

But first came LeAnne. Squeezing my hand, she led me back to the party. To where her husband Lynn (he worked for Radio Liberation) was talking to a middle-aged-looking young couple. Meanwhile LeAnne kept squeezing my hand. Her own was very cool. From her wanting to show she herself was cool, a cool hand, cool in the extremity; and from her clutching glasses with ice, palpable, also noisy and convenient, symbols of home. Holding onto my hand (her right hand, my left): too triumphant a sign to overlook, too tepid a one to provoke: LeAnne introduced her friends. Real Bavarians, the von Schons. Not minions of the U.S. she implied; like her husband and everyone else.

Back in the den, Merle Dankbloom was gazing at his shoes. They had buckles on them. He looked all at once very sinister in his vanity of detail. He took out his notecase and showed me one one-dollar bill. Its serial number had something to do with how you knew who he was. Eighteen months, he said, and in return I'd get out of the draft. Really? So Captain Dankbloom declared. Eighteen months working for the Company (as he called the CIA). I thought, no having to undress with men, older and longer schlonged. Yes, but doing what? And why me? Also I'd get a gun. Why me, though? Not that I asked. I was too vain.

And the offer made sense: an infidel business to go with my incurably infidel life.

True, to hear Captain Dankbloom was to indulge a puerile prospect of pleasure (I knew this even then) where others would be fixed by my secrets, where personal habits like lying would change into professional skills. Beyond that, however, as being pronounced then and there, in a faithless epoch and in a dishonored city; as coming to me in a manner so manly and special and chic, Merle Dankbloom's offer not only made sense. It was inevitable. In fact, it was everything I'd always known certain Jews could expect: in particular from the CIA, then beginning its degeneration from aristocratic plaything to everyday thing of use.

For in common with very many my age, not yet twenty-two, who read novels and went to the movies and grew up with money and art, I understood the CIA, for a time in the 1950s, as a shape of the nineteenth century, saying to youth in the words of Balzac's Vautrin: *No principles, only events.* Working for the CIA, even as "a contract employee," would finesse the question of what exactly my politics were.

LeAnne again, as I go. "Tomorrow night. Lynn's driving again to the border. OK? At your place. All night." Small frown. "If you want." No, I said, I'd much rather drive with Lynn into Austria and say to the refugees, *Go back.* "Are you being serious?" No, I said. No.

CONTINENTAL ARMS   Merle Dankbloom gave me a number to phone in New York if I wanted to work for the Company. Wasn't I going home? Very soon; to show off. (But how did he know?) For example, at Christmastime in New York, me to my mother and father (*very* cruel, *very* serves-you-right): ". . . people I now know, related to the Franz von Papens. . . ."

Self-exiled son of a self-made man, I went home now and then to draw blood.

I phoned the number from a phone in the Hotel St. Regis barbershop. I was given another number in Munich for when I got back. I walked over to Continental Arms, down the avenue from the St. Regis. I bought a "Chief's Special" revolver. The transaction was thrilling, muscular with equipment and craftsmanship. Its high point was hearing I needed a custom-made holster. I went to a special gunsmith west of Broadway, in the Forties: Chick Something-or-other, said to be the best holsterman in town. Unfriendly and fat, as became someone met on a slumming visit like mine, he showed me a letter. It was from the Havana Chief of Police: about how when arresting a suspect they had overlooked a wee holster Chick made, and two Havana policemen were killed, and the Chief of Police was writing to say, "¡Caramba! what a swell holster!"

I bought one, too; a small cartridge case; also a second holster that fit on my belt. Wanting Chick to smile (if not like me), I said, very man-to-man, "You realize most of my trousers are made only for suspenders?"

And fat, and with a holster of fantastic size over his ass: containing a long-barreled Colt of the kind called a Peacemaker, I believe: after a very long pause, Chick said (man-to-man, indeed!), "When you wear a gun, you dress for the gun."

Whenever I wore it, I felt I was strapping on a politics, too. Not the politics of America and the CIA, but those of a Dissident.

MY BAVARIA   Egon von Schon was American on his mother's side. His father was half American; Harvard 1909. During the Second World War, Egon served in the American army. There he'd had just one assignment: to be his father's jailer. Egon's father, Ernst (known as "Tui") von Schon, was infamous for his early support of the Nazi party. Then he became anti-Hitler in 1942. Arrested by the FBI, on a visit to the Warren Wampum, Seniors, in Bar Harbor, Maine, the summer before, Tui went from a federal prison to a comfortable sort of internment as an analyst for the U.S. Army Air Force, living in Bethesda, outside Washington. "It seemed I could tell exactly what Herr Goebbels intended the Allies to think," Tui wrote in his long, immodest book, My Own Struggle [Mein Eigen Kampf], after the war. "According to General George C. Marshall, my instincts about propaganda were 'miraculous and uncanny.' "

After the war Egon married and taught history at Columbia. His wife had gone to Smith. She was a magazine editor. Libby Sawyer, a plain intelligent girl who wasn't "exactly poor." They

owned a house in Stockbridge; they lived on the Upper West
Side. Yet all at once they pulled up stakes and settled in Germany. Now Libby worked for the family business: art-book publishers. It was a fine old prosperous house, including a bookshop
and art gallery, like the one in *"Gladius Dei,"* Thomas Mann's
story of Munich. Egon was now its director.

One afternoon Egon visited me at the radio. On the very spot
where the airfield had been: the porch, as it were, of the Munich
Pact: Oberweisenfeld. Things were getting back to normal.
Homes in the States had been found for most, if not all, of the
refugees; my affair with LeAnne had ended; I had a new girlfriend, a manicurist at the Vier Jahreszeiten hotel barbershop. I
owed lots of money, mostly for clothes; my trust fund was down;
I was thinking about getting married.

Egon disliked me and I disliked him. Still, he would talk, I
would listen. People Egon's age were susceptible to exactly that
kind of aggression; especially Germans craving a ceremony of
judgment. I also liked it that while Egon's path was longer and
stranger than mine, where they crossed it was with an eerie fit.
On the one side, Egon's insistence upon heading the family business; whereas, in his father's Munich, in the 1920s and 1930s, the
von Schons had been the wellspring of social connections for
Hitler, "old" money for the Nazis, and for once (as it seemed to
all then) *effective* polite respect. On the other side, my stress upon
beheading my family, so to speak; upon annulling my father's
career of "responsible" party politics.

Egon would talk of being a child, nine and ten and eleven years
old, when he played in the Munich Brown House or the Berlin
Reichskanslei. Hitler was good with children, Egon was that kind
of child.

"Hitler could mimic machines."

"You don't say?"

We were standing in front of a console in one of the studios.
They were transcribing a speech by President Eisenhower for
transmission to Eastern Europe.

"Practically *any* machine."

"Is that so?"

They were dubbing in applause. Where was the sound-effects
record from? Egon wanted to know. Yes, the applause record:

where was it from? They handed Egon the box. It read: "European Applause. *Reichsparteitag*. Nürnberg, 1934."

Egon said, "And they suppose that the Czechs and Ukranians won't recognize that kind of applause."

ERNESTA   Egon's American mother was a true high-toned managing matron of the Ethel Barrymore stamp. She "answered" to no one, as they used to say.

"Good evening, Ernesta."

"Missus von Schon to you."

Ernesta was one of just two women whom Hitler had wanted to marry. Cultivated enough, ladylike enough; beautiful and aristocratic. *Zu zehr kultiviert*, Hitler says of her in the *Table Talk*. So very cultivated.

Old women for whom famous men once burned were fascinating to me; like those rare books of which true collectors feel, according to Walter Benjamin in an essay dear to me, merely to buy and possess them is to give dead authors new life. I had once struggled hard to befriend an exceedingly boring old woman just because someone had told me that she had been the mistress of Maxim Gorky and H. G. Wells. "His penis was short but very thick," she said of Wells, "and it smelled of honey."

Ernesta had been all alone in the house on the night of the Munich *Putsch*. Hitler burst in and threw himself down in the drawing room at her feet. "The revolt has failed, Ludendorff is in jail— . . . Where is your husband?"

"On business, downtown."

She saw Hitler's arm was broken, his clothing was dirty and torn, he said he was wanted by the police. It was the ninth of November, 1923.

"He took out a big revolver and handed it to me."

Now Ernesta came to the part she liked best, with its apt effect of needless-to-say. " *'Shoot me!'* he cried. *'I'm a failure!'* . . . And I didn't."

ENFANT PERDU   My job had been mainly to help decide who of the many refugees should go where in America. I did this from English translations of interrogations conducted by U.S. Army or Air Force Intelligence. I was also supposed to stay alert for possible agents of AVO, the Hungarian secret police. Every two weeks I was paid in cash: twice in dollars and once in marks. At the end of six weeks, I was fired, having let through to San Diego a zookeeper named Szabo. I myself had questioned him with an interpreter in the room. Szabo had made no bones about working for AVO, declaring to me that he had also been reporting to the Cultural Freedom people. Szabo didn't tell me, though, that both he and his wife were agents of the KGB as well.

I left promptly for London, telling myself that I was like the "Enfant Perdu" of Heine's famous poem.

> *Verloner Posten in dem Freiheitskriege,*
> *Hielt ich seit dreißig Jahren treulich aus.*

[I fought to hold positions that were lost
In Freedom's war for thirty faithful years.]

The puzzle to me at the time was not that our government had hired an incompetent like me (no Magyar, little German). Nor even why I'd been paid in cash by the same U.S. Army historian at whose house I had met the von Schons. But rather why Merle Dankbloom was with me on the plane.

And why he was seated next to the Lisbon art collector, Carlos Cudell-Goetz.

> *Ein Posten ist vakant!—Die Wunden klaffen—*
> *Der Eine fällt, die Andern rücken nach—*
> *Doch fall ich unbesiegt, unde meine Waffen*
> *Sind nicht gebrochen—Nur mein Herze brach.*

[My wounds are gaping wide—A post's unmanned!—
One sentry falls, another takes his part—
And yet I fall unvanquished, sword in hand—
The only thing that's broken is my heart.][1]*

---

* Translated by Hal Draper.
NOTE: LeAnne, as noted, is Not Her Real Name; Lynn also is NHRN. Ernesta, Egon, and Ernst ("Tui") von Schon: these aren't Real Names. Neither is Libby Sawyer. Merle Dankbloom isn't a Real Name, of course, but I didn't make it up.

SPLEEN AND IDEAL

*My Politics • The Wit and Proprieties of the English
Are Known to But a Few • A Pleasant Little
Collection • I Hit Her, I Struck Her
The Horror! The Horror! • "I'll Marry You if You Want
Me To . . ." • La Consula
Ronda • Victor • "I Feel Free!"*

MY POLITICS I said to Merle Dankbloom, "Carlos Cudell-Goetz took me to hear Amalia Rodriguez sing fado." We were sitting in an office in a building in North Audley Street. "He wears two gold watches on his left wrist." I was sure this meant something sinister.

"Come and tell Ira Rich," Merle Dankbloom said. He was wearing a suit of cashmere and tweed. (Not too soft for the seat? I wanted to say but didn't.) I was wearing a brown tweed herringbone, from Henry Poole.

"Tell Ira Rich about Lisbon," Merle Dankbloom said to me. Ira Rich was one of those hard-soft types you saw in our Foreign Service then, young-old, blond-bald. He wore good-bad clothes and smoked a Barling pipe.

"Who is Amalia Rodriguez? What is fado?"

"Fado? The blues of Portugal." I tried not to hide my contempt. "Amalia Rodriguez is their Billie Holiday."

"I'm not much on popular music," said Ira Rich. "I like Oistrakh, Richter, Gilels. . . ." Of course you do, I thought, all being victims of Stalin.

Merle Dankbloom said, "Tell Ira Rich about the sculpture."

"Italian bronzes, Gothic madonnas, African sculptures, South Seas—"

"What sort of African sculptures? Bakuba? Bambara? Benin?"

I didn't know. I said, "Do you know the story about the family that inherits an oil painting of Uncle George? They have it cleaned and find underneath a portrait by Sargent. They clean the Sargent and find a Rembrandt underneath. And under the Rembrandt, a Leonardo. They keep on cleaning till under the Leonardo they find—a portrait of Uncle George!"

A pause filled by pipe tobacco smoke. My Mixture (Alfred Dunhill) from me. Mixture 79 from Ira Rich.

Out on the street I said to Merle Dankbloom, "Not much of a sense of humor, I guess."

"Ira Rich? Yes, he can sometimes be a little humorless. But, you see, Carlos Cudell-Goetz isn't just a collector."

Merle Dankbloom and I stood in North Audley Street. I looked north towards Oxford Street, he looked south towards Grosvenor Square.

"Not just a collector?"

"No. He makes pedestals." Now he looked north and I looked south. "Many, many public statues in Lisbon have his pedestals."

"Yes, I wondered at how many statues there are in Lisbon," I said. At long last I was in London, more or less where I wanted to be, smoking my pipe and dressed more or less as I wanted to be dressed, and listening to pipe-smoking men, pretending I understood. But weren't they fools? And wasn't I making a fool of myself?

"Most of the statues have pedestals by Carlos Cudell-Goetz. And," Merle Dankbloom looked down, I was looking up, "his pedestals are going in large numbers to Bissau." I pretended I understood. After a pause Merle Dankbloom said, "Ira Rich wants to know what your politics are."

"Tell him, Left-Wing Infantile." I was quoting Lenin. "Extreme positions loosely held." I was quoting A. J. P. Taylor, I think.

"I told him you were an artist," Merle Dankbloom said. Which meant he thought my politics were those of a ruling-class lackey? Merle Dankbloom looked at his watch. "I'm late for my fencing lesson. Do you want to work for us again?"

I watched him walk towards Grosvenor Square, admiring how high cut the vents on his jacket were. I hadn't said yes and I hadn't said no, and I hadn't told him about Senhor Benslimon and the pass he made at me. In point of fact, I wondered when and if Merle Dankbloom would make a pass, and I thought, "And what are *your* politics?" If mine were an artist's, then his were those of a broker, a panderer. Which was worse? "Tell him I am a Man of the Left," I said aloud. People turned my way. I had on suede gloves and a soft brown hat and was leaning on an unbrella (from Swaine). I didn't look like a Man of the Left.

THE WIT AND PROPRIETIES OF THE ENGLISH ARE KNOWN TO BUT A FEW.*   I was twenty-two when I got to London, with my small trust fund and high hopes. First, a literary career. And then, someone having told me that "there are only two or three men in London who really *like* women," I was also hoping to have my pick of the aristocratic young beauties I knew from the Sullys and Sargents that hung on the walls of 19 Gramercy Park. Meanwhile, until I met her: petulant, passionate, proud: to bring me out in London, I relied on the man I'm going to call Donald Maitland, an associate of my father's. He introduced me to his tailor in Dover Street, his bootmaker in Cork Street, and to his barber at Truefitt & Hill. He made me a temporary member of the Savile (where I shook hands with Cyril Ray, a famous wine writer, and glimpsed Peter Ustinov) and a permanent member of the Clermont Club, a casino, and White Elephant Club, a restaurant where actors and actresses went. He took me to a cocktail party at the *Spectator* magazine where he introduced me to Kenneth Tynan, among other journalists. When I next saw Kenneth Tynan, at an opening night, I greeted him as an old chum. "Ken!" I said, and he cut me dead.

One night a group of us were making fun of Maitland when our hostess, Elizabeth Ayrton, said:

"Well, as it happens, I *like* Maitland. I think he's awfully touching."

So we stopped. We'd gone for a nightcap to the Ayrtons' pied-à-terre in Fitzroy Street, after dinner at the Maitlands' house in Mayfair: Michael and Elisabeth Ayrton, my girlfriend Katherine and I.

Maitland was in advertising. He was paid lots of money but made it a point to tell you that he was "in the creative end." You met artists and writers at his house. Louis Le Brocquy, Selwyn Jepson. I once met the movie actress Ann Todd at a party there. She had starred in *The Seventh Veil*, with James Mason, in 1946. No one at the Maitlands' was "current": never Francis Bacon,

* John Dryden

never Graham Greene. Which made me wonder whether I ever would be "current" in London myself.

"I like Donald alright," Michael Aryton said, "but I don't much like him making me look down Gemma Maitland's dress."

"And," Elisabeth Aryton said, "I don't much like his looking down *my* dress, if it comes to that."

Maitland got drunk at his parties and threw his arm around you and pulled you over to his wife and made you look down her dress, saying, "The trouble with marriage is that the fucking you get isn't worth the fucking you get."

Katherine said (she worked for Maitland's firm and was also *in the creative end*), "I don't much like him making the girls at the office give him blow jobs after lunch." Everyone stopped and stared at her, so Katherine added, "I hear."

Well, as it happened, I *didn't* like Maitland. For one thing, he sent reports about me back to my father. For another, I owed him money, having let him pay some of my bills. And for a third, while to everyone else in London I was an exotic (I liked to pretend): the rich dark American Jewish heir to a fortune from borax, or steel, or rails: to Maitland I was only my father's son, "one of the very few young men lucky enough to be given one-eighth of a million dollars at the age of twenty-one," as he actually said to me once over lunch at The White Tower in Percy Street. He got drunk at lunch every day. "I'm no good in the afternoons," he'd say. He'd leer at the girl I was with and say, "I'm a *morning* man."

And, well, as it happened, I *liked* being made to look down Gemma Maitland's dress. She blushed a little, her scent came up; and distracted by the excesses of her very expensive frock, not to speak of her breasts (How not speak of her breasts?), I almost forgot about Katherine. I almost forgot how much money I owed Gemma's husband. One thousand pounds? Or two? How could I get her clothes off her and get her into bed? She'd tell me of the beastly things her husband had her do. Does he make you do *that?* She'd grow thoughtful, and ponder, and say, biting her lower lip, "No, I'd do *that*. If excited enough, I'd do any-thing. . . . Oh, but don't make me tell you everything. I don't want to lose *all* my self-respect."

Poor Gemma.

"Poor Gemma," Katherine was saying, "having to live in that house. What word best describes it? Chichi?"

"If *chichi* were not too robust," said Michael Ayrton, the painter and sculptor. The drawing room of the house was in greens, the dining room in reds, and the murals in the bedroom upstairs were by an art student who'd been told that what was wanted were Sydney Nolan colors and Reg Butler figures and an overall John Piper look, with portraits of their two pugs. Where exactly? " 'Oh, I leave that to you,' Donald will have said. " '*You* are the artist.' "

Michael Ayrton took him off beautifully.

•

No one in London liked anyone much. The longer they knew you, the more likely they were not to like you much. That was the London note. I aimed for it, but it's not easy to hit if you haven't been there long. For instance, I liked Michael Ayrton very much indeed. But everyone else had known Ayrton for years. First as the protégé of the painter Pavel Tchelitchew, then as the protégé of the composer Constant Lambert, then as the protégé of Wyndham Lewis (whose literary executor he was). "You are a careering shit," I once heard someone say to him. "If you want to be a painter, then paint, and don't spend your time running after famous people *to* paint."

"Look in his eyes," someone else said to me, "and you'll see he is dead." I had looked in his eyes and seen they were dull. Like ponds staled with algae, they gave back no light.

"Are you dead?" I said to Michael.

"As nail in door. Dead and forgotten," he said.

Everyone knew he was dying of a progressive hardening of the marrow in his spine. And everyone knew that *he* knew that he was a talented and disappointed man whose talent did not come across in his art but whose disappointment did. "Whenever they list British painters, they leave me off," he used to say. "Pasmore, Hamilton, Heron, Vaughan," he'd count them off on his fingers, "Bacon, Bratby, Le Brocquy (for chrissake!), but not me. I'm like the man at a theater bar unable to get a drink. The barman looks through me. . . ."

Later on in the sixties, Michael went on television. Everyone

found him to be a marvelous explainer and he was a success. No
surprise to those of us who knew his critical writings, collected in
Golden Sections, but a surprise to him, I believe. Michael came on
the screen with a scowl; he looked angry. Then he talked and he
wasn't angry. He talked about Berlioz, Inigo Jones, Kabirion
vases, or about the myth of Daedalus. He was obsessed with
Daedalus. He wrote a novel about him and built a maze for a
friend of my father's in the Catskills in New York State. The
following summer when I went to Greece, with another girlfriend, we joined up with the Ayrtons in Crete. He showed us
where the "original" maze had been. He knew such a tremendous
amount: about Knossos, the Minoans, the Mycenaeans, the Cy-
clades. When we drove with the Ayrtons to Phaestos and passed
Mount Ida, he told us such a tremendous amount about Zeus as
well. I remember that he kept using the word *numinous*.

Back in Athens, Michael got sick with hepatitis. I gave him a
small terra cotta of a satyr to cheer him up, and he later gave me
some drawings where that figure is dancing with a girl who looks
like my girlfriend. The figure has an erection. I ended our friendship over that. I was always looking for pretexts to end my
friendships then. The more profit I'd had, the more eager I was
for the friendship to end. I was always saying, *I know you all*, and
imitating the sun

> Who doth permit the base contagious clouds
> To smother up his beauty from the world,
> That when he please again to be himself,
> Being wanted, he may be more wond'red at . . .

Michael had once said to me that he had played Prince Hal in
his life many times to another man's Falstaff. Now he was playing Falstaff to my Prince Hal.

I saw him one more time after that, at a publishing party for
his Daedalus book. He was busily signing copies, but once he
looked up, and I saw that his eyes, merry with the lights of the
room, were no longer dead. Soon after that he died.

•

I dropped Katherine off at her mother's flat, in Bryanston
Square. When I got back to my own at Empire House, in the

Brompton Road, the band at the Rembrandt Hotel next door was winding up for the night. They were playing "For He's a Jolly Good Fellow." They played "For He's a Jolly Good Fellow" every Saturday night at two.

Katherine's father, the world-famous marimba player Maurice Swan, got into political trouble in the States sometime in the late forties. Someone in the American Legion called him a Communist, a concert of his was canceled, and he sued. He'd have won his case, my father said, if they'd kept him off the stand. But Maurice insisted on taking the stand; he made a speech and he lost. He and his family—Norma, his wife, and their children, Katherine, Christopher and Alice—left the States and settled in London. He'd always earned big money as an entertainer; in England, where he was known and esteemed as a serious musical artist, he earned less. And (worse) he was "MOR-ris" instead of "More-EESE."*

There were dozens of Americans in London with stories like Katherine father's. Displaced from California and New York by the blacklisting that followed the House and McCarthy committee hearings: screenwriters, movie directors, actors, designers and agents: they had earned millions in the States. Now they were living in London, some comfortable, all bitter. Occupations gone, they dwelt on appearances and keeping them up. Some had collections of paintings (they were the Hollywood Four Hundred and Ten): Schwitters, Matisse and Miró, Kandinsky, Kokoschka and Klee.

Katherine and I had gone out a few times, gone to bed a few times and then announced we were going to get married. (Well, after Sabina, what else could I do?) My parents and Katherine's were friends, old friends, and after the Swans were divorced, my father saw Norma Swan each time he came to London. I used to wonder if they'd conspired to set me and Katherine up. However that was, I bought Katherine a ring from M. Hakim, a jeweler in Shaftesbury Avenue: he told me the ring was Egyptian: and soon after that we broke up. Soon after that we were lovers again, and then we were friends, and then I married her younger sister. "As the French say," Katherine would say, *"Tout lasse, tout passe, tout*

---

* Maurice Swan is NHRN; Katherine, Norma, Christopher, and Alice are NRNs; "world-famous marimba player" is an invention.

se remplace." [All grows boring, all goes away, all replaces itself.]

When I first got to London people asked, "How come you stammer?": which I took to mean, Is that how you dodged the draft? Well, Henry James stammered, I used to reply, until once I overheard someone say that I was "the Jew-boy who acts Henry James."

But I hadn't been acting Henry James. I had been being British. I'd studied the British as sedulously as any wog in Cairo or Lahore. I was sure I knew their decorum better than the British themselves. I knew not to open my umbrella when it was raining unless I was with a woman; I knew not to whistle in the Burlington Arcade; I knew that if I wore a shirt with collar points which turned up, I was telling people that I was a left-wing intellectual (and I had several dozen shirts, from Hawes & Curtis, made so).

E. M. Forster says Italian is a language in which you can't condescend. English is a language in which it's hard to do anything else. That makes it good for insults. As Bernard Shaw says, it's impossible for an Englishman to open his mouth without giving mortal offense to some other Englishman. And on any subject whatever.

In London I learned to express myself with a sort of "innocent" anti-Semitism. It made me feel extra-British, and it let me pretend I was "as Jewish as I wanted to be." Why exactly I stopped had something to do with reading Jean-Paul Sartre, as well as with (to put it mildly) disillusionment with the British.

A PLEASANT LITTLE COLLECTION   Soon after my twenty-third birthday, I met Siriol Hugh-Jones. It was at the Maitlands'. Before dinner she and I talked about books, at dinner we talked about ourselves, after dinner we talked again about books, only now: *knowing* something of each other: we were flirting confidently. Next morning when I phoned her, it was as if we'd been talking all night.

"You won't remember what you said, but are you sure it's 'Cluff' and not 'Clow'?" We had been talking about the Victorian poet Arthur Hugh Clough.

"You never can tell with the English," she said, "and please remember I'm not English but Welsh, I heard a descendant of

Samuel Pepys being interviewed on the radio the other day and he said, sounding *very* cross, *It's Pep-is, not Peeps, it's always been Pep-is,* and before John Freeman interviewed him, Evelyn Waugh said, *It's Waw, not Wuff. I distinctly heard you say Wuff.* And what do you mean I won't remember? I very well remember my dreams, particularly the dreams that I know will end in tears . . . Anyway," she said, "I was on the point of ringing *you* to ask if you could come to supper on Thursday."

Siriol was in her early thirties. She was short and plain-featured, with short black hair, very far in looks from the fox-hunting beauty I was hoping to meet; very far even from the Gemma Maitland-type which I thought maybe I'd have to settle for. Yet when she and I talked, no one else in the room except Siriol existed.

She wrote me many letters, even when we were both in London and saw each other daily. When I was in Spain she wrote me two or three letters a day. To judge from them, and there're hundreds, from 1960 to 1964, I was always sending her flowers and books and presents for her small daughter, Emma. "How can I ever thank you?" she is always saying. We gave each other poems to read: "another important point of reference," we said. She paints herself in her letters as overwrought, "with too much to do and a spastic cat," and me as "mysterious" (always disappearing) and "magical" (always reappearing). It is late at night when she writes to me or very early in the morning. Her friends are always saying things about my "good manners" and my "good mind," and she flatters me by telling me how pleased and proud she is made by their praise: "but also a little cross." I am "dear child" in her letters. Ours was the very model of an *amitiée amoureuse.*

Her first letter to me was a postcard with *The Death of Chatterton* from the National Portrait Gallery on the back. "A man arrived here this morning with a bowl of freisias which Emma immediately assumed was for her. 'Didn't he send me the crayons?' Anyway, thank you, thank you. Please come to supper and meet Frankie. [This was Frank Hauser who ran the Oxford Playhouse.] Did you know that George Meredith posed for the figure of Chatterton? Did you know that the artist [G. F. Watts] ran off with Meredith's wife? Of course you did. You know everything."

She gave me a copy of *Modern Love*, something having come up that made the famous lines apposite:

> Then each applied to each that fatal knife,
> Deep questioning, which probes to endless dole.
> Ah, what a dusty answer gets the soul
> When hot for certainties in this our life!

Very soon she was like a figure from Meredith's novels for me, like Laetitia Dale in *The Egoist*, always keeping me from excesses, correcting my social errors, objectifying my girlfriends with phrases like "little rogue in porcelain"; masking her feelings with levity.

Giving presents was an art I learned from my father. Practiced by me with Siriol, it was, as with all forms of bribery, a kind of sadistic test as well, meant, at least at the beginning, to discover whether she could be enthralled. With Siriol it was easy: "given my well-known weakness for complicated and difficult men with dark hair and dark eyes, and your eyes slope down." Buying something for her, I would have in mind a phrase from "The Beast in the Jungle" where James says of the birthday present John Marcher buys every year for May Bartram that he was regularly careful to pay for it a little more than he could afford.

My circumstances were as follows: I spent half the year in the south of Spain, writing stories and hiding from my creditors. I had many girlfriends in London and two in Munich. My trust fund was now down twenty-five or thirty thousand dollars. I owed money to the tailors, Kilgour, French & Stanbury, Hawes & Curtis, Anderson & Shephard and H. Huntsman & Sons; to the florist, Edward Goodyear; the wineseller, Berry Bros. & Rudd; the tobacconist, Robert Lewis; and the shirtmakers, A. Sulka and Turnbull & Asser. I owed money to my bootmaker, C. J. Cleverly; to my booksellers, Bumpus, Heywood Hill and Blackwells; and to the theater ticket agents, H. J. Adams. I also owed money to the White Tower restaurant, Prunier's and Wilton's, not to mention the (by now) three or four thousand pounds I owed Donald Maitland. This last debt had to be paid in full, according to the peculiar code spelled out by Vronsky in Chapter XX, Part II of *Anna Karenina*. But when? Tradesmen could wait, but personal debts, like gambling losses and money owed your club, not that I had one, apparently had to be paid at once. On the question of lying, the code was not clear. Never lie to your friends, except husbands. Was Maitland a friend?

Siriol's circumstances were as follows: she and Emma lived at 5 Pembroke Studios, W.8. Emma's father lived there, too. He worked for the BBC and came in late at night and was away on weekends. I assumed they had an arrangement. Siriol wrote an advice column for the *Evening Standard*, "Ask Aspasia"; book reviews for the *Tatler* and articles for *Punch* and *Vogue*, where she had been features editor. She had gone with Norman Parkinson to "shoot" Edith Sitwell and with Anthony Armstrong-Jones to "shoot" the dancer Robert Helpmann. She told me that Spike Milligan (she'd met Spike Milligan!) had a silver frame on his piano with an eight-by-ten glossy of Jesus Christ, signed "To Spike, A swell guy, Love, Jesus."

Siriol said we couldn't sleep together, because it would jeopardize her divorce. Did I want to sleep with Siriol? I offered to once or twice when I was sure I'd be turned down. It was enough for me to feel I had only to crook a finger and Siriol would give up everything and come with Emma and live with me.

.

We went to the Merwins' for dinner one night. Bill and Dido Merwin lived near Primrose Hill. I'd told Siriol of my admiration for Merwin's *Green with Beasts*. It was one of a handful of books of American poetry I'd brought with me. (Others were *Life Studies* by Robert Lowell, *Heart's Needle* by W. D. Snodgrass and *Homage to Mistress Bradstreet* by John Berryman.) Siriol and Bill were friends from her days on *Vogue*.

Dido Merwin met us at the door. She was upset with the basement tenants. "They just had a baby and they weren't supposed to. It's in the lease."

"How inconsiderate of them," Siriol said.

"Yes," Dido said. "Well, they promised not to do it again."

With me and Siriol, there were the Merwins and Sylvia Plath and her husband, Ted Hughes, whose *The Hawk in the Rain* was another book of poems I admired. "There's almost no trace of Bill in the house," Siriol had said, "no wet raincoat hanging on the

back of the door, no pipe ashes, nothing. . . ." I was jealous of
Siriol's friends, and so I wrote in my notebook: with satisfaction,
no doubt: that at home Bill seemed "a sometimes very good,
sometimes very bad and always very precocious eleven-year-old
boy, vain of his goodness, of his badness, and of his charm and
intelligence." I told Bill I had been reading "Bartleby the Scriv-
ener," thinking he had something of Bartleby's "mulish vagary,"
and he asked me if I remembered the passage beginning *I was
thunderstruck* which he then quoted. I was annoyed by that, thinking, *Much as I like the story, I don't know it so well.*

Ted Hughes was tall and rough-featured and dark, with a dark
baritone voice. I never met anyone I admired so much who was
at the same time so approachable. I wrote in my notebook that
meeting him I felt like Hazlitt meeting Coleridge for the first
time: bowled over by his warmth and energy. Listening to him,
I did in fact fall off my chair. When he helped me up from the
floor, I wrote in my notebook, "He didn't stop talking and I felt
the vibration of his voice running down his arm." I asked Ted
about some detail in his poem "The Casualty," the handkerchief
perhaps, sure he would be flattered and impressed by my interest. He answered as though *why* I had asked didn't count and that
flattered and impressed me.

Sylvia was pregnant. She and Ted left soon after dinner. Dido
said something unkind about them and boasted of how good she
and Bill were being to them.

Siriol said to me later, "When Missus Darling sees Peter Pan
for the first time, Barrie says (this is in the novel), 'He was a
lovely boy, clad in skeleton leaves and the juices that ooze out of
trees; but the most entrancing thing about him was that he had all
his first teeth.' I love Bill and wouldn't change a leaf the dear boy
is clad in, but he *does* count on women being entranced by the
sight of his first teeth. And when he sees we are grown-ups, he
gnashes 'the little pearls' at us."

I wouldn't change a leaf he's clad in and *He gnashed his little pearls:*
these became catchphrases with us.

I saw quite a lot of Bill Merwin in London in those days,
always with great profit. We went once to the Greenwich Ob-
servatory Museum. On the way we noticed the gulls on the
Thames and he told me to which species the different gulls be-

longed. At the museum he spoke to me of the teredo worm and
how it ate the wooden planking of ships. I learned the words
gimbal and *widdershins* from Bill Merwin that day.

•

Peter and Wendy, J. M. Barrie's great satirical novel of 1911,
written seven years after the stage success of Peter Pan, was
Siriol's guide to England and the English, as well as to much else.
Laurence Olivier had told her (she said) that he longed to play
Captain Hook but despaired of ever finding an actress to play
Peter. His ideal was Jean Forbes-Robertson, the first Peter and
Barrie's favorite, the only one to have been truly "gay and innocent and *heartless*" (Olivier's emphasis), which are the last words
of the book. The daughter of the great Forbes-Robertson, she
was a notorious drunk. At the end of Act III, Peter is stranded on
the island, the waters are rising, he sees he will soon be sub-
merged. The curtain line is: *To die will be an awfully great adventure*, which Jean Forbes-Robertson uttered and dove straight off
into the water.

A part of the novel Siriol particularly liked is where Wendy
says, *trying to speak firmly:* "Peter . . . what are your exact feelings
for me?" And Peter says, "Those of a devoted son, Wendy." And
Barrie writes: " 'I thought so,' she said, and went and sat by
herself at the extreme end of the room."

That passage, so often cited, reflects the roles that Siriol as-
signed to us. I accepted mine readily, glad to be *gay and innocent
and heartless* with her, and to *gnash my little pearls* at her.

•

Siriol had been to Oxford; Somerville College, I think. Once
when I was in Oxford I went and had tea with John Bryson, a
teacher she often spoke of. Tea was at his apartment, which I
found quite luxurious. He owned a Degas drawing, a Cézanne
watercolor, and a number of Picasso etchings. He wore "the
softest-colored, most buttery tweeds," Siriol used to say. He told
me that he played the harpsichord and took lessons from Ernst
Gombrich's mother-in-law, who (I think he said) was the daughter of Fritz Busch. In a small oval frame, on a table near his
fireplace, was an Elizabethan miniature, the portrait of a languid

young man leaning against a tree. "Is that a Nicholas Hilliard?"
I said.

"Apparently it is," Bryson said. He told me he had bought it
for five or six pounds from an antiques shop in Portsmouth during the war. "How sad I was that morning," he said. "I'd seen a
young friend off on his ship the evening before. . . . Then I took
the little picture to the V and A and they told me that it was a
Hilliard. Leslie Hotson was here the other day. And he told me
that it was a portrait of Mister W. H."

"How amazing," I said. The question of the identity of Mr.
W. H., to whom Shakespeare dedicates the Sonnets, has eluded
scholars for centuries. Leslie Hotson, the author of *I, William
Shakespeare* (among many other works), had not yet published his
own *Mr. W. H.* "How on earth did he know?"

Bryson replied, "I didn't think it polite to ask."

"Divine understatement!" I said to Siriol later. "How I wish I
could say things like that."

Siriol said, "I much prefer your Russian style."

•

I gave Siriol dinner one night, at my flat in Empire House, and
read her "The Beast in the Jungle" aloud. She was crying quietly
towards the end, which was the effect I intended. Afterwards she
wrote me, "Dear child, you must be wary of reading aloud to
lonely women, especially after giving them so much good wine to
drink. Do you know a poem by A. Marvell called 'Mourning'?"

I looked the poem up. (We were always doing this.)

> How wide they dream! The *Indian* Slaves
> That sink for Pearl through Seas profound,
> Would find her Tears yet deeper Waves
> And not of one the bottom sound.

This moved me greatly, but "don't call me *Dear child*" was all
I said to her on the phone.

"What do you want me to call you?"

"*Ancient Person*," I said, "as in the Rochester poem."

"Which I cannot call *instantly* to mind but shall at once look
up." After which, in her letters, I was "Ancient Person of My
Heart."

Just before I was leaving for Spain, soon after our first meeting, she said, "I think I'm falling in love with you and I mustn't." How was I to know that she'd be in love only so long as I was away, only so long as I had girlfriends?

Obtuse! obtuse! . . .

•

From "Ask Aspasia":

I am really very fond of girls, of whom I now have quite a pleasant little collection.

I like their dear little voices and the tiny thoughts that sometimes wander through their minds and the way they trudge along behind one, carrying one's shopping so uncomplainingly in their little baskets. I make their lives so agreeable with a posy of flowers here, a telephone call there, and they are always grateful and pleased.

Sometimes I think I should settle for one and give the rest away to good homes. I have been leading this philanthropic life for some years now, and am beginning to wonder if it is not taking up too much of my time and energy.

Clovis D., W.1

No, absolutely not, dear child, you must press on in your enchanting, kindly way, bringing sunshine and happiness all round, I don't doubt. There being in England only about a dozen men—some now flagging slightly—who actually like women, no woman would be so unreasonable as to expect more than a modest share of your time and attention.

I took this to be about me. Siriol put up with my girlfriends, delighted in my vanity (I thought), and repaid my selfishness with compliments. Even when I had a romance with one of her best friends, even when I began sleeping with another of her best friend's daughters.

Siriol wrote me that she had cancer. When I next saw her, she'd moved to a house in Addison Avenue, W.11, with Emma and Emma's father. I saw I had been supplanted. A new "complicated and difficult man" was there in a chair by the window, and he had dark hair. Someone new to quote to from *Modern*

Love? Someone new to whom Siriol could say, *It will all end in tears?*

I can well believe now that then I made reflections such as these, drowned as I was in a deluge of vanity.

I HIT HER, I STRUCK HER   I met Sally Belfrage in the spring of 1961. We were both twenty-four. There were more men in Sally's life than there were women in mine. I was most bothered by this when we were at her house in Talbot Square. Men phoning up, dropping in, coming round; journalists, screenwriters, diplomats; back from Bulawayo, off to Macao. Sally made friends of her lovers; that really bothered me. The ex-speed-skating champion of North Korea, once a lover, was now a friend. Some lovers were friends and then lovers again. Some lovers never were friends.

I was still angry with Sally when we were at my place, in Ebury Street.* One morning she said something to me, I don't know what. And I struck her, I hit her across her breasts. What could she have said?

To make it up to her, I said, "Where in the world do you most want to go? And who with?"

"Berlin," Sally said. "And with you," she said.

And so to Berlin.

Sally had been given some names by Kenneth Tynan, then beginning his campaign on behalf of Brecht and his theater, and I had been given some names by Melvin Lasky, the editor of *Encounter,* a magazine subsidized by the CIA. From West Berlin we took the U-Bahn to East Berlin and saw the Berliner Ensemble in *Arturo Ui.* Another day we went and stood at the graves of Bertolt Brecht and Rosa Luxemburg. We went to a famous *Traviata* at the Komische Oper, in East Berlin, where the guests at the party in Act III behaved like capitalists in drawings in the *Masses.* Sally took me to meet a British journalist named John Peet. He had once been the Reuters bureau chief in Berlin and now worked for the East German government. He spoke about

---

*Actually, my block of flats was in Cundy Street, at the foot of Eaton Terrace. No one liked saying "Cundy Street"; once someone wrote above it on the street sign "Fulking and."

Walter Schellenburg, Himmler's Intelligence Chief, and Count
Bernadotte, assassinated in Palestine in 1948 by the Stern Gang,
no one knew why. But John Peet knew. He had been a British
soldier in Palestine at the time. He called the assassins "Ben
Gurion's people."

We had come to John Peet through Sally's father, the journalist Cedric Belfrage, who had co-founded the *National Guardian*, a
left-wing newspaper, in New York City after the war. Belfrage
was then expelled from the States as "an undesirable alien." I felt
at a disadvantage with Sally where politics was concerned; her
father's experience alone gave her much authority; and so we
stayed off the subject.

In West Berlin I took Sally to meet a journalist who was a
stringer for *Time* and CBS. "I'll be carrying a copy of *Encounter*,"
he said, "so you'll know who I am." He spoke to us about music.
He was rumored to be working for the CIA. Many in the CIA
spoke about music and art as he did, as though the Cold War
came down to the question of how our governments treated pianists like Sviatoslav Richter. Sally and I went to a nightclub,
Jack Bilbo's, where the theme was Chicago in the twenties. A
naked girl acted Al Capone. In "The St. Valentine's Day Massacre" she pointed a tommy gun at the audience and mowed us
down.

I said, "I feel better in East Berlin."

"You mean you prefer *The Resistible Rise of Arthur Ui* to 'The St.
Valentine's Day Massacre.' What a surprise," Sally said. A political argument threatened; I shut up. But there was something
I wanted to talk about, and if not with Sally, with whom? I
preferred to think of the Nazis as a coming together of capitalism,
to the function of which gangsters are necessary, as Brecht shows
in *Arturo Ui*. I didn't like thinking of the Nazis as an aberration
or gangsters as burlesque. It was also true that I despised West
Berlin for conforming to an America where there was no place for
someone like me, idle, rootless and mischievous. And I loved the
ideal of a society like East Germany's, where I supposed citizens
were protected impartially. I badly wanted to talk about this but
was afraid of sounding callow.

The day we were leaving, John Peet phoned and asked if he
and I could have drinks. We met in the Kempinski bar. He asked

where I lived in Spain. "Málaga," I said. "How did you know I live in Spain?" Did I know about the PAIGC? Did I know about Amilcar Cabral? Did I know where Bissau was? As it happens, I do know where Bissau is, I said. Bissau was one of the places in West Africa where Carlos Cudell-Goetz was sending his pedestals.

"In very large numbers, they said," I said.

"So they know," John Peet said to himself. They know what? And what did the "pedestals" mean? John Peet explained to me only that Amilcar Cabral was the leader of the anticolonial forces in Portuguese Guinea, the *Partido Africano da Independéncia da Guiné e Cabo Verde* (the PAIGC). He did say that public statues, of the kind Carlos Cudell-Goetz built pedestals for, were desperate manifestations of a dying colonial power.

I said, "And where did you fight in Spain?"

He said, "How did you know I fought in Spain?" From Sally, but I didn't tell him. "Ronda," I thought he answered me, "and Albacete."

Sally came in then. She looked excited. "You'll never guess who I saw in the lobby."

"Paul Robeson?" John Peet said to Sally.

"Paul Robeson is in Berlin?" I said.

"No," Sally said. "Marcel Marceau."

•

Back in London, I told Sally I wanted to go to Greece. I didn't want to go with her, afraid of becoming too attached, but we went together anyway. In Athens I chartered a yacht. Not a yacht really, a caïque. I was seasick as soon as we stepped on board. We sailed to Naxos and I was seasick. To Delos; I was seasick. We were stuck for days by bad weather in the harbor at Siphnos. I was seasick and it was all costing too much and I was running out of poems to recite.

"You sure know a lot of 'em," Sally said.

"So when they throw me in prison—"

"They'll never throw you in prison."

"Why not?"

They threw everyone else in prison. Why wouldn't they imprison me? Politically speaking, was my story to be a version of

"The Beast in the Jungle"? Was I to be the John Marcher of my time, *the* man to whom nothing on earth was to happen? Was I never to hear the cell door shut, never to see the greasy patch high on my cell wall, flecked with bloodstains of squashed mosquitoes, with the message scratched on it, "I shall not again see this world"? And my stint with the CIA: here I told Sally about Merle Dankbloom: did that count for nothing?

And why was Sally laughing?

When we got back to Piraeus we went to a bar and held hands and watched a young American couple I knew from Paris dancing the tango. They were Steven and Toby Schneider who lived in a big apartment in the *7eme* where they employed a chef. Steve was only a year or two older than I. Yet he knew all there was to know about Bordeaux wines and the Classification of 1855. Toby was a modern dancer, and I understood she had money. She had studied with Merce Cunningham and danced at the Judson Church in New York. She and Steve had been childhood sweethearts. Everyone in the bar applauded when they stopped dancing. Sally and I applauded too.

Steve and Toby came over to our table and sat down. Someone had once called Toby "the Buster Keaton of modern dance." Offstage, too, she looked snooty and cool; *auguste* is the term of art. Now she was sweating and looked excited. I tried not to look at her. Steve acted uneasy when I did. Would I ever know a woman I felt like that about? There was something violent in Steve, from which I didn't recoil.

In London I took rooms at a hotel in St. James's where I'd been told Henry James had stayed. I waited for my Alvis convertible which I had ordered some months before. When it came and we drove about London, people looked more at Sally than at the car or me.

I went to see the *Oresteia* at the Old Vic. I saw it again and again. The *Agamemnon* was gold and red, the *Libation Bearers* was gray and red, the *Eumenides* was white and gold. It was directed by Minos Volanakis, the sets and costumes were by Yolanda Sonnabend, the music by Elisabeth Lutyens. (All of them would soon become my friends.) The story of Orestes went straight to my heart. All in the story was just and unjust, as Nietzsche writes in *The Birth of Tragedy*, "equally justified in both." I fell in love with the actress who played Athena. Now I wanted to write plays like the *Oresteia*. No more *Dubliners*. No more Flaubert's *Trois Contes*. Now I wanted to dramatize, not narrate, and I began both to read things differently and to read different things.*

I left Sally in London and drove south. People stopped and stared at the car and me all the way to Málaga.

But what *had* she meant about prison? Yes, of course my secrets were cheap. Small change like the tips and items of the flacks and touts and runners who teemed in the gutters of my father's early career. And yes, such secrets must always be hoarded, jealously husbanded and discharged, always to petty advantage.

Did *they* know that? And was that why *they* wouldn't throw me in jail?

Spurned by the actress who played Athena, I grew lonely in Málaga and I asked Sally to come. When she stepped off the plane, men stared at her blond hair. She was wearing a stick pin that I'd given her. Men stared at her wide shoulders, narrow hips and long, well-shaped legs. I knew my life was going to fill up with people because of her, colorful noisy couples who quarreled and danced and drank.

•

One night we were going to a party at a house called La Consula. The house belonged to some people named Bill and Annie Davis.

"I don't really know who the Davises are. They are friends of the Tynans," Sally said.

"Ken Tynan, the world's largest rabbit."

"You're not jealous of Ken, too? There's no need."

"You're not going to wear that dress, I hope?"

"Yes, I am."

"No, you're not."

Yes, I am; no, you're not.

And I whipped the dress off her. I tore it off.

We picked up the Tynans at the Hotel Miramár. Ken and his

* The difference in my reading was that I stopped caring about realism. The different things I started to read began with the Dream Plays of Strindberg. August Strindberg became the one writer whose every work I felt I had to read.

wife, Elaine Dundy, had been quarreling, too. Ken broke Elaine's nose the day before.

"Who are the Davises?" I said.

"They know everyone," Ken said. "Hemingway stayed with them last year."

"Cyril Connolly was married to Annie Davis's sister, Jean Bakewell," Elaine said.

Ken said, "There's no one else *to* know down here."

Elaine said, "Ken quarreled with Hemingway, too. Didn't you, Ken?"

Ken told us that the quarrel had been over the wound some bullfighter had suffered. "He was saying it was two inches deep and I said Nonsense and he said it was two inches, he'd seen it, he'd stuck his fingers in it and I said I'd seen it too and he said I needed glasses and I got up to leave. 'Leaving before the check comes, Tynan, as usual? Where is your Parthian shot?' And I said, 'All I can say is, there are some men to whom two inches is important.' " Ken was a good mimic and like many people who stutter he spoke fluently when he was taking someone off. But this time he was so agitated that he stuttered badly when he said, "Leaving before the check, Tynan? Where is your Parthian shot?"

I said, "I don't go to bullfights."

Ken said, "They aren't sports events, you know. They are ritual sacrifices."

La Consula was a big white house with Doric columns along the front. It sat in a park on the road between Churriana and Alhaurín de la Torre, near the airport. As we approached, Elaine told us that when the Davises lived in Paris, Bill Davis had a rotten reputation. He used to get drunk and get into fights and was always going to brothels. Now people spoke of the Davises as if they were Gerald and Sara Murphy. They spoke of La Consula as if it were the Villa America and we were all on the Riviera with Scott and Zelda Fitzgerald.

That night at La Consula we spoke to Orson Welles and his wife, Paola Mori. Ken was telling Orson that he admired Alain Resnais' *L'Année Dernière à Marienbad.* "Then you are a cunt," Orson said to him. I was flirting with Paola Mori. She was beautiful and young, she told me that Orson often left her alone with their little daughter, Beatrice, and with Becky, Orson's daughter by Rita Hayworth. Ken was saying that he admired *L'Année Dernière* because of Orson's own films. "Then you are even more of a cunt," Orson said.

From the little I saw of them that evening, Bill and Annie Davis seemed a pleasant enough, middle-aged American couple. Bill Davis did not drink; I remember noticing that.

Sally soon went back to London. I went to Paris. My father was there. Sabina was there as well, and she and I went to bed together for the last time. I was always telling Sally about Sabina, but I didn't tell Sabina about Sally. Instead, I told her of my love affair with her best friend, LeAnne, in Munich. "You have humiliated me about as much as it is possible for a man to humiliate a woman," Sabina said. We were in an apartment in the rue de l'Université. I saw myself in the mirror. I liked looking at the seducer to whom Sabina spoke. Cheese and biscuits were on the table. I looked at myself in the mirror and smiled, eating a biscuit.

My father, in his usual suite at the Plaza-Athénée, asked me to deliver a package from Cartier to an actress in London.

"From you?"

"Dear boy," he said, "when other men have love affairs they put on a raincoat and a soft hat. They arrive in a taxi and no one asks who they are. It's harder for me. I go everywhere in a town car with a driver, I wear funny clothes and a bowler hat, I have a funny mustache. . . ." The delivery was for a client. He didn't have love affairs? He told me of one, with his secretary when my mother was pregnant with me. I told him I was thinking of how to have one with Paola Mori. "You scoundrel," he said.* I told him that, it being October, the automobile show was on in London and I had nowhere to stay. He made a phone call and, *presto!* I was booked into the Savoy. His parting words to me were always to take a sitting room when I stayed with a woman at a hotel. "That way they won't bother you." The mirror in his suite also showed I was a Seducer, a *Coureur de Femmes*.

---

* I know of only one other love affair of my father's. It was more an infatuation, but it disturbed my mother. It started sometime in the early sixties when he began seeing an intelligent, aristocratic, middle-aged Englishwoman of bohemian habits, who incidentally was a friend of the Davises and whom I liked a great deal.

At the Savoy, Sally told me that she was pregnant. An abortion cost 200 guineas (about $800). Half of it had to be paid the next day in cash.

THE HORROR! THE HORROR!   After her abortion I bought Sally a necklace from M. Hakim, who'd sold me the Turkish ring I'd given to Sabina, also the Egyptian ring I'd given to Katherine. He told me the necklace was Greek.

Before driving back to Málaga with her I told Sally to take the necklace to the British Museum. "They'll tell you where exactly it is from in Greece."

"They laughed at me when I said it was Greek," Sally said later. " 'Maybe the *blue beads* are Greek,' they said. 'But the bulla is Etruscan-type.' "

"What were you wearing?" I said.

"They were laughing at the necklace, not me."

"Why do you stay with me?" I said. "I'm sure you often ask."

"No, as it happens, I *don't* often ask. All my friends do, though," Sally said.

I was astonished we were still close. I'd thought the abortion would be the end.

One November day in Málaga, I was approached by a young man who asked me if I'd "make a delivery" to someone in Portugal.

"For Amilcar Cabral? For the PAIGC?"

"No," said the young man, shaking his head yes.

"A delivery of what?" I said. At least I think I said that. I'd lived in Spain for almost two years, but my Spanish was not great. I'd once told a waiter that if he brought me something I'd make him very famous when what I meant was I'd be very grateful.

"You have a fast car?" the young man said.

"And I have a pistol," I said.

"Saturday night at eight," he said. Was he wearing two watches on his left wrist, like Carlos Cudell-Goetz? No, but everything else was right.

On Saturday night at eight I met "Pépé" and "Paco." They put a long heavy crate in the trunk of my car. Machine guns, no doubt. I was to drive to the Portuguese border through Estremadura. Or explosives? At the border "Mateus" would meet me and give me instructions. At one point I was supposed to drive very fast with no lights. Coming back, the same drill.

"*¡Yo volveré!*" [I will return!] I said, confident of my meaning as "*Yo no volveré*" was the first line of a poem I knew by Jiménez.

I drove to Sevilla and from Sevilla to Badajóz and from Badajóz the short distance to the Portuguese border. I kept saying the poem "*Yo no volveré*" over and over and worrying about where to get gas. I had never done anything so exciting in my life, yet it all felt familiar to me, from Eric Ambler and Graham Greene, from the opening pages of *For Whom The Bell Tolls*. All would go smoothly up to a point, then something would go wrong. A young woman in love with me would get killed. Dolores. Killed because of me. I would go on and do what I had to do. Afterwards I wouldn't talk about it. People would ask and I'd hold my head in my hands and say, "The horror! the horror!"

I was wearing cream-colored corduroy trousers with wide wales, made for me by Huntsman, with a button fly; a green houndstooth-checked hacking jacket, also by Huntsman; a green Shetland sweater from W. Bill and a green-and-white gingham-checked shirt of cotton taffeta with my collar open and the tongue for the guide-button hanging out à la Douglas MacArthur. I was specially proud of my shoes, brown brogues made for me of pebbled leather by C. J. Cleverly of Cork Street, W.1. My Chief's Special revolver by Smith & Wesson was in that ankle holster made for me by Chick Something-or-other of New York.

The drive was long, the road was empty. Life alone with Sally was strained. Living with her at Granja Amos was like being on the boat in the harbor at Siphnos. Sometimes we were happy, but most often it was as I wrote in my notebook: "Sex without endearments, closeness without intimacy." Sally had been many places, many more places than I. Moscow, where she had lived for a year by herself when she was nineteen, Ulan Bator, Peking, Beirut . . . Whenver she spoke of her travels, I was sure she was really speaking of men. There were men in her stories whom she didn't name; I was sure of that: men hidden in the landscapes, encrypted in the names of hotels. I punished her by alluding to books I knew she hadn't read. I played music I knew she didn't like. I criticized her cooking. I grew angry whenever we drove to

Bill and Annie Davis's: we went frequently to La Consula: so I could change my attitude as soon as we were with others and make her feel responsible.

All went smoothly on my drive, nothing went wrong. I wasn't searched at the border. The heavy crate was taken out, at a town on the other side, and I drove back without incident. The sun came out and there was no need to drive without lights. "Mateus" hadn't been wearing two wristwatches.

"I have returned," I said the next day to the young man in Málaga, unsure how to say *volver* in the past perfect tense. "What was in the crate?"

•

"What was in the crate?" I asked Merle Dankbloom when Sally and I got back to London.

"I can't say for sure, but we'll find out."

"What do you think was in the crate?" I wrote to John Peet.

"I can't say for sure," he wrote back. "Explosives? Machine guns? The PAIGC needs small arms." We were corresponding about Carl Goerdler and the German Resistance to Hitler. No such resistance existed, according to John Peet, except the Communists.

"We know what was in the crate," Merle Dankbloom said to me at last. "It was clay."

"It was clay?"

"Cudell-Goetz uses only a special clay from Málaga to make his pedestal models."

"It was clay?"

"Only clay."

Sally told me that she was pregnant again, but now an abortion cost two hundred and fifty guineas.

"I'LL MARRY YOU IF YOU WANT ME TO . . ." I left Sally in London for her abortion and went to New York for my birthday presents. Behind me the heavy front door slammed shut, sounding as it always had. "Good to have you back," said the butler. "Nice to see you again, Mister Ben," said the maid. All was before, as it would always be. I was twenty-five.

Well, not all was the same. My rooms were neater and more

formal, more like the rest of the house. My books and records had been put away. But everything else was the same: the chef was in his kitchen, with the kitchenmaid; the laundress was in the laundry room; the houseman was in his little room next to the elevator; the upstairs maid was upstairs . . . I began to doubt I had changed. And my mother and father, they were the same.

"I have nowhere to take my friends," said my mother.

"Her friends?" jeered my father when we were alone. "Poor relations, acquaintances from the old days, lonely resentful women, none as well off as she." Still, it had been painful to hear her complain.

"I'll marry Sally if she wants me to," I told my mother, to make her feel better.

"I'll marry Sally if she wants me to," I told my father, to make him think better of me. We were sitting in the library. He was reading as usual, some new life of Samuel Johnson no doubt; I was facing Biography again: Emma Goldman, *Living My Life*; *Byron In Italy* . . . Waiting for him to turn to me, I started to work on an anagram for *My Past and Thoughts* by Alexander Herzen, four volumes, which was new.

He got to his feet and said, "I have some men coming for dinner, dear boy. I have to get dressed and go to work."

So I went to my room and phoned Sally. "I'll marry you if you want me to."

•

My father got me and Sally rooms at the Tuscany on East Thirty-ninth Street where he knew the manager. The Tuscany? Who stayed at the Tuscany? And why couldn't we stay at Number 19?

In point of fact, I was glad. I hated the way the house made me behave. The worst I behaved was when a friend from London came to stay. "Let's dress tonight," my friend said. We were going to see *Who's Afraid of Virginia Woolf?* and I sneered. "No one dresses for the theater on a weeknight," I said, "unless it's an opening." My friend dressed formally anyway (he didn't own another suit) and we had dinner with my parents. We went to the theater and I was embarrassed. The house made me act that way.

Collectors' sons will tell themselves that, as if far from the precincts of their parents' passion, the humps are lifted from their backs, the casts go from their eyes, they don't stutter or come prematurely, they don't limp, and women love them for themselves alone. Collectors' daughters must tell themselves: *At home I am plain, I am lead. Away? I'm like fire, I fly!*

Before Sally came, I went round the galleries with my friend Michael Train. I was never happy going to galleries with Sally. Mike was a painter like the ones in Henry James's stories of artists and writers: which is to say, very talented though he was, his inhibitions were greater than his talent, and of his inhibitions, the social ones were the worst. He believed that being a gentleman, he couldn't be a success, and being a gentleman was something he understood too well.

I first met Mike in 1960. He had had a sports jacket made at Henry Poole in London and a friend of his asked me to take it to him in Paris. He was short and dark. To me he looked like one of Picasso's acrobats.

"Your friends say you are the funniest man in the world," I said to him.

"Really? And what do your friends say about you?"

He told me that sometimes his name was Migué and sometimes it was Monk. In a very short time he told me an astonishing amount about himself. Sometimes he sounded like W. C. Fields, sometimes like Groucho Marx.

We drove south together from Paris, stopping at Lacan de Loubressac, in the Dordogne, to visit the Merwins. I had to drink several whiskeys before I could face Dido and Bill. "Bill always makes me feel undereducated," I told Mike.

"How do I make you feel?"

"Like I know everything."

In his Groucho Marx voice: "I bet you don't know who wrote 'The Syncopated Clock.' "*

Everything at the Merwins was just so, same as in London, and, as in London, a genius showed in the arrangements. But the genius was Dido's. Bill's genius showed on walks out of doors, same as in London. The first morning we were there, Bill took Mike and me to the ruins of a Romanesque building, an abbey,

---

* I said Morton Gould, Mike said Leroy Anderson. He was right.

I think. As we walked he spoke of birds, of plums. Everything he said made me restless, irritable in fact. He told us of the hawks he watched from a spot near the Abbey: buteos *and* accipiters: and I recited "The Swallow" by Francis Ponge. *"Tu t'écris vite,"* goes the poem, *"en encre bleu."* [You write yourself quick- / ly in blue ink.] He told us how the farmers at Lacan made their *prune* eau-de-vie; having nothing to say about fruits and vegetables, I was annoyed. At one point we stopped and he pointed, showing us a plain. He spoke of the armies that had fought there, Roman, Gaulish, Moorish, Spanish, French, until we heard the clash of battle; and I declaimed this from Robert Browning:

> Oh heart! oh blood that freezes, blood that burns!
> Earth returns
> For whole centuries of folly, noise and sin!
> Shut them in,
> With their triumphs and their glories and the rest! . . .

I hated myself for behaving like that.

Mike and I drove to Montauban, to see the Ingres museum, and to Albí where on a rampart of the Bishop's Palace I affected to be entranced. I quoted one of Pound's versions of Arnaut Daniel (or Bertran de Born?): *Breathing, I draw the air to me I know comes from Provence.* There were roses there on a trellis, I held out a rose to Mike. Sounding like W. C. Fields, he said, "Yessir, a real smell-a-roo."

•

Soon after Sally came to New York, I met someone else and Sally and I broke up. That was Maria, an actress. She lived on Jane Street in the Village, not far from the White Horse. Her father knew my father. "I just don't want to get married," I told Sally. We were going down in the elevator at the Tuscany. I was carrying a bottle of champagne wrapped in paper from Sherry-Lehmann.

Mike came to stay with me at Granja Amos the next summer. So did Maria.

Once at La Consula, Annie Davis said to me, "That Maria's a beautiful girl."

"Touches more than quickens the heart," I said in my long-practiced old roué voice. "Beautiful is Ava Gardner, Silvana Mangano—"

"Well, if she isn't beautiful," Annie said, "she's right next door."

She was indeed a pretty girl. Her only flaw was she wasn't prepared to be as interested in me as I was prepared to be interested in her.

One day Mike told me that after I'd left New York he'd gone to bed with Sally. "Nothing much happened," Mike said, "but coming out of the White Horse Tavern one night, Sally and I met—" He mentioned a writer we both knew. "He smiled at Sally, she smiled at him, so I left them together." He said, "I gave her to him."

I was hurt but said nothing. Then one night I drove Mike and Maria to Granada. I drove on back roads, expertly. I bribed a guard at the Alhambra to let us into the gardens. I did that expertly, too. It was August. We walked alone in the gardens. The moon came up. My arm was around Maria's waist. A nightingale? Why not? My arm is around Maria's waist. The moon is full. A nightingale sings. Mike is walking behind us by himself. That was my revenge on Mike.

Sally's revenge on me was that in the year after we broke up, I fell in love with her.

LA CONSULA　　Not only had Ernest Hemingway stayed at La Consula. So had Cyril Connolly, whom Bill Davis called "my brother-in-law," though Annie Davis's sister Jean was long dead; so had Sinbad Vail, Peggy Guggenheim's son; and Caresse Crosby, who with her husband had run the Black Sun Press and published James Joyce. After breaking up with Sally, I started to go there a lot.

Bill Davis looked American. He wore blue deck shoes and white duck trousers and that kind of short-sleeved shirt which everyone wears nowadays but which then used to remind me of the polo player Tommy Hitchcock. Bill's trousers all had button flys. He was bald and tall and built like an athlete, with that sort of deformation athletes sometimes have. A slightly elongated right arm: from too much polo perhaps? A deafness in the right ear: from too much shooting? And Bill Davis sounded American. "I'm going to give you the gen on Granada." Most American expatriates tried to sound British. We spoke of "school hols" and "a spot of chat." But Bill knew about swimming and tennis; he knew about bullfighting; and he spoke about books as he did about sports. "Let me run down the form on Bill Faulkner for you."

Another American thing about Bill: his mother's family had been the model for the Ambersons in Booth Tarkington's novel. He remembered the old Waldorf-Astoria, when it was where the Empire State Building is today. "When my mother ran away from my father to be with her lover, who happened to be the scapegrace heir to the Pinkerton fortune, we all lived at the old hotel," he said, "the happiest years of my youth. Ah! the bliss of an absent father, luxury, adultery, room service and a happy mother. An Amberson Abroad."

Bill kept much of his past a mystery, with lightning flashes of detail. After Yale, a spell on the *Herald Tribune:* stories of drinking at "Blake's." Then a Mexican period when he first met Hemingway. Then a time in New York in the early forties when he was Peggy Guggenheim's lover and helped her with her gallery, Art of this Century, and knew Ernst and Pollock and Gorky. Bill's first wife was a Peabody (pronounced PEA-biddy). His war was making training films about VD or something like that. I know he wasn't an officer. He said that not to have been one, "you had either to be an idiot or an awful snob."

The money to run La Consula was said to be Annie's. She was a Bakewell from Baltimore. Which meant that her "people" had money? She was certainly rude enough, often enough. But she would have given Bill everything, however much or little she had. That was the truly important thing. They both had that air of recklessness which people who marry in middle age sometimes make up for themselves. With Annie and Bill Davis, I'm sure it was genuine. It took the form of living not on income but principal, and what could be more reckless than that?

Bill had an obsessive interest in the very rich and their "arrangements." Of the famous society murder that had taken place a few years before, he said, "To understand the Woodward murder, you have to know that after she blew off her husband's head and told the butler, the first person the butler phoned was Missus Woodward Senior, and the first person *Missus Woodward* phoned was her old beau, Averill Harriman, who happened to be Governor, and *he* phoned Cissy Patterson who owned the *Daily News*, and only then was the butler told to phone the State Police. . . . This gen is from Bill Woodward's sister Ethel. I like it because it shows beyond a doubt that the very rich *can* get away with murder."

Bill told me what Ernest Hemingway had told him about his famous exchange with Scott Fitzgerald. "Ernest didn't say, *Yes, they have more money.* What he said was, *Yes, they don't give a fuck,* and a hoor who was sitting at the bar with them said, *Neither do I!*"

Hemingway had stayed at La Consula during the Dangerous Summer (so-called) of 1959. Bill had been his chauffeur, driving from *corrida* to *corrida* so that they could see Antonio Ordóñez *mano a mano* with his brother-in-law, Luís Dominguín. Bill had dressing-room stories about Ordóñez which I'm afraid were wasted on me. I do remember Bill telling me how exceedingly lightly Hemingway moved. "The most graceful man I ever saw."

"With a beautiful tenor voice," Annie said.

"Graceful," Bill said. "Balanced at the hips."

"Like a dancer," Annie said.

Hemingway's sixtieth birthday party had been at the Hotel Miramar in Málaga the year before, when he'd shown signs of madness that no one could mistake. A year later, in August 1960, he was again at La Consula (that was the summer he quarreled with Ken Tynan), and Bill was "shocked at how ruined Ernest was." Bill told me, "I don't think Ernest ever knew how damaged he'd been by the two plane crashes."*

Another time Bill told me Ernest gave him the wristwatch he was wearing. "Ernest said, 'You don't own a thing really and truly until you give it away.' "

* In his 1987 biography, Kenneth Lynn writes that in the summer of 1960 "Bill Davis was staggered by the psychological changes that had taken place in his friend in less than a year. [Hemingway] couldn't sleep, in spite of the pills he gulped, and everything worried him—including the idea that Bill was plotting to kill him by wrecking the automobile in which he drove him about. Feelings of loneliness, guilt, and remorse swept over him in enormous waves, along with a terrible frustration whenever his memory failed him."

Bill's stories were the real scoop, the true gen. And how amusing of Bill to say that to be very rich was "to have a hard-on and nowhere to put it"!

It was all *very* American.

.

Bill's English houseguests were titled, swept up by him from the bar at White's, where he was a member, or from a country-house party somewhere. His American houseguests were famous, one for "having revolutionized the modern game of backgammon," another for being "a three-figure man." One was famous for something he'd done at Yale (Bill was Yale '29), one was famous for having been in the U.S. Army Ski Corps in the Second World War, when he'd invented a maneuver that downhill skiers still use.

In the games room at La Consula, against a wall of books about American social history, I used to see men and women I'd only read about, in Henry James and John O'Hara. Their good manners: dispassionate, uniform, especially to servants: were those of professional houseguests. They looked like skeletons. I saw through them to *The Gilded Age, The Robber Barons* and *America's 60 Families* on the shelves at the end of the room. They behaved to one another with such cold-blooded courtesy, it was hard to believe they were ever hot. Skeletons. Yet of one of them, Bill said, "He'd sleep with a snake if he couldn't get a woman." Of another, a woman notorious for her very many rich lovers, Bill told me she'd put their names in a book, together with their "grades." She kept the book at her bedside. "She calls it her fucking book," Bill said. " 'Where's my fucking book?' "

I once wrote down in my notebook the names of all the people I met that summer at La Consula. I was thinking of writing a story about two small children growing up in a house given over to guests. They would be a brother and sister, aged about nine and seven, like the Davis children. The houseguests would be leeching away the children's futures.

At La Consula, then, in the summer of 1962, I met Sir Robert and Lady (Isabel) Throckmorton; the British painter and sculptor Eduardo Paolozzi; Rupert and Jeannie Bellville (he had flown for Franco; she was American, with money); their son

Hercules Bellville and his girlfriend, Charmian Montague-Douglas Scott; Rupert Lycett-Green and his girlfriend, Candida Betjeman; the Marquess of Bath and his sons, Christopher and Valentine Thynne; Anthony and Violet Powell and their son, Tristram; "Puffin" Asquith and David Niven, Xan and Daphne Fielding, Georgia Tennant who was staying with Gerald Brenan; Jonathan Gathorne-Hardy, who was writing a book on the British nanny; Patrick Kinross, who was writing a life of Ataturk; Kenneth Wagg, who had been in love with the American actress Margaret Sullavan and then married the Horlick heiress; and Sarah Courtauld and her brother, Simon, and his friend, Bozo Ivanovic.

The Americans I met that summer at La Consula were Ted Basset and Inez ("Inky") Millholland Rupp; the abstract expressionist painter José Guerrero and Roxy Guerrero; A. E. Hotchner and his family; Harvey Breit, John Crosby, and Mr. and Mrs. Montgomery Patterson Ford.

From Churriana, down the road, came Lucia Gold with her younger sister, Dorothy, who liked swimming naked; and from up the road, Ethel Woodward de Croisset and her sons, Charles and Patrick de Croisset; and the American painter Bayard Osborn, his wife, Anita, and his daughters, Margaret and Io.

Also, one day, from Estoril, came the Prince d'Orleáns (who was not French but Spanish). He wore plus-fives and a Norfolk jacket of very heavy tweed, and was holding two big brown and white springer spaniels. Finally, there was young Timothy Willoughby d'Eresby, the heir of the Duke of Ancaster, who owned a discothèque in Torremolinos, who was good-looking in a Byronic way and generous with money and was drowned the next summer off Cap d'Antibes while sailing to Corsica.

La Consula had been a convent. Now it was a place where men and women with pedigrees could come and play cards and fall in love. However empty and boring they were, they would still be known and esteemed there for their antecedents. I could bring my friends to La Consula and not apologize. I could come and go there and fall in love and not have to explain. The boring, pretentious and empty talk? A small price to pay for meeting beautiful young girls and boys with names like Iope Oldcastle and Endymion Porter.

Bill had a collection of Henry James. "I'm lacking *Confidence*," he said, a late James novel which James hadn't liked. I found a copy and gave it to Bill. In return he gave me a Henry James letter, not dated but from when he lived at 34 De Vere Gardens:

My dear Marriott [?],
   I have a great wish to visit face to face with the tributary Three, with nothing more disjunctive than a dining table between us. Will you, to this end (which I have been baffled & hindered in arriving at), give me the pleasure of dining with me on Friday March 20 at the Reform Club, Pall Mall, at 8 o'clock? I am asking only Harland & Crackenthorpe, who I think are able to come. I greatly hope you can join us. Believe me yours ever
                                                    Henry James

Like all good presents, this one was half compliment, half reproach. The reproachful half said that, as I knew more about riding clothes than I did about riding, more about auction prices and collections than about art, so I knew more of "the mere twaddle of graciousness," as James called such letters, than of the passions and disappointments underlying a London "season."

For at one time I had told Bill, "I am socially very ambitious." I can't believe now that I said that, and I can't think what I meant. That I wanted to marry Iope Oldcastle? That on my mantel I wanted crested invitations? That I wanted to be a member of White's? Thanks to Bill, I did get invited to Chatsworth by "Debo," the Duchess of Devonshire, and to Longleat by Henry, the Marquess of Bath, and to two or three other great houses for fashionable weekends. But I never got invited back. As Wilde said of Frank Harris, "Frank is invited everywhere—once."

I never discovered exactly what my gaffes had been. Chesterton says somewhere that while a murderer may expect divine absolution, there is no forgiveness in heaven for having chosen the wrong fork. I never did anything quite like that; but what was it I did wrong? Only once did a social error of mine meet with a prompt, explicit and condign rebuke. It was when, joking with Princess Margaret at Kensington Palace, I likened something (I forgot what) to the American attitude to George the Third. "*King* George the Third," Princess Margaret said.

In that phase of my life: briefly among the Right, the Real, the Royal, and even (sometimes) the Right Real Rich: I remember turning up my nose at the tacky coziness of certain domestic arrangements in the great houses I went to: the electric heater, the cheap storebought lamp, the general air in private quarters of a third-class hotel in a second-class place; while outside, in the spacious public rooms, there were decorations by Gibbons and Adams, paintings by Holbein, Bellotto, Marshall and Stubbs and family portraits by Van Dyck.

And, oh! the boredom of being in the English countryside. The embarrassment of sitting at luncheon with this MP and that ex-cabinet minister and having nothing to say. And, oh! the pain of feeling I would never belong to the so-despised group. False ennui plus true disappointment. Result: spiteful disapproval.

•

That same summer at La Consula I met an American man of about Bill's age who Bill said had worked for the CIA. He was retired and was building a house with a swimming pool across from La Consula. We talked obliquely when we first met. Bill said, "Ben lived in Munich for a time." The man knew the Institut für Zeitgeschicte and its director, but he didn't know any of the other people I knew. He wore a small military-type mustache. He was fit, if a little overweight. He smoked cigarettes and drank quite a lot.

The next time we met, at his invitation, for drinks at his new house, we sat by the pool and he spoke to me more "confidentially." He told me of Beirut, where he'd just been posted, of Kim Philby, who'd just escaped to the Soviet Union. He told me of seeing the photograph of Mount Ararat that the famous spy used to hang in his office. "No one noticed that it'd been taken from the Russian side."* He asked me in some detail about the Ukranian Section of Radio Liberation. Many of the Ukranians there were openly pro-Nazi, I said; many were ex-Vlassovites and had fought for Hitler. Their anti-Semitism was alarming. I

---

* An old chestnut now, but a green one then, a story told well by many, including Graham Greene and the journalist Murray Sayle.

told him of an incident at Radio Liberation when poison was put in the salt cellars in the cafeteria. The culprit was a Ukranian who had wanted revenge on a Jew from his village. That seemed to me typical of what was wrong with the Munich radios. My host said, "It's often true that the policies of very large organizations are determined by the vindictive heat of very low-level agents."

I asked if he knew Merle Dankbloom. No, he said, but the name reminded him of "Vivian Darkbloom," the anagrammatic nom de plume used by Vladimir Nabokov in Berlin in the 1920s. I also asked if he knew Ira Rich and he said no. Then he asked me about the Szabos, the zookeeper and his wife, whom I'd let through to the States and who'd turned out to be Soviet agents. "Did Szabo tell you what they did about the animals in the zoo?" No, I said: I hadn't thought to ask. He told me that the animals had all been released before the Russian tanks came. "Better dead than Red, I suppose," he said. He told me that it was a variation on what happened at the Royal Zoo at Vincennes in 1789 when in the name of the Revolution the sans-culottes demanded that the animals be freed. "For decades the poor animals roamed the forest at Vincennes."

He asked me why I'd been fired. I said, I guess because of my politics. "They wouldn't have let you go for that," he said. "They like having wide-ranging people like you, rootless, intelligent and detached. So long as they collect gossip." I loved thinking of myself like that. But why didn't they just rely on the small talk of journalists? He said, "I've often wondered that myself."

His name eludes me. I came to know his house well. Next summer I swam in that pool every day. A few years ago I saw him on TV in New York, still fit, still with a smoker's cough, commenting on some recent convulsion in the CIA.

RONDA   One June morning I drove to Ronda from Granja Amos. The first time I'd driven there, to meet friends of Siriol's, I'd taken the road from Marbella, and Ronda had been hard to approach. Franco was still punishing Ronda for its devotion to the Republicans in the Civil War by not improving the roads, it was said.

The second time I drove to Ronda it was for the bulls which in Ronda, during the *féria*, are fought on horseback as in the eighteenth century. That time I drove in from the east and the approach was easy. I'd never been to a bullfight before, but I wanted the girl I was with to believe I'd seen dozens of them: hundreds! This time I was taking the road from the south. I wanted a hard drive. I was going to Ronda to find out what I could about John Peet when he fought in the Spanish War, before he went to East Berlin. That was the sort of thing I did, to stay in touch with Sally somehow, in the year after we broke up. Maria, the girl I'd left her for, the one I'd gone to the bullfight with, hadn't lasted long. Nothing was going to last long any more; I was sure of that.

Ronda is high in the mountains. A deep gorge, the Tajo, runs through the town. Men kill their enemies and throw the bodies into the Tajo, people said. I stayed at the Reina Victoria, where Rilke once stayed, and asked in the bar whether anyone there remembered a tall fair Englishman during the Civil War. "*Muy rubio,*" I said, "*muy alto.*" Very fair, very tall. It was the wrong place to ask. I was met with hostility and suspicion, disguised as boredom. The bartender whispered to me to go to a wineshop near the station and ask there. Yes, yes, they said at the wineshop. They remembered the tall Englishman. They remembered him well. He had come to Ronda during the war and while he was there an entire family of Anarchists had disappeared. The authorities found blood on the walls of the family's home, but no bodies were ever found. Look for them in the Tajo, they said. And the Englishman? *¿Quién sabe?* said one. Anarchists, Reds, said another, they're all the same! And he spat on the floor.

"*¿Puedo invitarles un trago a todos?*" I said. ["May I buy drinks for all?"]

Universal acceptance. After one round I said it again. Universal compliments on my excellent Spanish. A guitar was brought out. I said it again. And so on and on. . . .

I was hung over next morning. On the drive back, I saw a woman on a white horse. She was crossing the road, and her large floppy hat showed her to be English. So did her posture. Coming nearer I saw it was Penelope Chetwode, the wife of John Betjeman, on her horseback tour of Andalucía. She was staying at La Consula. I like to think of that moment, me driving on that steep twisting road in a long low fast open foreign car, crossing paths with an Englishwoman on a white horse. Penelope Chetwode and I, both of us blinkered, eccentric, intent.

At La Consula, Bill was having a drink with Gerald Brenan, who lived down the road in Churriana. Gerald was the most famous person I knew in the south of Spain. Long before we met I'd read his books. *The Spanish Labyrinth*, about the Civil War; his *Literature of the Spanish People* . . . He and Bill were talking about orgasms. Gerald was saying that for him they were the same as when he was seventeen. He was then about sixty. Bill said that for him they were the same "but less intense." He said that now he liked a woman who knew how to hold him in her. Gerald said that that didn't matter to him.

I waited for them to look at me to see if I knew what they were talking about, but they didn't look at me. They talked instead about the best sex they had ever had. I can't remember what Bill said, but Gerald said the best he'd ever had was with a farmer's wife in a hill village on his first walking tour of Andalucía when he was in his teens.

Again I waited for them to look at me, and this time they did. I said nothing.

After a pause, Gerald said, "His best sex is to come." Then I told them about Ronda.

"So it seems that John Peet was an executioner for the Reds," I said in conclusion. Then Gerald told me that the "Englishman" the men in the wineshop remembered had in fact been a Danish journalist named Ole Something, who hadn't been tall.

"And the Anarchist family?"

They later turned up in Ronda as tourists from San Francisco, Gerald said, where they had been living for twenty-five years.

"And the blood on the walls?"

"Ah, the 'blood on the walls'!" Gerald said and laughed. Bill laughed, too.

I was angry at Gerald for implying that I'd been made a fool of, which was undoubtedly true, and I was angry at Bill because he'd heard it.*

---

* According to his autobiography, *The Long Engagement, Memoirs of a Cold War Legend*, published posthumously in 1989, a maybe too-boyish but charming and believable book, John Peet fought for the Spanish Republic in Albacete where he was wounded and after which he returned to England. When in the Kempinski bar I'd asked him where he'd fought in Spain, he must have answered, "Around Albacete," and not "Ronda, Albacete," as I'd heard.

There were always young girls in Gerald's house: well-born,
even aristocratic, beautiful young English girls: Pakenhams, Ten-
nants and the like: whom Gerald had invited to stay. He was like
an old ram among them.

Soon after we met, I gave him Bill Merwin's *Green with Beasts*
and his translation of *El Cid*. I gave him *The Hawk in the Rain*. Gerald gave me a set of the *Autos* of Calderón printed in Madrid in
1717. I read the Spanish poets he liked and we used to talk about
them. John of the Cross and Góngora, Jiménez and Machado. He
told me how very many Spanish poets, including John of the
Cross, had been Jewish. *Conversos*, crypto-Jews. Teresa of Ávila,
Santa Teresa, had been Jewish, too. (Francisco Franco was Jewish, everyone knew that.) He told me of the novel *La Celestina*,
written in 1499 by Fernando de Rojas; and he told me that Rojas
had been a converso. *La Celestina* has a distinct bearing on the history of the Jews in Spain, Gerald said. "The plot of *La Celestina* is
very simple," he writes in *The Literature of the Spanish People:*

> A young nobleman called Calisto falls suddenly and violently
> in love with a girl of high rank called Melibea, whom he has
> met through an accident. Since, by the custom of the age, she
> is secluded and never leaves her house, he calls in the services
> of a bawd called Celestina to help him to press his suit. Ce-
> lestina is successful, Melibea falls in love and agrees to meet
> Calisto by night in the garden of her house. The tryst takes
> place, but on a subsequent occasion there is an alarm and in his
> hurry to descend the ladder, Calisto falls and is killed. Melibea
> in despair throws herself off a tower and dies also. Her parents
> are left to weep and moralize.

La Celestina is indeed a marvelous book. The character of the
bawd is like no other in literature. But in talking to me about it
Gerald always stressed its importance to "an understanding of
the history of the Jews in Spain," as if to say, "Being Jewish,
you'll know what I mean." In the *Literature of the Spanish People*,
Gerald writes:

> [It] may have been written for a little circle of humanists and
> conversos, who met together to read it aloud and perhaps made

suggestions for improving it. Now it is a common tendency for
Jews to exaggerate the characteristics of the nation they belong
to. Intensely Spanish and Castilian as this book is, I believe
that in the uncompromising tone of its language, the crudeness
of many of its scenes and the unflinching way in which the
tragedy is carried through to its final consequences, there is
something one may call Hispano-Semitic . . .

I resented Gerald's emphasis as condescending. I also disliked
his emphasis in telling me this story. In 1935, he told me, the
second Republican government, wanting to celebrate the eight
hundredth anniversary of the birth of Maimonides, invited Jewish scholars from all over the world to Córdoba. There they were
given an elaborate luncheon, all with great ceremony, great self-
congratulation on the part of the government. Many of the laws
excluding and disabling Jews were still on the books, and the
Republican government meant to show how it was going to re-
peal the laws, some dating from 1492. The banquet table was
heavy with food, beautifully arranged, including many artful and
colorful salads of langostines and shrimp. "Shellfish!" Again Gerald implied that being Jewish, I'd know what that meant.

Gerald had been in love with the painter Carrington who had
committed suicide and had herself been beloved by the *Jewish*
painter Mark Gertler who had also committed suicide (Gerald's
emphasis); Carrington had been in love with Lytton Strachey
who had been in love with Ralph Partridge, Gerald's best friend,
who had married Carrington, and Duncan Grant whom Lytton
had been in love with and who had at one time been the lover of
Virginia Woolf's sister Vanessa Bell— . . . Was I getting it right?
The Bells, the Stracheys, the Stephens, all marrying one another, all sleeping with one another. It was a Pastoral. And that
was England. And with it all the First World War, the Spanish
War, the coming of the Second World War. I was never sure
really that I got it right, or wanted to. Besides, it was all in
Virginia Woolf's *Between the Acts*.

I was better friends with Gerald's wife, Gamel Woolsey. She
was a sister of the Judge Woolsey whose statement exculpating
Ulysses from the charge of obscenity was for many years printed
as a preface to the Modern Library edition. It stated that the
novel was not pornographic in effect but "emetic." He had meant

"cathartic," surely? Everyone assumed that. But Gamel said no, her brother had meant that *Ulysses* made him want to throw up.

Gamel was *once-beautiful*. This quality, so well known to me from novels and poems, I was just beginning to discern in living people. *Once-beautiful* and *soon-to-be once-beautiful*. Gamel's carriage was that of a belle, her conversation and ways with a cigarette had been learned at some long-ago cotillion. She had *once-beautiful* features in a *once-beautiful* face: thin, lovely lips, a long philtrum and bright, flirtatious eyes. But her skin had that thin, crepey, old-paper look, and she drank and was unhappy.

Gamel was a poet. She had recently sent a sequence of sonnets to Faber & Faber and they had been rejected by T. S. Eliot, "Tom," the modern poet she most admired. She was pleased that I remembered reading a poem of hers in the literary magazine *Botteghe Oscure*. "Such a pleasure to talk to someone who is interested in poetry, really cares for it and understands it." Words I had been hearing from women for years. Her poems were Georgian, much influenced by D. G. Rossetti. They can't ever have sounded fresh, even when first written. She spent several weeks in North Wales every year, visiting J. C. Powys, whose lover she had been, and Bertrand Russell. She told me how vain Russell had become. "Well, of course, he was always vain, but now he turns the spoons around so he can see himself reflected in the backs and he purses his lips and primps."

VICTOR   That evening, at Granja Amos, thinking of the best sex I'd ever had, I thought of Nora.

The youngest, prettiest housemaid when I was nine or ten years old. Black hair, blue eyes, fresh complexion. Like most of the maids at that time in our house, Nora was an innocent-seeming girl from Ireland who went to confession and mass. *Fresh off the boat*, my mother said. She must have had brothers: she wrestled with me after school every day and seemed to enjoy it. I sure did. Once, alone with Nora, I took a piece of porcelain up from off the table. "Lift up your skirt and take down your underpants or I'll drop this and tell them you did it," I said. She lifted her skirt up and showed me that she wasn't wearing underpants. After looking and looking, I looked in her face. Then, I let the porcelain fall. It smashed on the floor. Nora dropped her skirt and she smiled at me. Then she came and gave me a hug.*

Nora went and told the steward that she'd broken the orna-
ment. She offered to pay for it. "Not at all, Nora, you're a good
girl," the steward will have said.

And so she was.

I had done such a typical thing in such a typical way. Its
aggressions: on servants, women, possessions, the house: and on
myself: these do not speak to me now of good sex. Instead they
remind me how I hated being nine or ten, in that house, with
those things. But how artful I was. How inventive. I suppose I
must add how appalled I am, too. I'm not, really.

*"I FEEL FREE!" (or I GET HIM TO CRACK HIS KNUCK-
LES)*   Donald Maitland rented that house with a swimming pool
across from La Consula. He left Gemma there with their children
and a nanny, and went back to London, meaning to return in
August for the *féria.* I took Gemma to dinner one night. We went
to the restaurant I'd gone to with my father. Only tonight it was
crowded, there was music, you could have any of the dishes the
place was famous for: the braised barbel brains from Valencia,
the roast baby boar from Asturias, the nectarines from Spanish
Morocco; and the unfamiliar-tasting wines from all the familiar
vineyards of Spain.

"Cheer up," I said to Gemma over coffee, lighting up a maduro
cigar. "Donald will be back soon." Meant to *not* cheer her up, of
course. But she burst into tears and people started looking at us.
"I always knew you were unhappy," I said, hoping she'd calm
down, "because you were always so cheerful." I knew? How
perceptive I was! how deep! And she'd been sure I'd never noticed her. "Not notice you? Not notice that ravishing frock with
the . . . What do you call 'em?" Buttons? "Buttons, exactly."
How keen my eye was! "I was unhappy myself, you know. Yes,
an unhappy romance with Charmian Scott." The beautiful niece
of the Duke of Buccleugh? "I was in love with Charmian and
Charmian wasn't in love with me." How was that possible? Her
tiny hand on my big one, she told how she hated Charmian Scott
for having made me suffer.

* In the play *Victor ou les enfants au pouvoir* [*Victor or the Children Take Over*] by Roger
Vitrac (1928), the opening scene is a little like this.

The night was warm, I put the top down, and we drove back to her house very fast. She threw back her head in the car and laughed and said she felt free, *free!* "Like Nicole Diver in *Tender Is the Night,*" I said. (How well read I was!)

"And to think that tonight is my tenth wedding anniversary," she said when we got to her house. "I was never *disloyal* to Donald before."

By this time I owed her husband between four and five thousand pounds.

I began staying at La Consula and slipping out after the house was asleep to go each night to Gemma Maitland. She showed me exciting English country-house-party skills: how to make your bed look slept in when you spent the night somewhere else. "Crease the sheets like this, press them down like that." I used to leave her house before dawn. No one saw me. No one. But if they had, they'd have admired my luck, my grace, my stealth, my shoes, my shirt.

One day we made an excursion to Míjas, another town like Ronda being punished for its fidelity to the Republican government. "But why are they so unforgiving?" she said. Patiently I explained. On other days she came to Granja Amos or we went for two or three hours to a house that I knew was empty: no one there but the servants. I boasted to her of past love affairs.

"You can have any woman you want, I suppose?"

"Alas, yes," I said (I'd been waiting to say this for years, ever since I first read it in a story by Barbey d'Aurevilly) "because of my looks, I have never had the profits of my timidity."*

We frequently went on picnics with Bill and Annie Davis.

"Gemma's in love with you, isn't she?" That was Annie one afternoon. Gemma and I had disappeared and come back to the picnic smiling.

"Yes, and she's leaving her husband," I said, trying to sound like Count Vronsky in *Anna Karenina.* "We're all going to live somewhere in the south."

"You're already in the south," Annie said. "And what about the children?"

---

* *"Le plus bel amour de Don Juan"* in *Les Diaboliques: "Grace à un beau visage, je n'ai jamais eu les profites de ma timidité."*

"I'll educate the children myself." Gemma and Donald had two, a son of three and a daughter of five. I liked them alright. "What will Donald say?" That was Bill. We were in his dressing room. I was looking at his trousers and belts and admiring how the buttons were fastened on his shirts. I said I knew exactly what Donald Maitland would say, having a scene from *Anna Karenina* in mind. Donald would sound like Alexéy Karenin, cracking his knuckles as he spoke. Bill said, "You'll have to find money somewheres, I guess. . . ." True, but all I was thinking was, *Gemma puts powder on her thighs with a powder puff and I've never known a woman who does that each morning after her bath.* "Now don't get me wrong, Ben, I'm not saying I'd ever kick Gemma out of bed, but hairdressers, dressmakers. . . . As the song says, 'Romance without finance is a nuisance.' "

"Do you think we're doing the right thing?" Gemma said. We were in the woods. There was a mill and a millstream. She was crying and she was twisting a little white handkerchief to shreds. Their car and driver had come down from London the day before. It was one of those boxy limousines with a sphinx on the hood, not as good as a Daimler, but better than an Austin Princess. Donald was coming back the next day.

"Why don't we say nothing?" I was thinking we could see one another in London, with me living in rooms in Half Moon Street, a few blocks away from Gemma, near where John Reginald Christie used to pick up prostitutes before taking them to his house at 10 Rillington Place and murdering them. I would be a famous philanderer. *His mistress is the beautiful Gemma Maitland,* they'd whisper at Wilton's, as I was leaving the restaurant. Meanwhile Gemma stopped crying. She gave me her handkerchief, wet with her tears.

"Yes, yes, let's say nothing!" she said.

But she was eager to tell Donald, and tell Donald she did.

The scene with us three soon took place. It didn't go as I'd planned. Did I want my legs broken? Did I want my hands nailed to the floor? That would happen if I saw Gemma again. "A vacation love affair . . . all very well if you're twenty-five, and single," Donald said harshly, adding (suddenly lyrical), "and it's summertime in the south of Spain. . . ."

I was afraid he was going to cry, but he said, "Unlike you, I believe in the family." Hypocrite! I looked at Gemma, she looked at the floor.

"I see it's cold chicken in *Gatsby*," I said. I was thinking of the scene where Tom and Daisy Buchanan are reconciled. It wasn't the zinger I needed, but still . . .

"Where can I write you?" I managed to whisper to Gemma before I left.

"You can't write me—*ever!*" she whispered back. "It's over!"

"Couldn't you take a post office box? Or let me write care of Elspeth." Elspeth was her best friend.

"Post office boxes are squalid, *I* always think."

"Well, maybe Donald's right and we shouldn't—"

"*Write care of Elspeth!*" were her last words.

Maitland showed me the door, sounding at last like Alexéy Karenin. "My secretary will be sending you a memorandum of your account."*

---

* Gemma and I corresponded, but soon her letters sounded false and my own grew bitter, and after a while we stopped. Helen sent me the money I owed Donald Maitland; I never had to ask my father.

There is no such scene as I'd imagined in *Anna Karenina*, among Alexéy and Anna and Vronsky, after the love affair begins.

THEATER

THE ABOMINABLE SNOWWOMAN *Jane Street* was my first play. It was about two girls living together in an apartment in Greenwich Village. They have an extra room which they have to rent. One of them, Pearl, is pregnant: will she have an abortion? The other girl is Dido: will she find a husband? Enter Jo and Stu, prospective tenants. The room doesn't suit them. They go. Enter Norma. She is an abortionist. Pearl doesn't like her. Exit Norma. Pearl says, "Flat-chested girls are nympho, some of them." Dido reminds Pearl that they have to rent the room, so Pearl and Dido go out to find Norma. Enter Lester. He is Pearl's boyfriend. Enter Milt. He is "from out of town." Lester has told him he can fix him up with Dido. Lester is obsessed with the Abominable Snowwoman of the Himalayas who he says represents the vengeful spirit of all the women he's broken up with. Milt is obsessed with poon-tang and with finding his runaway daughter, May. Re-enter Pearl and Dido. Dido and Milt go out for coffee. Pearl and Lester quarrel and make up. Re-enter Dido and Milt. They are engaged. Re-enter Norma. She turns out to be Milt's long-lost daughter, Norma May. Re-enter Jo and Stu. They've changed their minds about the room. Enter the Abominable Snowwoman. She carries Lester off, to be "shot down by police over Gansevoort Street." Jo and Stu decide to devote their lives to racial equality. "Whatever we can't support we will destroy." They won't be needing the room. They go. Milt and May also go. Pearl tells Dido she is no longer pregnant and the play ends.

Mike was staying with me at Granja Amos and as I wrote it I gave him each page and he laughed. I dedicated the play to him with a line from Theognis: Κύρνε, κύει πόλις ἥδε . . . [Cyrnus, this city is with child . . .] And I decided that writing plays was what I wanted to do.

When I got back to London I gave *Jane Street* to Siriol's friend

Frank Hauser, who ran the Oxford Playhouse, and he laughed when he read it.

Next I gave *Jane Street* to Minos Volanakis, who lived with Frank, and after he read it, he dedicated his translation of *The Parliament of Women* by Aristophanes to me. So I decided that writing plays was what I was meant to do.

I see now that I got into *Jane Street* much of my feeling about Sally and her abortions, attenuated by gags. My feelings for her grew stronger, now that she lived in New York and I was living in Spain. Both Pearl and Dido were Sally, Lester of course was me. Norma May, the abortionist, was modeled on a girl I'd picked up at the Central Park Zoo cafeteria, the worst-dressed young woman I'd ever seen.

She was reading a copy of *The Noble Savage*, a literary magazine. Her clothes were filthy and torn. Her nails were dirty, her fingers likewise, her hands and forearms were yellow-stained. She told me she was a photographer. I went home with her. She lived on West Twelfth Street, near the river. Her husband came in while I was there with her, her little daughter also. Neither was disturbed by my being there. I admired the way her desires seemed to rule her household. Her desires seemed to rule everything. Artists can live like that, I thought. I myself could live like that.

She was a good photographer, with a national reputation. She'd been brought up rich, like me. "I'd like to go slumming with you," I thought. When I got back to Granja Amos, she wrote me of going to a basketball game between the Go-Getters (paraplegics) and the Flash (spastics): I put that into *Jane Street:* and of meeting a young woman who was Queen of the Amputee Ski Race in Aspen that year: I put that into another play.

DUPLICITY (I) Minos had directed Sheila Hancock in *The Parliament of Women* and Constance Cummings in *Lysistrata* and Diane Cilento in *Naked* by Pirandello and Sean Connery in *The Bacchae* and Joan Greenwood in *Hedda Gabler*. His production of *The Maids* was the first Genet play to be put on in London. He was friends with Genet, and he told me that when Genet first came to London what he'd liked best was seeing a policeman in uniform embracing a sailor in uniform in a doorway near Picca-

dilly. Minos had been engaged to a woman who had died suddenly the year before. He was dark and slim and didn't smile
much. From time to time, for no apparent reason, he would burst
into tears.

Minos took me to meet Elisabeth Lutyens who was living in a
garden apartment in Hampstead. She was a composer of twelve-
tone music and had worked with Minos many times. Her living
room was big and dark and smelled of that incense people burn
when they own cats. She played a record of hers for us and I
asked to see the score: which I saw won her heart. She was in her
mid-fifties. Big nose, thinning hair: the sort of woman of whose
love affairs you're always surprised to hear. She used to speak of
her love affairs, which were many. Her husband, Edward Clark,
would come in and out of the room as she spoke. He was a
serious, courtly man, a friend of Stravinsky's, a student of Schoen-
berg's; he had worked long years for the BBC, then been fired.
There had been some sort of scandal. Elisabeth said that Edward
hadn't worked at a job for years. On many occasions, in different
words, over the years when I knew her, she said, "When a man
earns a living, it's a compliment to his wife. When a wife earns a
living, it's a compliment to neither."

Minos took me to meet Elias Canetti whose play *The Numbered*
he had directed. Canetti also lived in Hampstead. His apartment
was filled with books. Many, many anthropology books, books of
folktales, travelers' tales. I saw *Scatalogical Rites of All Nations*,
Premature Burial, *Magic and Witchcraft Among the Azande*, *Blood
Sacrifice Among the Jivaro Indians of the Amazon*. I told him of the
books I owned: Levy-Provençal on the Jews in Spain, Sacy on
the Druses. I told him of the *canero*, a parasite that enters the
urethra of swimmers in the Amazon and lodges there, putting out
little spines. I couldn't stop showing off. Canetti spoke of Bertolt
Brecht, John Heartfield and Karl Kraus, and I remember thinking that none of them would have spoken as intimately of him.
After we left, Minos told me that Canetti had a second apartment
in Hampstead. A mistress? Another life? To me it mainly implied more books.

Edward Clark died and Elisabeth asked me to choose a book
from the bookcase in his room. The bookcase, a beautiful two-
sided piece, was by Elisabeth's father, Sir Edwin Lutyens, who'd

designed it for his own library. I chose a volume of poetry by Léon-Paul Fargue. It was inscribed to Edward.

Merle Dankbloom asked me to ghost the life story of a violin-bow maker from Odessa who'd just defected to the West. It began, "Leopold Auer would not have liked Odessa in the winter of 1959." The CIA has an interest in publishing this? I said. I'm not going to do it, I told him. It's trivial. Merle Dankbloom looked annoyed. He next offered me a "mission" of sorts. I was to go to Lisbon and "make contact with an agent-in-place" whose name and address I wrote down, which I'm sure was not the right "drill." In any case, on my way to Lisbon I found that I'd forgotten the slip of paper. I knew a young Portuguese woman of excellent family; her politics were anti-Salazar, and so I spent a few days with her at the Avis Hotel at the Company's expense. "He wasn't 'in place' after all, I guess," I told Merle Dankbloom when I got back.

Elisabeth gave a party for my twenty-sixth birthday. December thirtieth, 1962. I was feeling blue. Who was I going to go home with that night? And the next night was New Year's Eve. I'd asked Sally to come to London, but she wouldn't come. Anyway, now when we saw each other all we did was fight. She used to say, "I can't forgive you for saying *I'll marry you if you want me to.*" For my part, I couldn't forgive her for going on with her life. I'd had one short vengeful love affair with an actress who'd starred in a movie with one of Sally's lovers.

Canetti was at my party. He was short and fat, he dressed badly; yet young women were drawn to him. No young woman was being drawn to me. I'd tried being in love with Minos's friends, with an actress in his production of Montherlant's *Queen After Death*, with Yolanda, the designer of the *Oresteia*. . . . Yolanda was at the party. We'd gone to Paris together a few times, she'd come and stayed with me in Spain. "Your world is money and power and fast cars," Yolanda had said to me. "Hard, beautifully dressed women, polo ponies, baccarat. My world is masks and illusions. Your world is commerce, my world is art. . . ." A very good joke. Yes, an excellent joke. But I wasn't going to go with Yolanda that night.

At the party I said to myself, "You're not as important to anyone here as they are to you. They will remember you hardly

at all, while to you they will be as vivid as Karl Kraus and Bertolt
Brecht are to Canetti." And who *was* I going to go home with?

Ted Hughes was at my party and towards the end he recited
a long poem: Chesterton's "The Rolling English Road," I think:
and afterwards we walked from Belsize Park Gardens, where
Elisabeth lived, across Regent's Park to Half Moon Street where
I was living.

> My friends, who will not go again or ape an ancient
>   rage,
> Or stretch the folly of our youth to be the shame of
>   age,
> But walk with clear eyes and ears this path that
>   wandereth,
> And see undrugged in evening light the decent inn of
>   death . . .

So Ted was the one I went home with.

When I think of Ted in London, I think of our walks. Once
walking with him in Regent's Park: he was pushing a baby carriage with his daughter Frieda in it: Ted was telling me of how
Sylvia wouldn't go out of the house, she relied on him for news
of the world. "When I come home she *wrings me out*." Of writing
his poem "The Jaguar," Ted told me that he had had trouble with
the end until, one day there at the zoo, he had seen a fly go into
the jaguar's nose and he saw the jaguar throw back his head and
from that came his last lines:

> His stride is wildernesses of freedom:
> The world rolls under the long thrust of his heel.
> Over the cage floor the horizons come.

I can't have liked Sylvia Plath very much, I remember so little
about her. Sally and I went to dinner at the Hugheses', when
they lived in Chalcot Square. I remember thinking that Sylvia
expected too much applause for the dinner she'd cooked and too
much approval for the economy of her and Ted's arrangements.

•

Frank and Minos used to give parties to which they invited me.
Most of their friends were queer (*queer* is the word they pre-

ferred). At these parties I was *with* them but not *of* them. I could say of them, quoting *Henry IV, I know you all.* . . . And they would have known I was saying *I know you all* . . . from *Henry IV.* With them I felt I was Prince Hal, King Henry, Falstaff and Poins all in one. Sometimes I brought a girlfriend with me. That was to show that I wasn't queer and it showed the girl that I wasn't the slave of desire she took me for: I had sources of pleasures apart from her. I had to have to hand at all times a mysterious and even threatening company to oppose to the company I was in: queers in the case of women, women in the case of queers, friends with no evident ambition in the case of my parents, and East German Intelligence (or anyway John Peet) in the case of the CIA. This arrangement of life allowed amply for pleasure, if not for much else, so long as strong feeling kept out of the way.

Frank was exceptionally musical. "He's the most musical person I know," said Elisabeth. His opinions on music were nothing if not emphatic. Once I was praising Schnabel to him, some performance I knew he disliked. But I could never win with Frank, not about music, at cards, or at anything else. As soon as I had a strong hand, so to speak, he made me laugh. *A certain loosening of rhythm,* I was saying, a *certain hardening of tone* . . . "A certain this, a certain that," he replied. "A certain Greek, a certain cat . . ." Merrystep, their cat, had had kittens behind the refrigerator. Minos was going back and forth between the living room and the kitchen, so was Merrystep. Minos brought in a kitten and then went back for another, Merrystep then took the kitten back, and so on and on. . . .

Frank and Minos were my university. Because of Frank, I looked deep into works I thought I already knew. His productions at the Oxford Playhouse were the education I'd scanted. I can't speak of their effect on me without sounding dumber than in fact I was. Besides, I was more conceited than dumb, and I always talked as though I knew what I was talking about.

Because of Minos I looked into works I'd never known before. *Le Cocu magnifique* by Fernand Crommelynck was the most important of these. I saw Minos's *Hedda Gabler* very many times, I saw his *Bacchae* many times in many different productions. His work had the effect on me that earthquakes are sometimes said to have: afterwards you can still walk, but you prefer to dance.

I loved going to Paris with Minos. He was stagestruck, as I was: however dreadful the production, however silly the play, we could not walk out. We saw plays in Paris by Pirandello, Claudel, Valéry, Valle-Inclán. Sometimes we saw as many as three plays in one day. One day we saw Hugo's *Ernani* and Kleist's *Penthésillée* and Ionesco's *La Leçon* and *La Cantatrice chauve*. Other times we saw Pierre Fresnay in Diderot's *Neveux de Rameau*, Edwige Feuillère in Pirandello's *Les Regles de jeu* (or was it *Commes Tu me désires?*), and Lolah Belon in Giraudeaux's *Judith*. Michel de Ghêlderode's *Mademoiselle Jairus*, Brecht's *Puntila* at the TNP-(with Georges Wilson and Charles Denner as Matti), Robert Hirsch as Néron in *Britannicus*. . . .

In Paris all drama was to me without national boundaries. No historical boundaries either. Each production was compact with all other productions of that play. Directors, actors and audience saw each play with its history in mind, whereas in London and New York, each new production was discrete. Or so I thought, because in Paris stage productions were numerous, tickets were cheap, and theater-going itself . . . Why, it was as it should be: continuous with restaurants, sex, and politics.

I told Minos of how troubled I felt, politically. Having no skills, no objectives, I said, I was susceptible to men like Merle Dankbloom, whom I described. He had lately sent me to Lisbon and twice before to Munich. Trivial errands, more like tests, and for what? "I have no imperatives," I said.

"I have nothing but imperatives," he said. He'd grown up in Athens during the German occupation, with the imperative of resistance, and after the war his father had been abducted and murdered by the Communists. "My imperative then was exile," he said.

I took him to meet Steven and Toby Schneider. They had recently bought a gloomy seventeenth-century house on the quai de la Tournelle. Minos and I had been to see *La Double inconstance* by Marivaux, so we wanted to talk about politics. "I'll tell you what politics is," said Steven. I leaned forward. Steven's authority with me was great, given all that he knew about wine, about fencing, about fishing. He also knew a lot about guns. He used to go to Gastine Renette, the gun shop where Maupassant and Proust used to go (now in the avenue Franklin-Roosevelt), and he had once told me that he was involved with some Corsicans in an arms deal.

I wanted to hear what he had to say. But all he told us at that time was, "Politics comes down to what your friends are doing."

SAMUEL BECKETT, A DIGRESSION   I met him for the second time in a Romanian restaurant in the rue Sainte-Anne in Paris in 1964. I was with Minos, and Beckett was with the French director Roger Blin. Being friends of Genet, Blin and Minos began to talk about him. For some minutes, then, I was alone with the author of *Malone Dies*, one of my favorite novels.

What to say? I could have mentioned our first meeting in London the year before. I was leaving the Old Vic, after a dress rehearsal of his one-acter *Play;* he and Kenneth Tynan were coming into the theater as I was going out. Their combined thrust in was more forceful than my polite push out, and they'd knocked me down. Speak to Beckett of that? No, instead, I said, "I've been collecting jokes that can't be translated into French. For example: *A man goes into a bar where there's a piano player with a monkey. The man orders a martini. The monkey comes up to the bar and puts his tail in the man's martini. The man says to the piano player, 'Do you know your monkey has put his tail in my martini?' 'No,' says the piano player, 'but maybe if you hum a few bars I can fake it.' "*

After ten seconds or so, Beckett said, "I think I can translate that." But just then Blin and Minos finished their conversation. We went to our table across the room and I never heard Beckett's translation.*

DUPLICITY (II)   One afternoon, in London, talking with Minos and Canetti about duplicity, Canetti told us this story. It happened in Prague in 1941. There were two brothers, neither of them Jewish (obsessed with the *Epic of Gilgamesh*, Canetti liked stories of brothers). The two brothers were in love with the same young woman. She wasn't Jewish, either. She married the older brother and started an affair with the younger one. Her husband found out that she had a lover, and he denounced her to the Ge-

---

* The difficulty is that the verb *to know* is translated into French by two verbs, *savoir* and *connaître*. The martini man's question employs *savoir*, but the piano player's answer is to a question that employs *connaître*.

A sequel to this story appears in a footnote on page 202.

stapo as a Jew. She was arrested and sent to Auschwitz. The husband told this to his brother, adding that he had also told the Gestapo that the lover, whoever he was, was a Jew as well. "Oh, my god," said the brother, "I was her lover and now they're going to send me to Auschwitz. Not only that, but if I am a Jew, then of course you are, too." After a pause the older brother replied that if he had it to do over, he would do the same. Canetti said that duplicity healed itself through treason and that the brother's reply was the only sort of heroism which duplicity could attain.

Minos told me afterwards that he couldn't think of duplicity as a wound. "Anyway," he said, "duplicity gives a *useful schizophrenia.*"

Duplicity not a wound? Schizophrenia a beneficence? I was stirred by these ideas.

THE DRESDEN GALLERY   Merle Dankbloom next asked me to go to Portuguese West Africa. For the Company? Or for U.S. Air Force Intelligence? I knew he was attached to both. To go to Bissau, posing as a collector of Ivory Coast art. For what purpose? Merle Dankbloom couldn't say. Again I told him no, again I said the jobs you offer me are trivial. "Besides," I said, "our policies in West Africa are evil."

"Evil?" he said. "You don't say?" Which told me I would never be taken as a Serious Person politically. Certainly not by Merle Dankbloom. My own notion of such a person came first from Silone and Sartre, then from Gramsci and Fanon; and I knew that I wasn't serious because (a) I wasn't wretched, poor or oppressed, (b) I couldn't work with a group, (c) I liked mischief and (d) I was drawn "fatally," as I put it, to women. At least the women I was drawn to were fatal to a serious politics. In September 1963, for example, I determined to go to Dresden. The Berlin Wall was up. As an American, I could still go to East Berlin, but travel into East Germany was forbidden. All the same, I longed to have a "crystallizing" political experience such as I was sure would occur in Eastern Europe and only there. I wasn't going to tell Merle Dankbloom of this; I'd ask John Peet to help me; and I'd tell him only that I wanted to see the paintings in the Dresden Gallery, adding perhaps, "Dresden is where Richard Wagner met the anarchist Mikhail Bakunin and where Bakunin was arrested during the revolution of 1849, Wagner having fled the city." In fact, I may have been thinking of writing a play about Marx and Wagner with Bakunin as the seriocomic victim of the clash between these two universal forces. Mostly, however, I wanted to go to Dresden because it would be difficult, if not impossible: just the sort of challenge that privilege sets for itself. Ill-conceived, worse-digested and confused, my political purposes were at least not vulgar.

I went to the Courtauld Institute, then still in Bloomsbury, to find out what I could about the Dresden Gallery and its history, and there, in the library, a young woman caught my eye. She was talking to a slightly built, very well-dressed man whom I thought I recognized. After he left, I went up to her, and she told me that she was a specialist in the work of Hercules Seghers. "You will never have heard of Hercules Seghers," she said, "but it is rumored that six at least of his canvases were in the Dresden Gallery before the war, more there then than anywhere in Europe, including Amsterdam. During the war, along with all the Dresden treasures, the Seghers oils were stored in a salt mine. All were taken by the Russians in 1945, then restored to the East German government. In the collection today all the Rembrandts are there, the Georgione, the Raphaels; the Gemäldegallerie is intact. But where are the Hercules Seghers?"

Her accent was foreign, German or Portuguese, or Magyar or Danish or Dutch, and she had a gap between her two front teeth. Her clothes were post-graduate-student style: the nymph Daphne in disguise. "Hercules Seghers," she explained, "an exceedingly important, though too little known, landscape painter. Dutch. He lived from 1589 to 1633."

"Or 1638," I said. Color came to her cheeks. "As it happens," I continued, "I know not a little about Hercules Seghers." This was true: Seghers had been a particular favorite of Hans Dreier. "On my first trip to Holland," I told her, "I made it my mission to see every one of his landscape paintings in the Dutch collections." This was true, too. Almost all his paintings had been destroyed in the explosion of a gunpowder factory near his studio in Amsterdam, and he had died soon after, in a drunken fall down a flight of steps. Or so his biographer, Hoogstraten, alleged. Today only three or four of his oils hang in the Dutch museums. I told the young woman, "There is a Hercules Seghers in the collection of the Hispanic Society in New York." True. (She was growing excited.) "I myself own a folio volume— printed in Leipzig in the nineteen-twenties—of his landscape etchings." This was not true (but now her excitement caused her to lean against a library table). "Is it possible that somewhere in the Soviet Union there are six of his oils? Why don't you and I go to Dresden and find out? I was planning to go anyway."

"You know about Hercules Seghers! . . . My name is Agnès, by the way," she said.

"Agnès," I said, "what a ravishing name. An-yes, An-YES." She must have been about thirty, yet her hair was completely white. She told me that her name originally was Rachel. She was French, her parents were Jewish, and during the war they had given her for protection to an order of nuns in Grenôble. Hence, Agnès.

"I identify with Ribera's *Saint Agnes in Prison* in the Dresden Gallery. Do you know it? I'm sure you do," she said (I didn't), and she showed me a plate in a book: a naked figure in a cold dark cell being clothed by an angel in a sheet.

"Or is the angel taking the sheet away?" I said. Our hands touched on the table.

Agnès smiled and said she was married. Her husband worked in the Treasury and they had a son. "We have a cocker spaniel as well. I love her. Her name is Cressida."

Before leaving with her, for tea at the Ritz, I asked, "Who were you talking to when I came in?"

"My teacher here. Sir Anthony Blunt."*

Agnès used to speak to me of El Greco, particularly of the influence on him of Titian, Tintoretto and Palma Vecchio. I remember telling her one afternoon of El Greco's portrait of the poet Góngora that hangs in the Prado. There is a black spot, a birthmark, I said, on the left side of Góngora's head. I wrote down in my notebook what Agnès replied: "Many painters of his day went to Venice in search of the secret of color, but El Greco went to Venice in search of the secret of *blackness*."

Another afternoon, at the Dulwich College Collection, before

---

* See note on page 151.

a thrilling *Landscape with Cows* by Cuyp, talking of how we must soon say good-bye, she said, Not to worry, there'll be someone else soon. And I said, I'm sick to death of Someone-Else-Soon, maybe I should get married? And she said, "No! no!" She said: "Forgive my vehemence, but you mustn't get married. You like women liking you too much."

And so never to Dresden. Never to be a Serious Political man.

"WHY NOT AFTER ALL?"   I moved from 5 Half Moon Street into an apartment on the top floor of 26 Mount Street, down the block from the Connaught Hotel. Now I owed money to the contractor and upholsterer, as well as to the usual tradesmen. A good time to get married, and this time I did.

I married Katherine Swan's sister, Alice, who was seventeen. Now *that's* a pretty girl, Bill Davis said. *IT WILL KILL ME IF YOU DO THIS*, Sally cabled from New York. "Don't you *ever* marry anyone, you just have lots of splendid children instead," Siriol wrote. "But then, of course, you might manage to marry someone and go on being nice to them forever, why not after all?"

But first I had to end my affairs with Chloe and Atalanta. As neither was deep-rooted, this was hard to do. "Are you going to take marriage seriously?" Chloe said to me. It was late in the afternoon at her mother's house in Belgravia. "Else why bother?" Chloe and I used to go riding in the mornings in Richmond Park. "What very *brown* boots," she'd said to me the first time in the car. "I don't know when I've seen such very *brown* boots before."

"Yes, well," I'd said; I was mortified, "they are *polo* boots, my *hunting* boots are in Spain."

Chloe's mother was related to the Earl of Ancaster, who they said owned more land in England than anyone except the Queen. Her father's people claimed a barony that was the oldest inherited title in England. To know Chloe was to turn the pages of a fat Peerage and Companionage.

Why, with such very compelling claims, didn't I marry Chloe? Well, for one thing, she didn't much like me and I didn't much like her. (I could never have forgotten the incident with the boots.) For another, she was more like a sister you fight with than like a lover. In fact, she lived with her sister and their mother in a house in West Halkin Street. I knew a number of households like Chloe's. Mother and daughters living together, luring men in, then stunning them and eating them up. The floors of Chloe's mother's house were littered with the casings of men they'd chewed up and spat out.

"I am going to take marriage seriously," I said to Atalanta. It was early evening at her mother's house in Edwardes Square. "Else why bother to get married?" Atalanta was a student at the Slade. She was related to the Huxleys, the Stracheys, the Darwins, the Garnetts, the Wedgwoods. To know Atalanta was to turn the pages of a fat *Dictionary of National Biography.*

I hadn't married her because there was Someone Else, from her Past, in her life, and in such situations I was beginning to find it better to withdraw until powerful enough to reappear and crush my rival with a single anonymous act of annihilating magnanimity.

Atalanta sang as I left, "Just seventeen, If you know what I mean."

Anyhow, take marriage seriously? Who did? "I'm going to take marriage seriously," I told Alice, "if you know what I mean."

"Me, too," she said.

"I'm going to destroy all those photographs and letters."

"I could destroy all my stuffed animals, I suppose, if you really want." How darling she looked as she said that. "Flopsy, Juniper, Grey . . . No, instead I'll destroy all my memories."

Siriol died on March 11, 1964. She was thirty-nine.

Alice and I got married at a registry office a little later that month. I didn't tell my family and Alice didn't tell hers, so it all felt like an elopement. She wore a short-jacketed two-piece suit of rose-colored tweed, a pink and orange silk chiffon blouse (the blouse with a jabot), and a broad-brimmed crimson straw hat. I was wearing a grey flannel suit from Hawes & Curtis and a grey-green shirt from Lanvin in Paris and a green silk paisley-patterned tie from Charvet *et fils.* My shoes (C. J. Cleverly) were black calf. Frank and Minos were there, so was Alice's best friend.

After the wedding we went to Paris for the day and had lunch at the Grand Véfour. "I used to see André Malraux lunching here," I said to Alice in the restaurant. Then I explained who André Malraux was. After lunch, in the gardens of the Palais-

Royal: "Colette lived over there, there lived Jean Cocteau. I myself used to stay at this hotel, the Hôtel de Beaujolais. . . . Cocteau made a portrait drawing of me but crumpled it up before it was finished. [That was true.] He said that I looked like Raymond Radiguet. [That was untrue]" Then I explained who Raymond Radiguet was. Then we went to the Hittite exhibition at the Petit Palais.

At the moment before I got married was this undercurrent of revulsion. Having said good-bye to Agnès, when I was seeing both Chloe and Atalanta, Chloe was also seeing someone else, and meanwhile I was infatuated with Iope who was engaged to marry Endymion who was himself infatuated with Chloe's younger sister, Cleo, who in her turn was infatuated with an Italian movie director who had been a lover of her mother's and with whom Chloe later ran off. That clot of adulterous parasites, with their second-rate talents and vile characters. Yet I envied them. Marriage would save me from that.

And the fear caused in me by Siriol's death. Once she had said to her daughter, "Ben is leaving town again. Whatever are we going to do?" Emma's answer: "I plan to grieve." Postponement of feeling: how childish that was. Yet I did it, too. Marriage would change that.

Salvation, protection, reform: these are what marriage would bring. Not forgetting redemption. Literally, for my debts would all be paid.*

•

We went to Spain for our honeymoon. We stayed at La Consula. I picked up my Alvis in Gibraltar and we drove north. Outside Jeréz I smashed the car into a truck and we went to the hospital. Then we went to Venice. "There are no cars there," I explained.

In Venice I got a letter from Atalanta. How pleased she was I had "*found* someone." One afternoon, on the Giudecca, we saw Ezra Pound walking with Olga Rudge. "You know who that is, don't you? That is *Ezra Pound Walking With Olga Rudge*," I said to

---

* Chloe, Cleo, Atalanta and Angès are not their real names. Neither are Iope Oldcastle and Endymion Porter.

Alice, as if reading the title of an oil painting in the Accademia: sure I'd have to explain, *pleased* I'd have to explain, *only too ready* to have to explain.

We had dinner with Peggy Guggenheim. "You had an affair with Bill Davis?" I said, and she said: *Best technique, best equipment, best everything.* Then we all went to a rooftop nightclub and watched Peggy Guggenheim dance with Doris Duke. "Naturally," I explained to Alice. "The two richest women in the room . . ."

I was disturbed, not always unpleasantly, by how men looked at Alice. I could hear myself saying to a man some day, "Some men can pay attention to another man's wife in such a way it is a compliment to them all. . . ."*

•

Spronce was a word much used by girls in London then. To spronce meant to show off. Someone sproncy was someone who wanted you to stop talking and look their way when they came into the restaurant. It was sproncy to go to South London and sleep with a Jamaican. You got the Jamaican to say "sproncy," and back in Bayswater or Chelsea you yourself said "mon" and smoked "ganja."

I bought Alice a car for her eighteenth birthday. A black Mini-Cooper-S with wicker on the sides. That was sproncy.

We had two dogs. Chiang and Poppæa. Chow Chows, a deep blue in color. Sproncy. We walked them in Hyde Park.

And we went to sproncy restaurants and shopped in sproncy shops.

•

At seventeen and eighteen, Alice was a lovable child. She looked love at me and she looked like me, too, with her big dark eyes and dark brown hair; and her very white skin was like paper

---

*I in fact believed that adultery was essential to marriage. Joyce's play *Exiles*, Dostoevsky's "The Eternal Husband," Goethe's *Elective Affinities*, together with *Women in Love* and *Cosi fan tutte:* these works summed up all there was to say on the subject of the infidelity essential to marriage, with its vital homosexual component. Or so I thought before Minos introduced me to *Le Cocu magnifique*. Crommelynck's play showed me clearly what the other works lacked. A posthumous essay by William Empson (*London Review of Books*, January 24, 1991) shows this to have been Joyce's experience, too.

for me to write upon. I thought sometimes of Sophia Schliemann in the famous photograph where the very young Sophia is wearing the treasure of Clytemnestra, excavated by her much older husband, Heinrich, at Mycenae. So Alice would be bedecked with my knowledge, I thought. She was a show-business child, what is more, with the darling weakness such offspring have for the punch line, for whatever "works." Funny and quick-witted, she was more like Frank and Minos and their friends than like Agnès, Chloe or Atalanta. Something of Alice's spirit would rub off on me.

What a darling couple we looked. I was a little overweight. Not much; but I was a little. But I wore beautiful shirts and suits. My shoes were works of art. And my pretty young bride! So *dolly*! Like a fashion model, the fashion then being young and popular. And only seventeen!

My father came to London, and Alice and I went to dinner with him and Alice's mother. Old friends though her mother and my father were, that evening, at the White Tower, he was rude to Norma.

"Maybe they used to be lovers?" Alice said later.

"No, he's always like that with relatives," I said. "Maybe she owes him money?"

"Why not? She owes money to everyone else."

I asked him about it when I saw him the next day in his suite at Claridges.

"Do I tell you how to write plays?" He was getting dressed for the evening. A "shindig," he said, at Lord Bossom's for David and Evangeline Bruce, our ambassador and his wife.

"You acted like someone meeting a bawd at a diplomatic reception."

"By the way," he said, "I paid your tab at Robert Lewis."

"Thank you," I said.

"And at Dunhill."

"Thank you."

"And Lansdowne, and the White Tower."

"Thank you, thank you."

"And Wilton's. . . ."

Norma Swan had a dress shop, in Brook Street, near Claridges. It was called "So You Want to Be Young" and sold

American-designed clothing to young Englishwomen who
wanted to dress differently from their mothers. I used to drop in
there after lunch. Henrietta, Fiona: that sort of girl. Arabella,
Anthea, Althea. "Ben, what do *you* say? . . . More *poitrine*? . . ."
More was shown. "There speaks a man-of-the-world." From
the back of the shop came giggles. Says Falstaff's Hostess in
Henry V:

> We cannot lodge and board a dozen or fourteen gentlewomen
> that live honestly by the prick of their needles, but it will be
> thought we keep a bawdy-house. . . .

I used to leave the shop feeling like a dandy in a painting by
Caillebotte or Manet: heartless, idle, insouciant. A dandy, a
flâneur, a fop.

In point of fact, I admired Norma and resented my father's
rudeness. A *once-beautiful* girl (she'd been a Powers model),
Norma was now a vivacious, resourceful, hospitable woman with
habits of kindness and many friends, some of these Old Lefties.
Yet I'd say to myself, in a sort of drawl, *Like many single women
with marriageable daughters, Norma Swan often acts desperate and loud,
and when she's drunk, as she often is, she loudly proclaims Edwardian
standards of propriety. There's a certain Missus Warren-like lewdness in
that. . . .*

Her kindness to me was reflected in numberless compliments,
and in letting me sleep with her daughters of course. Pronounc-
ing so hostile a judgment on her does nothing but satisfy a wish
to pay women back for not complying, always and in all things.
"Men are like that," I told Alice. "Admire *me*," we say, "and me
only. If not, *prends garde à toi!*"

("Which means, Watch out?" Very *good*, Alice.)

•

I was asked to edit a book about the assassination of President
Kennedy. I felt I knew something about this because on the day
Oswald was shot to death by Jack Ruby I was in New York,
watching it on TV with my father and Abe Fortas. My father
said, "Whoever shot Kennedy, you can be sure it wasn't Oswald." And Abe Fortas agreed.

About the assassination itself, my feelings were mixed. Detestation of the Kennedy administration was uppermost. Also, when it occurred, I was with Maria at the Bronx Zoo and we heard about it in the cab going back to Manhattan. She was upset. I thought only, "There goes the evening."*

A word about my father and Abe Fortas. Their friendship went back many years, to the second Roosevelt administration, when Abe had been in the Department of the Interior. They had many clients in common. I admired Abe for his pro bono work, the Gideon case in particular. My father admired him for his sinister pliancy, the quality that made him apt as "Lyndon Johnson's hatchetman." *Your eyes drop millstones when fools' eyes fall tears*, as Richard the Third says to the Murderers. My father often boasted of his many powerful political friends. Abe was but one of them. He said to me, as we were going down in the lift that afternoon, *Your father is a magician. He has done me many favors.* Newspapermen often said the same, adding (famous enemies of power) *It isn't easy for me to accept favors from someone like your father.* After Abe was forced to resign from the Supreme Court, in 1969, for accepting a comparatively insignificant gift of money from a retired businessman (also a convicted felon), my father said to me, "You'll never understand what money means to someone brought up poor like Abe."

I took a tiny office in Albemarle Street to work on the assassination book. I tacked my calling card to the door. One morning I found that someone had drawn a swastika under my name. I used to act tired when I got home, the better to enjoy the tyranny of the fatigued. Sometimes, when I got home, Alice wasn't there.

"Where *were* you?"

"I was hit by a bus in Oxford Street. A number twenty-five. I wasn't hurt much. Only my back."

Another time she told me she had fainted in the lobby of the Westbury Hotel.

* Compare "Thank goodness it happened on a Friday," i.e., when the Market could close for the weekend, which I heard from a banker friend of my father's. Compare also Malcolm X's remark, "It's a case of the chickens coming home to roost." I'm not sure how much I knew then of the Kennedy policy of "selective assassination," but Merle Dankbloom had shown satisfaction over the death of Patrice Lumumba in 1961. He went about as though he'd caused the awful event himself, as is said about Natasha and the town fire in Act Three of *Three Sisters*.

"What were you doing in the lobby of the Westbury Hotel?"
"I thought you'd ask me that. I was having a drink with Peter
Finch. He wants me to go to the Caribbean with him and work
on his new movie as a press agent."

The CIA was not involved in the book I was editing. When I
told Merle Dankbloom about it, he said, "My god! Can't they
leave that poor man alone?" Kennedy? Oswald? Earl Warren? It
turned out that the "poor man" was an obscure White Russian
émigré who lived on Cape Cod (where, as it happened, I once
met him). He was at the very fringe of the Warren Commission
investigation.

•

Debt was a bad thing about married life, making certain side-
walks impassable; before I was married, I'd never really minded
about debts.

A second bad thing was Alice's friends. One was living with
Paul McCartney. When the four of us went out, the talk was of
nothing I cared about. Another friend of Alice's was Deb of the
Year that year. I had nothing to say to her either. Meanwhile,
Alice was a hit with my friends. She flirted with them, even my
queer friends, and she seemed to expect me to flirt with hers, so
we could quarrel about it afterwards.

I did not know how to talk to, much less make love to, a girl
of eighteen. If you know what I mean.

One afternoon, looking at photographs, I said to Alice, "I was
trying hard to look like Montgomery Clift, as the young woman
by whom I was then *sidéré* had just made a movie with him. . . .
Yes, well, I may as well tell you it was Susannah York." And
then I told Alice this story which Susannah York told me. Clift
played Freud to Susannah's Martha Bernays, Freud's fiancée, in
John Huston's film, script by Jean-Paul Sartre. Susannah and
"Monty" did not get along. When it came to the wedding scene,
"Monty" kept muffing his lines, so Huston stood in for Susannah
and then the scene went smoothly. A funny movie story, I
thought; it always went over well, and I liked the way I showed
myself in a not altogether flattering light. "So, you see, my efforts to look like Clift went for naught." But Alice wasn't laughing.

"You had a thing with Susannah York?"

"A *romantic* interest, Alice," I said. "Not a *thing.*"

"But you slept with Susannah York?"

"Lips sealed, gentleman's code, and so on . . ."

But I saw at once that such subjects were best not brought up, however urbanely, however disguised in gallant ambiguity.

•

Alice and I lied to each other. My lies were crude: name-dropping, boasting, the usual thing. "I used to know Christine Keeler. Bill Astor introduced us. She lived around the corner from me. . . ."

Alice's lies by contrast were motiveless, less studied and more fun. The possibility that one day she might be a great liar came up on a short drive we made to Penshurst Place in Kent, the house of the Sydney family. I was looking forward to showing Alice the house and quoting to her "spontaneously" from one of Ben Jonson's great "To Penshurst" poems. I was planning the lines I was going to remember, when suddenly she told me that since the age of thirteen she had been having a love affair with a man whom she described pretty much as Emily Brontë describes Heathcliff. The warmth I felt! the excitement!

"Since you were thirteen?" Thirteen was when I'd first met her, a sweets-loving, pasty-faced schoolgirl, Katherine's little sister, whose most guilty secret I'd imagined to be the pack of cigarettes that fell from her duffel-coat pocket when once in horseplay I'd picked her up and turned her upside down.

"Yes, and I'm finding it hard to break off. You see, he wants to marry me—except his wife has cancer."

"What sort of cancer?"

"*Terminal* cancer."

"But that first time in Half Moon Street, weren't you— . . . ."

Whereupon she burst into tears and said it was all a lie. "I invented it because I was afraid that you were bored with me."

I was disappointed not only at her expectation that the truth would interest me more than her lie, but also at her furnishing a motive. I began to fear that with Alice my own lies were wasted, or (worse) translated into the banal terms of a system of interpretation.

•

We went to Greece. In Delphi, a tour guide stopped in mid-sentence to watch Alice as she walked by. All the tourists turned to watch her, too.

Alice got pregnant and miscarried and then got pregnant again. With her doctor's permission, we went to Sicily. In Selinunte, near a marble quarry, I bought an archaic bronze figure of a woman from a local man. How good it would be to start collecting "seriously." To travel the world and buy small archaic Greek bronzes, or Minoan pots, or Belgian mannerist drawings: something like that. I already had a "serious" collection of Ezra Pound, my James collection included an *American Scene* inscribed to William and Alice, I had my firsts of *Ulysses* and *The Waste Land*. If I collected art, my credit would soon be as good at Colnaghi's and Sotheby's as it was now at the booksellers Bertram Rota and Quaritch.

The archaic bronze woman turned out to be fake.

"But it's so beautiful," I said to the London dealer Hans Calmann.

"Have you ever seen a fake that *wasn't* beautiful?"

Meanwhile, Frank Hauser gave me one hundred pounds to translate *Le Chandelier* by Alfred de Musset. It was put on, a "first-class production." Minos directed it. But I felt sick to my stomach when the audience laughed. Making people laugh was more aggressive than I wanted to be. Maybe a life in the theater was wrong for me?

•

In September 1965 our daughter Susanna was born. "You go back and get some sleep," they told me just before and when they phoned and woke me up I was ready and ran down the stairs and drove our car as fast as I could through the black, wet, shiny trafficless streets to the London Clinic. A black nurse was holding Alice's hand, turning her wedding ring round and round, a Roman child's ring on a hand that still looked like a child's, the fingernails always bitten down. I had bought the ring from M. Hakim. I watched our daughter being born. She slithered out like a fish.

"I did it," Alice said, laughing and crying before falling asleep. "Ben, I did it for you."

I went back home to walk the dogs. Next I went to the Connaught for breakfast. Other men had had children, had watched while their wives gave birth, and then had slipped back into their lives, as though nothing extraordinary had occurred. I told myself, Don't let that happen to you.

After breakfast I ran into Ken Tynan, who lived across the street. "I'm a father," I said to him.

"Congratulations," he said. "Have you heard from Tsai?" Tsai had been a girlfriend of his, then I went out with her once or twice. (Or had it been the other way round?) Ken had once said to me about Tsai, "Oriental women are more like sisters than like mothers if you think of them as wives." I said I hadn't heard from Tsai.

"I haven't heard from her either," Ken said.

He pointed to a house on the other side of Carlos Place and said he was going to consult a trichologist there. This news depressed me. I didn't know why. I was sure I didn't see England as depicted by Beatrix Potter and Kenneth Grahame. It wasn't populated for me by small lovable animals: John Stoat, Amanda Vole, Piers Badger, and so on. No, I was sure I saw England as it really was: in harsh, unlovely, satirical terms. And yet now, I was thinking, here is London's tallest rabbit worried about losing his hair and I'm depressed.

"I'm going to leave London and live in New York," I told Ken.

"New York is not the antidote to London," Ken said.

"What is?"

"I wish I knew," Ken said, and groaned.

I went to the shop where I used to buy toys for Siriol's Emma and bought a stuffed squirrel for Susy. It would be her first toy. At the London Clinic I held her for the first time. The room smelled of lilies-of-the-valley. I handed Susy back to Alice. She began to nurse. How beautiful she looked. How happy we were going to be. In a few days Alice and Susy came home.

THE HINGE The moments when I got up at night and fed Susy were the happiest of my life. It seemed to me when I was alone with her that there was no question but that all would be well as soon as we got out of England. We'd go to New York and I'd write plays. My father would buy us a house and give me the "wherewithal" to run it. I'd be faithful to Alice.

First, though, I had to be harsh with myself. "Face up to myself," which as I was two-faced was hard to do.

"What has my life been?" I said to Alice. We were at the White Tower. That was a good place to be harsh. The owner had come over and told us of the ortolans he had, I had ordered the wine from Yorgos. "Evasions, equivocations. My life has been a *comédie à tiroirs.*"

Alice of course had to ask what that was: was it something funny with drawers?

And "No," I had had to say, dryly. "Not drawers, *episodes.*"

"But it is something funny? . . ." I looked at her or did not look at her. "Why are you angry with me?" she said.

"I'm not angry," I lied. "But you see," I said, "Chloe, Gemma, Atalanta, Sabina, Sally, Agnès . . ."

"Who is On-YES? Oh, Agnes, is it? AGG-ness." I had made a show of destroying my photographs, love letters, souvenirs: burning my memories, too, like her. Yet here I was listing them, boasting penitentially. And who was Agnès? I'd never mentioned Agnès. How many others were there going to be?

"You don't understand," I said, dryly, with becoming bitterness.

There were little glass screens between the tables. Behind one screen I saw Lucien Freud. The young woman he was with was crying and he was looking straight ahead.

"I was offered a job at the BBC," Alice said.

"You're not going to take a job," I said. Lucien Freud and the young woman walked out. She was still crying. "We're going to go and live in New York."

Yorgos came and clipped my cigar. Now Alice was crying. I smoked my cigar and looked straight ahead.

THE LAST INCARNATION OF MERLE DANKBLOOM One afternoon, before I got married, Atalanta and I had been going through some boxes of hers. Drawings of insects, bats, Etruscan masks . . . I turned up a photograph. It was of Merle Dankbloom in field boots and a U.S. Army tunic.

"Who is this?."

"Sidney Freeman. He was a teacher of mine at the Courtauld."

"What did he teach?" I said. "Housebreaking?"

An American intelligence officer I knew had told me of being given a course in espionage skills by the British at a house somewhere in Hampshire. One instructor he'd had was a convict who taught them how to rob an English country house. "All you have to do is go there on a weekend night wearing pajamas and if someone stops you in the hall you say you're looking for the bathroom."

"No," said Atalanta. "He taught us Italian Mannerists. He knows more about Parmigianino than anyone in the world, apparently."

"Then why is he dressed like a cavalry officer?" In fact, he looked like a British officer on the staff of General Haig in the First World War, Sam Browne belt and all. His field boots had those little pieces of leather that the spur straps go through. I was sure I knew who had made those boots.

"I don't know," Atalanta said. "He told me he was in American Naval Intelligence at the time."

•

"Who makes your boots?" I asked Merle Dankbloom the next time I saw him.

We were in a pub in Jermyn Street, down from Paxton & Whitfield, near where the Cavendish had been. He had just come from Sotheby's.

"Maxwell's in Albemarle Street. At least they used to make my boots. I have my field boots from them. I got my last pair of hunting boots from Mister Cleverly in Cork Street. Do you know him? Reversed calf."

"Who bones them for you?"

"I bone them myself."

A man came each week to my apartment from Mr. Cleverly. He polished my shoes and cleaned my calf boots with the shin bone of a goat. But I told Merle Dankbloom none of that and he told me nothing explicitly about his art-history teaching. "Maxwell's in Albemarle Street" was enough: that alone confirmed

that he was "Sidney Freeman." But why had he been teaching at
the Courtauld?*

•

Some months later, after I married, I went to the American
Embassy to pick up a visa for the nanny Alice and I were taking
to New York. The visa had been impossible to get until my
father pulled strings. "Thank you," I said to the chargé.

"What else are we here for?" the chargé said. I saw Merle
Dankbloom going into the ambassador's office. I hadn't seen him
for weeks. "Is that Merle Dankbloom?"

"No, that is Carlos Freedberg, our man in Djibouti," the chargé
said. (Or did he say Jakarta?) "He went to Yale with the ambassador's son."

"Carlos Freedberg" was wearing a suit of green plaid, a sort of
horseblanket material with narrow stripes in it of red and yellow
and blue. I myself had an Inverness cape of the same material,
made by Huntsman; but to have had it made into a suit— . . .
That was genius!

I was never to see Merle Dankbloom again.

---

* In the early 1960s, nothing was known publicly of Anthony Blunt's importance as
a Soviet spy. He was known only as a respected art scholar, an expert on Poussin and
Picasso, Surveyor of the Queen's Drawings, and head of the Courtauld Institute. Sir
Anthony Blunt, FRS. He may or may not have been the reason that Merle Dankbloom was at the Courtauld.

A book on Parmigianino by a Professor Sidney Freedberg was published sometime
in the 1960s. Sidney Freedberg had been a romantic interest of Siriol's and had
worked in U.S. Army Intelligence during the war. I met him once at the Fogg
Museum when he was teaching at Harvard: plummy voice, made-up accent, buckle
shoes. But he looked nothing like Merle Dankbloom.

PART TWO

A DESIRABLE CALAMITY

Alice was unhappy when we got to New York. It was my fault completely. "This is my fault completely," I said. "Your unhappiness is the price we all have to pay."

"For what?"

"Yes," I heard myself saying, "your unhappiness is—"

She threw an ashtray at me. The ashtray smashed on the wall. "For the coming Revolution!" I cried. "Yes, it's the price we all have to pay." Then I explained to Alice about the Black Panthers. "Read Fanon," I said. "Read Malcolm X." As every young man in the States had a beard, or seemed to then, I shaved off my own.

We moved into an apartment on Sullivan Street in Greenwich Village. Edgard Varèse had lived nearby. In the mornings I took the dogs and walked across Washington Square to the office I had on Eighth Street, *I haven't failed; I've merely not achieved*, I told myself. That was from "Old Trails," a poem by E. A. Robinson which is set in Washington Square. [*F*]*ive years he toiled*, goes the poem, *In Yonkers—and then sauntered into fame*. Some day they would say that about me: *sauntered into fame*.

I was writing a play about a rich young man who collects African art and lives alone with his collection and a black manservant on the Upper East Side. It is Sunday morning. The young man, Joel Mole, has visits from his broker, his art dealer, his mother. Each is shown in and ushered out by the black manservant. Enter his analyst, Dr. Tuco Paz. "I've found you a girl." She is a very young girl. "A mystery," says Dr. Paz. She is waiting at the zoo cafeteria in Central Park. Joel, alone, contemplates his collection and quotes Garcia Lorca rhapsodically: "*Negro! Negro! Negro!*" Three negroes pop up in different parts of the room as Joel Mole exits to the zoo. At the zoo Joel meets his intended, but their rapture is interrupted by a band of black revolutionaries. "Free all the animals!—the *African* animals!" Actually they are old black juvenile delinquents who took refuge in

Central Park after the Harlem riots of 1943. They have been waiting for the coming of the King of Harlem. Enter Dr. Paz. He scoffs at the revolutionaries and denies the possibility of a King of Harlem. Enter the King. He is Joel's black manservant. Joel's bride-to-be follows him to Harlem. In the next scene, at the wedding, the guests assemble: the bridegroom is there, Dr. Paz is there, Joel Moel's mother is there, so are his art dealer and stockbroker. All await the bride. She comes in, "like an army with banners." When she takes off the veil, she narrates the murder of the King of Harlem which she witnessed at the Audubon Ballroom on 132d Street and Broadway (where Malcolm X was assassinated in 1965). The assassins come in during her speech and lay their weapons down at the feet of Dr. Paz. The bride dies, the wedding goes on, there's dancing, and the play ends.

I wrote until midafternoon. Then I went home. Alice and I would get Susy up and bathe her and feed her and play with her and then I would read to her and put her to bed. Otherwise our life differed little from what it had been in London.

My bills in London had been paid. I was looking forward to being given a proper income in New York: twenty or thirty or forty thousand dollars a year. Meanwhile, not having enough money from my father to pay all our bills, I paid none of them. Instead I bought first editions from Seven Seas and antiquities from Mattias Komor. From time to time, to make up to Alice for the angry phone calls she'd had to deal with, from the butcher or liquor store about unpaid bills or bounced checks, I bought her a piece of ancient gold jewelry.

For once in my life I liked going to 19 Gramercy Park, going there with my wife and baby daughter. My mother and father loved Alice, and I loved showing Alice where I'd grown up and showing off to the servants. One afternoon, watching Susy, on the needlepoint rug, in the paneled library, I remembered how once at a dealer's, a decrepit old collector came, with his young wife and new baby, to inspect a white-figure wine jug of the fourth century B.C. The baby pulled at something, the lekythos nearly fell, and from the way the collector looked, I knew if he had had to choose between the vase and his baby, the baby would be dead. I'm not like that, thank goodness, I thought, watching

Susy on the rug, watching my parents watching me, turning my foot from side to side, catching the light on my shoe.

Alice and I looked at townhouses on Charlton Street, Bank Street and Stuyvesant Street. Federal houses, not grand in scale, needing not too much help, with room for more children, and space for my books, and my paintings, and my clothes. Our house would be thronged with artists, authors and famous musicians. Our lives would be filled with children and pets and art, like the lives you see in Vuillard and Bonnard, rich, extravagant lives, innocent in their greed: calm lives but with a muted turmoil underneath.

I took Alice to a fund-raising cocktail party for something or other (*not* the Black Panthers) at Leonard and Felicia Bernstein's on Central Park West. "You won't remember me," I said to Felicia Bernstein, "but we met years ago when you were living at the Osborne. I was with Posie Salter, you know. *Being a poet* . . ." Self-deprecating chuckle. *Of course I remember you*, she said, *weren't you a friend of Paul Feigay's?* She didn't remember me, that was clear. *I know Paul is here, let me get him for you.* "Paul Feigay was Lenny's roommate at Harvard," I said to Alice. He'd kissed me in a taxi cab once.

"Did you ever sleep with a man?" Alice said.

It wasn't the first time she asked. "No," I said, also not for the first time. I flirted with men, I said. With Lenny, with Paul, with Dimitri Mitropoulos, with Francis Robinson, the assistant general manager of the Met. "I liked women to wonder if I was queer."

"Men, too, apparently," Alice said.

•

Together with Virgil Thomson, Alice and I gave a party for Elisabeth Lutyens at 19 Gramercy Park. The guests were mostly Virgil's friends: well-known composers, world-famous musicians, rich patrons-of-the-arts. A tenor sang, from Elisabeth's *Rimbaud Cantata*, "*Ô saisons! Ô châteaux!*" The life of a woman composer in England was hard, I told my parents: a woman composer of twelve-tone music, a woman composer of twelve-tone music with strong opinions and left-wing views, who was not beautiful.

To thank me for the party, Elisabeth took me to the Pierre Hotel to meet Stravinsky and his wife. Stravinsky talked in an animated way about Edward Clark, Elisabeth's late husband.

"I'll tell you a wonderful story about Edward," Stravinsky said.

But Elisabeth said, "I poked my head into the bedroom the night before he died and said, 'You know, I'm glad I have someone like you to talk to,' and he said, 'Someone to sharpen your tongue on, you mean.' They were his last words to me."

Stravinsky said, "I've long been afraid that my own last words would become *le dernier cri*."

When I told Virgil of our visit to the Pierre he said, "Stravinsky is always shaping Great Man stories about himself." We were having dinner at Foo Joy, a Fukienese restaurant in Chinatown. "And as for Great Man stories, I prefer the Sibelius ones."

Here is the Sibelius story Virgil told Elisabeth, Alice and me: "Sibelius used to get his cigars delivered from a shop in Helsinki. One day he heard that the delivery man, who was very old, had worked for a music copyist in Bonn and had delivered scores to Beethoven. 'What was he like?' said Sibelius. And after thinking about it a long, long time, the old man said, 'Very hairy hands.' "*

"Don't you hate the smell of Finnish cigars? They smell like mouse droppings," Elisabeth said.

"Mouse Droppings would be a good title," I said.

Virgil said, "There are many books where the interest lies in the title and nowhere else. This is often true of autobiographies. Eddie Cantor's autobiography was called *My Life Is in Your Hands*."

Virgil's recipe for autobiography was as follows. It needed a space large enough for a span from the rapture of memory to the rigor of record and back. From *I remember! I remember!* to *You*

---

* Alexander Cockburn tells a Sibelius story that he heard from his father Claud. "A man writing a profile of Sibelius called on the great composer and spent an agreeable afternoon noting down his views on art, life and the state of the world. Later Sibelius took him to the station and put him on the train back to town. The man was settling into his seat when he heard a bellow from the platform. Sibelius was dashing along beside the carriage, determined to impart a final piece of information he deemed essential to the understanding of his creative wellsprings. 'I forgot to say,' Sibelius panted, 'I have an enormous prick.' "

could look it up. With the truth lying (old well-loved English pun!) somewhere in-between. It was best accomplished at that time of life which, in *My Past and Thoughts*, Alexander Herzen calls "grey-haired youth." Artists should be careful when writing their lives about including too many banausic details.

Was that it? (*N'est-ce que ça?*) No, Virgil said. Alice Toklas taught him that always in giving a recipe, good cooks deliberately withheld the one secret that made the dish truly great. Well? Well, Virgil went on, great events, great works, great love affairs.

"I hope some day you write about growing up in the Gramercy Park museum," Virgil said to me.

"If I do, I'll call it *Lost Property*," I said. "My model will be Aubrey's *Brief Lives. My life in others' words.*" But what great events? What great passions?

"I'm calling mine *Old Scores*," said Elisabeth.*

"I'm calling mine *Virgil Thomson by Virgil Thomson*," Virgil Thomson said.

"What will you call volume two?" Alice said.

In the cab I asked Virgil what he thought about the Beatles.

"The lyrics are better than the tunes."

The cab driver said, "Do any of you people know 'In My Life,' by John Lennon? It goes *tum-tum-tum-tum, tum-tum-tum-ti. . . .*"

I said, "I don't listen to popular music myself." I was disappointed that Virgil hadn't been more disparaging about the Beatles.

•

"A successful evening, don't you think?" I said to Alice when we got home.

"You had a good time. I felt stupid. You all know so much. What does *banausic* mean?"

"I'll take out the dogs and walk Nancy home. I'll tell you when I get back."

Nancy, the baby-sitter, was about Alice's age. She lived on

* Elisabeth called her autobiography *A Goldfish Bowl*. Her version of Edward Clark's last words is somewhat different there. She remembers our visit to the Pierre somewhat differently, too. She gives good sketches of Virgil, also of Minos, but not, I regret to say, of me.

Thompson Street. "You better button up. It's cold. Here, let me—" . . . To button her up and then walk with her, bumping against her from time to time, the dogs pulling! . . .

She played the cello, she told me, she studied at N.Y.U. You live here? I said. I live here, she said. We grinned at each other. It was cold. The dogs pulled. I went home.

What *did* banausic mean?

"I thought better of you than that," Alice said when I got back with the dogs. She was giving Susy her bottle, so she couldn't shout and neither could I.

"What do you mean? I don't know what you mean. Do you mean Nancy? Don't be ridiculous. And what about that unctuous runt I find here every afternoon?"

"You mean Ray? Or Earle?"

"I mean Earle. Who's Ray?"

"Because Ray isn't a runt."

Well, whoever Ray was, neither he nor Earle was the sort to whom I wanted to say, "Some men can pay attention to your wife in a way that is a compliment to all. . . ." Neither was the sort of man to whom I could imagine Alice saying, like a character in the *Princesse de Clèves*, "I wanted to pay myself the compliment of not being married to a cuckold. . . ."

Before leaving New York, Elisabeth dedicated a wind ensemble to us all, *À les Sonnenbergs* [sic], and gave me the score. I'm the trumpet, Alice the clarinet, Susy the flute, my mother and father the oboe and bassoon.*

•

One day my father came for tea.

"We have two kinds of tea, Lapsang Souchong and Formosa Oolong."

---

* I was astonished to read in *A Pilgrim Soul*, the 1989 biography of Elisabeth by Meirion and Susie Harries, of how anti-Semitic Elisabeth was. I'd never noticed it. Neither had Katerina Wolpe or Yolanda or Frank or Harold Lang or Canetti, nor, so far as I knew, Luigi Dallapiccola or any other of her many Jewish friends. Her anti-Semitic attitudes seemed to me at worst the quaint properties of the class into which she was born, Edwardian, upper middle-crust. They were no sooner uttered than they were disowned. It is painful to read of how in old age Elisabeth blamed the Jews for her exclusion from the English musical establishment.

We had little tea sandwiches and little tea cakes. During tea we told my father about the houses we'd seen.

"The Bank Street house is Georgian."

"It's the one we liked best."

"Architecturally, it is the best."

"Definitely."

"But the house on Stuyvesant Street makes more sense."

"Definitely."

"I mean, you could run it without a staff. It is the old Schuyler house."

"Tell about the cellar."

"Yes, well, you see, gun powder was stored there—"

"During the Revolution."

"During the Revolution, and—"

"It blew up."

"The cat did it! You see—. . . ."

It was darling, the way we talked, finishing each other's sentences, excited, avid, noisy, greedy of course but lovable.

"And Stuyvesant Street costs less."

"Yes, it costs twenty thousand less."

"Maybe you could talk to the broker?"

Greedy, lovable, but responsible.

But my father was not going to buy us a house. "It wouldn't be a favor to you," he said to me when Alice was out of the room. "I'm telling you privately," he said, "because I never like to humiliate a man in front of his wife." All the same, when Alice came back, he said, "I was just telling your man here that he mustn't mistake my Largesse for License. He has to find a way to *increment* his income."

After he left, Alice said, "I thought he was going to buy us a house. Didn't you say that he told you that he was going to buy us a house?"

•

Alice and I went to New Orleans to stay with the author of the book about the Kennedy assassination which I had edited. He and his wife had taken an apartment in the French Quarter. He was working on some new lead. There it was that Alice told me that she had had an affair with him in London at the time I was working on his book. It had continued for some weeks in New York, and now it was over. "It's over now," Alice said. And here we were staying with him and his wife. Alice felt bad about that, she said.

I can't say exactly what I felt. I *can* say what houses we looked at along the Mississippi, with their *pigeonniers* and aisles of oak. I remember one in particular with a grand center stair and I remember feeling surprised that more of them didn't have grand center stairs.

•

Alice was pregnant again. We were happy, choosing a name for the baby, making plans.

And I got a job, "landed" a job, reading scripts for a Broadway producer, going every morning to an office above the Palace Theater. Now when Alice and I went to the theater, I could say I was "scouting" new material. Often we were "comped." I was in the "business." At last I was doing something "gainful."

I took Nancy to lunch a couple of times. She still baby-sat for us now and then. Nothing happened between us, nothing. I didn't tell Alice about it, though. Soon after, Nancy stopped baby-sitting.

One day I forgot to tell my boss that someone important had phoned and when he spoke to me sharply, I waited a couple of days and then quit.

Then one day my father told me he was giving me a million dollars. Just like that? Just like that.

Something had happened. This, I think: the Pepperidge Farm bakery was bought by the Campbell Soup Company in 1961. The Rudkins, who owned Pepperidge Farm, were among the people we used to rent from in the summers when I was a child. (See page 33.) In return for some services to them, including inventing the story of how the first loaf had been made, my father had been paid in stock, and so when the bakery was sold he felt he had some "real money" for the first time in his life. He bought a Degas drawing, at about this time, and one by Ingres. (Both were a little dull, I thought.) He bought a rare and expensive "Windsor" Gothic triple-back settee, late eighteenth century, made of elm and yew and beech. But *real money*? What sort of money had he had up till then? Earnings weren't *real money*, and he'd saved nothing. "I mean to die poor," he often said. *Real money*: that was what Bobby Lehman had. Paul Mellon, John Loeb, Bill Paley, Jock Whitney, Marjorie Post Davies: they all had *real money*. *Real money* usually was inherited, he noted with scorn, or it was made in the days before the income tax, as with Albert Lasker. And what about me? Was my money *real*? "You?" he said, also with scorn. *Real money* was money you couldn't *piss away*. "Let us see," he said, "dear boy."

Alice and I started looking at houses in Dutchess County, New York, and Litchfield, Connecticut. One in Lakeville, Connecticut, had a music room. Another in Kent had a stable with twenty-four stalls. All had many hundreds of acres.

We decided on a house near Millbrook, New York. It was big but not grand. Its grounds, overgrown, had "potential." "Potential," "possibilities": these were everywhere. There was a gigantic horse barn. I could make a theater there. There could be a lake in front of the barn.

As I drove up to the house with my father, deer started away from the car. Deer, like possibilities. "Now whose dogs are those?" my father said.

Remodeling the house was going to cost as much as the house itself. The architect understood that while the house had "integrity," it was not an "historic" house. My father said he'd make us a gift of a "spiffing" new master bathroom. "My daughter-in-law should be able to bathe luxuriously," he said.

Alice and I chose handpainted tiles for the bathroom and handmade bricks for the kitchen floor. There was to be a bedroom downstairs where I'd keep my clothes, the shower there would have black slate floors. There were to be hundreds of yards of shelves for my hundreds and hundreds of books. Our bedroom was to be upstairs; across the hall were the children's bedrooms, a nursery and a "sewing" room for Alice (not that she sewed). Downstairs were to be a formal sitting room and a dining room large enough for a dining table *and* a billiard table; and there was to be in the oldest part of the house, where the fireplace was dated 1765, a study for me with a bow-window that I'd bought in Bath. The bow-window would look out over the fields to the barn and the lake and the new *plantation*, and maybe there'd be

Charolais cows. Or Merino sheep. Or Nubian goats. And maybe
there'd be a ha-ha. A hall led from the kitchen to the garage, with
an apartment above for the caretaker and his wife. My father said
he'd make us a gift of a period mantel for the fireplace in the
sitting room. "I want my daughter-in-law to entertain in a stylish
setting," he said.

Alice and I went to London to buy furniture. We bought
deliriously: oak refractory tables of the seventeenth century and
fruitwood chairs of the eighteenth. I bought a "gout" chair, Victorian, like the one Evelyn Waugh reclines in in the famous
photograph, and a two-kneehole architect's table, late eighteenth
century, like the one in the John Soane house. Alice bought an
"amusing" wrought-iron four-poster bed from a shop in the
King's Road. "On a whim," we would say. "It's a whim—a
caprice. A bagatelle." We bought Georgian mirrors, a beautifully
joined Regency traveling desk, and a diminutive oak rocking
chair for Susy.

Alice's sister Katherine was getting married and so, our delir-
ium spilling over, as we bought presents for Katherine, we also
bought more for ourselves. Alice bought me a new silk dressing
gown from Beale & Inman in Bond Street, and I bought Alice a
Castellani necklace from S. J. Phillips, and she bought me a
leather case fitted just for shoes from Mr. Lansdowne in Duke
Street, St. James's.

But when we got back to New York, Alice, now in her fifth
month, did not eat. She would not eat, and the doctor made her
go into the hospital.

The summer before, in Provincetown, a neighbor had said,
You sure know how to pick 'em, Ben. This summer no one would say
things like that, Alice was positive. She spoke of how, when
pregnant with Susy, she didn't exist for men. Even after Susy
was born and she walked with her in her stroller in Washington
Square Park, she was invisible to men. "My life is over," Alice
said.

My life wasn't over. There was the house.

"She says her life is over," I said to Nancy one afternoon. We
were at her apartment, listening to the Debussy cello sonata.

"I think I can play that section," Nancy said. She played, I
turned the pages, going *tum ti tum* for the piano part. This was
to be my first infidelity.

"She says her life is over," I said to LeAnne one afternoon. LeAnne had had two more children since Munich. Now she lived in Washington.

"Not too bad for a woman of forty," LeAnne was saying about her own body. A record of Handel songs was playing downstairs, to remind us of Munich. Getting dressed, LeAnne said, "I married so as not to be lonely. But it wasn't until I got married that I discovered what loneliness is."

I wasn't lonely, my life wasn't over. There would always be new interests like Nancy, there would be old interests as well (if I may so call LeAnne). There would always be Susy. And there was the house. More infidelities followed.

In September of 1967 our daughter Emma was born.

•

We moved out of Sullivan Street in the summer and went to Provincetown. The house in Millbrook would be finished in a couple of months. I rented a Cadillac convertible and drove from Provincetown to Millbrook and from Millbrook to Provincetown two or three times a week. I bought Alice a red Triumph convertible as a house present, to surprise her the day we moved in.

The setup in Provincetown was this: my mother's house, at 571 Commercial Street, was on the bay; our house, my sister's and mine, was across the street. Helen and I spent a month there with our families in the summer, all expenses paid. Helen: with her husband and their three children: in August, me in July; sometimes the other way around. Our mother's house was as friendly and cheery as 19 Gramercy Park was imposing and grand. "I feel myself here," our mother liked saying. Which was to say, she felt angry and lonely and sad but at least on her own turf. "Your father hates the country. [Provincetown was the country?] There's no one important here. I hear him telling people, 'My wife has a little house in Wellfleet.' " They both used to boast of the house having belonged to John Dos Passos. *Susan Glaspell had lived across the road. The original Provincetown Playhouse had been on a pier right next door. Eugene O'Neill, Carlo Tresca . . .* Everyone important was dead? Well, not everyone important, of course. Norman Mailer lived next door. Edmund Wilson lived not far away.

"Found a job yet, young Sonnenberg?" Dwight Macdonald said to me one July Fourth. No, I said, I'm thinking of selling out. "Too late," Dwight said. "And you'll find the market goes down with age."

But living like that: all expenses paid: was debilitating, I thought. I never thought that except there, in Provincetown, in the summers. The rest of the time I thought being a writer was justification enough for the way I lived.

Meanwhile *Jane Street* was put on in New York, off-off Broadway, for four Saturday nights. The audience liked it well enough, the actors seemed to like it. But, as with my Musset translation (which I called *The Firescreen*), I was frightened when the audience laughed, I felt sick to my stomach, and had to leave the theater. I told no one about the production.

One morning in Provincetown I saw in the *Village Voice* that Jean Genet was going to be in New York.

"I have to go to the city," I said to Alice.

"I have to go to Boston to meet my mother and her new husband," Alice said.

So I went to the city, to a benefit for the Black Panthers at the Village Gate. Genet did not turn up. A young civil liberties lawyer spoke, beginning: "Power to the People."

"Louder!" said someone behind me.

The lawyer said, "You say it your way, I'll say it mine." Then he went on with his speech.

That was me, my attitude exactly I thought: *You say it your way, I'll say it mine*. And I smiled like the lawyer exactly, smug and self-satisfied. The winter before, Alice and I had given a party at the Village Gate for Melina Mercouri, to benefit the resistance to the dictatorship in Greece. I felt more attached to that cause than to any in America. "That Greece might still be free!" Mine was Byron's cause. I'd marched with Melina and Minos to the U.N. one winter night in 1966. I'd never marched on the Pentagon.

So, I was political, in my way: except my way came from a love affair with a Greek actress in Paris, a lifelong Communist. She grew up in one of those villages in the Northern Peloponnesus that had been destroyed by the Germans during the Occupation. Politics often followed from sex, even with serious women and men; I remember her telling me that. Anyhow, my delighted interest in Greek politics distinctly followed from sex with her, as well as from knowing Minos.

Next morning, first thing, I went to the framer's to pick up Alice's birthday present: a painting by a friend of ours of a hillside with fruit trees in Sicily.

"You're English?" I said to the girl in the shop, the same expensive framer's that my father used. "My wife was brought up there."

"I know," she said.

"This is a birthday present. I'm taking it to her in Provincetown. My wife is going to be twenty-three."

"I know," she said.

"Your name is . . . ?

"Antonia," she said.

"Do you know my wife?"

"No," she said, "but I know a great deal about you."

On the plane to Provincetown I thought about that *I know. . . . I know. . . .* She'd also said, "People say I look like a Romney." Romney had in fact painted an ancestor of hers, it was one of the Romneys in the National Portrait Gallery. A beautiful girl. Best not think of her. I thought instead, How pleased Alice is going to be with her birthday present, I thought of the house, I thought of the children. *I know. . . .*

A TRIAL SEPARATION

"I want a Trial Separation," Alice said to me in Provincetown, before I could give her the present.

I was flabbergasted, so I said, "I'm not surprised." And then I said, "Of course I saw this coming."

She was giving Emma her bottle. It was early evening. I don't remember where Susy was: reading somewhere, probably.

Alice said, "I'm sure I don't want to move into the house."

"I'll sell the house," I said. "Is it Dick?"

"Dick?" Alice said, and laughed.

"So it isn't Dick?"

"Dick is short."

"Dick is ugly."

"Dick is a gnome."

"Like Max Lerner without the charisma, like—. . . ."

I was laughing, Alice was laughing. The phone rang. I picked it up . . . Then I handed Alice the phone. "It's Dick," I said.

"Hold Emma," Alice said, and she went into the next room. When Alice picked up the phone, I hung up. Holding Emma, I thought, How like me she looks. Alice came back. We put Emma to bed. "She looks just like us, doesn't she?" I said. Alice said nothing. I said, "I want to stop taking money from my father."

Alice said, "I still want a Trial Separation."

"I understand. Truly. And let me say, I admire you," I said. "A moment ago you were a millstone around my neck. Now you are superb, a—"

"Pygmalion, Act Three."

"I've no one to blame but myself."

"Nina Simone."

"It's nobody's fault but mine."

"Ray Charles."

"Fuck you!" I said.

Alice said, "If you're going to shout, let's go downstairs."

Downstairs I said, "I'll murder you if you leave me and kill the

children and myself. Headline: MAN SLAUGHTERS WIFE AND CHIL-
DREN, KILLS SELF."

"Slaughter *Emma?*" Alice said. We laughed some more.

•

"A real woman doesn't walk out," said my father when I phoned
and told him. And next: "You're lucky you and Alice never moved
into the house." Lucky for me, brave of her, I thought. I mean, the
institution of married life— . . . Alice, the anti-bourgeois. I was
proud of her. Next I thought of Antonia. Then of how much I was
going to miss living with Susy and Emma.

My mother said: "Dick?!" She was incredulous, Dick was so
homely. Here began my pleasure in defending Alice from the
bad opinion of others.

"Short homely men have this power," I said. "Look at Mus-
solini. Look at Billy Rose. Look at Louie Lepke." Look at my
father, if it came to that.

I moved into a loft in the city, on the corner of Mulberry Street
and Grand. The loft belonged to a dancer. There was hardly
anything in it. There was a low wooden platform on which I
arranged my shoes, shoetrees in each pair. *Early Penitential* style;
very alluring.

I took Antonia to Millbrook and showed her the house. She
was engaged to be married to a man in England. Break off your
engagement, I told her. She did. Then I broke off with her. I did
the same with other girls. New York City that summer seemed
made for someone like me. Unattached young women were everywhere. "I'll break your heart," I liked saying to them. Alice
and the children moved into the Croydon Hotel. Whenever I
picked up the children, no matter who opened the door, and
whatever my mood was, I'd burst into tears.

Soon after, I moved to the Chelsea Hotel, on West Twenty-
third Street. Bedroom, sitting room, kitchen: $600 a month, maid
service included. My style there: *Middle Penitential. Distressed
Émigré*, I liked to think, almost *Deposed Monarch*. Alice and the
children moved into an apartment on Seventy-fourth and Lex-
ington. Its atmosphere: like a bordello's before the customers
come. "Dick never phoned, you know," Alice said. Did she think
I cared? I believe she did.

I began taking the children on long city walks as my father had done with me, narrating the city to them. *That is vermiform rustification . . . That is Joseph Pulitzer's house. A secret passage runs under the house to the house where his mistress lived. . . .*

•

Late one October afternoon, I was walking back to the Chelsea when my left leg scissored in front of my right and I fell down on the sidewalk.

I fell down!

I got up in a panic: *who saw?* I was outside of a Bickford's. Old people ate there. The restaurant was shut. Inside was a cleaning woman. She smiled at me. A benignant smile. How I hate the benignant smile. I walked rigidly back to the Chelsea.

Other such incidents followed every six or eight months. It turned out that what I had was multiple sclerosis. I was thirty-four years old.

Multiple sclerosis is a disease of the central nervous system. Something eats away the material that sheathes the nerves. The material is called myelin. MS demyelinates the nerve: it's one of a class of diseases called *myelinoclastic:* and the uninsulated nerve can no longer function. MS progresses, as a rule, from the outside in. My finger muscles would grow weak, I wouldn't be able to tie my shoes, I wouldn't be able to type. First fingers, then hands, then arms . . . Or maybe with me it would progress from the bottom up. First legs, then balance . . . Useless, unused, my muscles would slowly wither away. Only certain automatic things, like digestion, would be unaffected. If you think of multiple sclerosis (sometimes called *disseminated sclerosis,* sometimes *insular sclerosis;* all unsatisfactory terms) as a speeded-up kind of aging, which I maybe too promptly did, then probably you'll think of Thomas Hardy's poem "I look into my glass":

> But Time, to make me grieve,
> Part steals, lets part abide. . . .

I went to many doctors for tests; none was conclusive. Could it be I didn't have it? No doctor was going to say. So far, the diagnosis of MS was mine alone. It was to be months, years in fact, before my diagnosis was confirmed. Meanwhile I learned that, far from being a rare disease, as I'd always supposed, MS was not uncommon. Everyone's sister had had it. Or they had had it themselves.

Fortunately, from my point of view, MS was at least idiosyncratic. Bespoke, as it were, fitting no one the same. MS was ambiguous, too. With many, its symptoms would vanish, then just as sportively reappear. With others, however, it marched on and on; every change a deficit.

My MS was of the type that has *episodes* and *remissions*. After each episode: panic, astonishment, shame, and bitterness about women. How soon before I couldn't walk? How soon before I'd be impotent, incontinent, insensate, blind? And who was going to take care of me?

I liked reading that MS didn't occur spontaneously in mammals other than man; I liked reading of its discovery by Freud's teacher, Charcot, in the 1860s; I liked reading of its *baffling distribution* and *mysterious origin*. In one (now outdated) textbook I read that the cause of MS might prove to be a case of *"orphan antigens in search of a disease."* I liked reading that MS seemed to choose victims with a distinctive character. We were cheerful and uncomplaining. "Typically," I enjoyed reading, in that same old book, we were "lovable, young, attractive and bright."

"Your ailment," my father used to say. "How is your ailment?" MS was almost a darling disease.

•

Jane Street was put on by a small theater group in Aspen, Colorado. I wrote a curtain raiser. A young woman gets sawed in half by a magician and spends the rest of the play trying to pull herself together. The parts were the Woman's Head, the Woman's Feet, and the Magician. It was called "The Courtship of Rita Hayworth." But nobody showed an interest in *Joel Mole*. Nobody. I couldn't interest even an agent. At its core, my work was of interest to no one but me, it seemed. I struggled to make a virtue of this.

Minos showed up in New York, to direct *The Screens* by Jean Genet. I was in Mount Sinai Hospital. One of my doctors, a Dr. Malis, had said, "Your symptoms haven't *advanced enough* for us to make a diagnosis, but a myelogram is *indicated:* to make sure there isn't a tumor on the spine."

I told Minos about the MS. "So what you've got, *if* you've got it," he said, "is a *maladie à tiroirs.*"

The Attica riots were on the TV. They'd been going on for days. I said, "I'm reminded of what Lermontov said about the genius of the Russians for 'forgiving evil where evil is inescapable'. 'That clear common sense of theirs— . . .' " Minos couldn't hear. I had to shout over the noise of gunshots on TV. "Em Ess will be my politics now," I said. "True, it is politics understood as being acted upon. As fate, not as action. But what else is there?" I had to shout more. "But what else is there? If I have Em Ess, the question doesn't arise."

Now the TV was showing some passengers whose KLM flight had been skyjacked by South Moluccan "terrorists." A famous folk singer was among the released hostages. "Oh god," I said, "can you imagine five days and nights of 'Buffalo Gals' in Hebrew, Swahili and Portuguese?"

Minos said, "Now *that* is politics understood as fate, not as action."

"Or 'Buffalo Gals' as-Beethoven-might-have-composed-it? Can you imagine anything worse?"

•

My rooms at the Chelsea were on the tenth floor, apartment 1026. Virgil lived on the floor below. We talked about my producing *Four Saints in Three Acts* at the Friends Meeting House on Gramercy Park. My father had bought the building, to keep it from being torn down. I walked Merce Cunningham through the place, talking about his directing the opera. I had grand plans for the building.

I went to concerts with Virgil and once he took me to the Century, on Central Park West, to meet Fania Van Vechten, the widow of Carl, author of *Nigger Heaven* and *Parties*, who'd named the Harlem Renaissance. At concerts Virgil would fall asleep as soon as the program began. If, during the concert, I made the mistake of waking Virgil up, he'd start to applaud.

Once I went with Virgil to a recital by William Warfield. For an encore the great bass-baritone for a reprise sang Jerome Kern's

"Ol' Man River." I said, "It must be painful to have to sing 'Ol' Man River' again and again."

Virgil said, "Success is never painful, for a performer."

"Is he queer?" Gregory Corso said that to Virgil. He was looking at me. We were all going up in the elevator at the Chelsea. "Him? Oh, no, a new girl each week," Virgil said. He and Corso got off at nine. I was seeing a girl named Haydee (not her real name) who lived on West Twenty-first Street. Her father had worked for the CIA, been a Deputy Director for Plans, and now he wrote and lectured on nuclear disarmament. One evening I had dinner with Virgil and Pierre Boulez in Virgil's apartment. "Ben is a friend of Lizzie's," Virgil said, meaning Elisabeth Lutyens. Boulez looked at me with respect. He and Virgil started talking about the composer Henri Sauget, who Virgil had told me was the literary executor of the poet Max Jacob. I can't remember what they said: I was impatient to get away. To Haydee for whom I had less regard than for Boulez, need I say? I walked Boulez to the corner of Twenty-third Street and Eighth Avenue and asked him about René Char, whose long poem "*Le Marteau sans maître*" he'd set. I can't remember what Boulez replied. A cab came and he got in and I ran from Twenty-third Street to Haydee's apartment on Twenty-first. I well remember that: it was the last time I ran anywhere.

Once in Paris with my father, in a café in Montparnasse, near the *impasse* where Brancusi's studio was, I heard my father say, "Ossip!" and an old Russian gentleman came and sat at our table. "Ossip Zadkine, this is my boy . . . Tell me, do you ever see Man?" And Zadkine had said, *Man Ray today is like a dog who has seen too many people's feet*. I'd always admired my father for conjuring people up like that: like Glendower, *I can call spirits from the vasty deep*. I was sure that had we been on the Right Bank, at Chez Francis in the place d'Alma, he could have called up Aurélie, the Madwoman of Chaillot. I'd looked forward some day to sitting at a café with Susy and calling out "Pierre! . . . Pierre Boulez, this is my daughter Susanna. What news of Virgil? of René?" In fact, one afternoon in Paris, sitting with Atalanta, I think, or maybe Sally, at the restaurant Méditerranée, I saw Jean-Louis Barrault coming from the Odéon. I had met him once or twice. "Jean-Louis!" I called, and he looked at me and walked on.

•

Soon I was living at the Chelsea with Susan de Verges and Stephen, her three-year-old son. I met Susan in the New York way. A friend of mine was subletting his apartment and moving to London and I went to say good-bye. Susan had answered his ad in the *Village Voice*. Everything about her declared that she was unattached. I took her back to the Chelsea, foreknowing all, as Eliot says. I could not have foreknown her little child or the attaching power of a fatherless boy of three.

Susy and Emma came and stayed on weekends at the Chelsea, and they and I and Stephen walked all over downtown. I narrated different neighborhoods now. *That is Friends Seminary where Helen and I used to go to school. . . . That is Washington Irving High School where your grandmother went. . . .* Because of Stephen, Emma changed to a middle child. Her skills of spite (so like mine) changed to skills of guile. She'd always been a naughty child, now she was well behaved: covetous as ever but subtle, jealous but now still.

I moved with Susan and Stephen into a loft on Great Jones Street. My allowance was stopped. I'd sold almost all my drawings and didn't have any money. What had I done worse than usual to be cut off in this way? I wrote my father but got no reply.

> *Genus, Aucte, lucri divites habent iram:*
> *odisse quam donare vilius constat.*
> [The rich know anger helps the cost of
>   living:
> Hating's more economical than giving.*]

The "million" I'd been promised? Vanished when Alice and I broke up. After some weeks my mother told me, "None of us is getting younger, you know."

And some weeks after that my father said, "Your mother thinks I ought to do something about this catarrh I have." Quaint word, *catarrh*. Like *ailment*.

---

* Martial, *Epigrams*, *XII, 13*. Translated by James Michie.

Having sold off whatever I could, I was now living off Susan.
She worked in leather. She made guitar straps for rock musicians, and handbags and jewelry. She was a talented artist. Everything she undertook: embroidery, leather work, clothes: she
did in a talented and original way. She was a good photographer,
too. For a time she and Alice went into business together, Alice
buying antique beads at Sotheby's, Susan stringing them. Alice
got some stationery printed with the name *Juniper Traders* and
sold Bloomingdale's one or two necklaces. I was having an on-
and-off affair with a Japanese woman who waited tables at the
Mie restaurant on Second Avenue.

The Screens was put on at the Brooklyn Academy of Music.
Minos was going to stay in New York. He directed Irene Papas
in the *Medea* and was planning the *Bacchae* for the Repertory
Theatre at Lincoln Center. He introduced me to Jules Irving who
was running the Repertory Theatre, and Jules gave me a job. I
was made Literary Manager. Then I moved with Susan de
Verges and Stephen, now four years old, to a loft on the Bowery.

On weekends Susy, Emma and Stephen and I went to movies
in Chinatown and the Village. I took them to see *Freaks.* "An
important point of reference," I said to Susy, just as I had once
said it to Siriol. *The house of Edna Saint Vincent Millay, the narrowest
house in the Village. . . . That's where Al Smith was born. . . . That's
the bank designed by Stanford White where my father first saw my
mother when they were fifteen and sixteen. . . .*

"You get more of a kick out of your children than I ever did out
of mine," said my father: which to me meant that *he* had had to
earn a living, that *he* hadn't had a rich father. I was getting an
allowance again, the house in Millbrook having been sold. "Had
you moved in with Alice, half the money would have gone to
her." His *catarrh* had gone away. He stopped smoking, however.

I loved bringing Susy to rehearsals at Lincoln Center and
showing her that I had an office. I loved reading plays and think-
ing of eventual productions. I looked forward to our doing old
French and Italian and Spanish plays, like the ones I'd seen in
Paris; and to our doing new German and Australian plays. I
didn't much care for "classical" American plays, except *The
Torchbearers* by George Kelly and *June Moon* by Ring Lardner and
George S. Kaufman, and I hated almost all modern American

plays, except those by Rosalyn Drexler and Ed Bullins. I'm baffled now by how closed-minded I was, given my experience with
Frank and the Oxford Playhouse. It had something to do with the
high-mindedness of the people at Lincoln Center. One day I told
my father of some trouble Jules Irving was having with his board
of directors. "What do you think Jules wants?" said my father. I
think he wants to resign, I said. "Are you sure?" I looked sage; I
said I was sure. At that moment at least Jules *did* want to resign.
The next day Jules's troubles were on the front page of the *New
York Times*, the Repertory Theatre collapsed, and I was out of a
job.

I didn't reflect on the mischief my father and I had done.
Instead, I was proud of his power, of his having been able to
phone up the managing editor of the *Times* and dictate a story to
him, and I was pleased to have acted together with him, after a
fashion, however self-destructively.

Then he gave me four thousand dollars. To atone? Or was it
a test? I left Susan and Stephen in New York and I went to
London and stayed at the Connaught Hotel. I owed money to the
lawyers and, as ever, to the Eighth Street Bookshop; I still owed
money to the Chelsea Hotel. All the same, I went to London and
stayed in a suite at the Connaught. I saw Sally in London. She
was married now, with two children, and wouldn't go to bed
with me. Neither would Agnès. I saw Atalanta who also was
married now. We went to the opera. Over supper I told her of
my troubled life in New York and of having had to sell the house.
"But soon you'll be rich?" Atalanta said.

"Yes," I said, "I'll soon be rich." After dinner, however, I
grew depressed, and so no Atalanta either.

When I got back to New York, having spent the four thousand
dollars, Susan told me that she was pregnant and was not going
to have an abortion, so with Stephen, now five, our two new dogs
and a songbird, we moved to Woodstock, New York. In June I
went to Boston and at Massachusetts General Hospital my multiple sclerosis was at last diagnosed conclusively. Steven Schneider was living near Boston. He and Toby had separated. I stayed
with him for a night or two. This was the first time he told me
about his being an alcoholic. He also told me that he had once
prepared a refutation of the Labor Theory of Value, which again

made me feel the poverty of my own politics. He also told me of Schneider's Law: "No person defines an aristocracy from which that person is excluded." Talking to me about politics let Steven dance away quickly from the subject of alcohol and me from the subject of MS.

Susan de Verges and I got married in July 1973 and in November our daughter Saidee was born.

•

Soon after this Alice got married and Susan Sonnenberg (as she was now) made me angry by going to Alice's wedding.

Then Susan got sick, very sick indeed. One afternoon she had convulsions. She was found to be suffering from a "subdural haematoma." It was a blood clot on her brain, caused by no one knew what. But I knew. We'd quarreled that summer, over money as usual. She'd said, "Talking to you is like hitting my head against the wall." And she had hit her head against the wall, again and again and again.

Susan was treated with steroids. She seemed to be getting better. But she said she felt she was going mad. Steroids will do that. "Oh! what joy it is to go mad!" Nietzsche once wrote to Strindberg. My wife's going mad was no joy for me. As best I could, I tried to keep house and look after Stephen and Saidee. I was frightened and felt that yet again I was being tested, appraised, weighed in the balance, and found wanting.

Minos was doing Genet's *The Maids* in London with Glenda Jackson, Susannah York and Vivien Merchant. I translated Genet's radio talk, *L'Enfant criminel*, which I hoped Susannah would speak as a curtain raiser. I translated Fernand Crommelynck's *Les Amants puérils*, which I hoped Elisabeth Bergner would want to do in London. Neither was done. I felt obscure. Obscure even by the standards of Woodstock, New York, a refuge for the obscure in art. I was sick of being obscure.

One afternoon, Susan having recovered, I got in the car to go and pick Stephen up from school. I could not turn the key. I blew the horn until Susan came out. I started sobbing, and with each sob a little man came up out of my throat and stood on the tip of my tongue. He stamped his foot Rumpelstiltskin-like. Then he reached down and pulled up another little man from my throat

and jumped off my tongue and disappeared. And so on and
on. . . .

Catenary was the first word I spoke at the end of my fit. No
light came with the word. My own sickness coming out, perhaps? How angry the little men were. Whatever had happened to
me, my marriage to Susan was at an end. I started seeing Haydee
again. Susan started seeing someone, too. At home I remember
an atmosphere only a little less grim than that of *Dance of Death*,
Stephen going between us, trying to stitch us together as small
children will at such times.

I moved in with Haydee who now lived on Hudson and was
studying acting. I told her my current philosophy was from the
Dance of Death: Cancel and move on. One day I overheard her say
to a girlfriend on the phone: *The love of my life has come back into my
life*. Meaning me! It was swell hearing things like that again.
Haydee praised my learning, my looks, my *savoir vivre*; I told her
that her acting was good. "Excellent. Superb!" Now I walked
with a malacca cane which I sometimes forgot in a restaurant or
cab. How jaunty I was. How insouciant. The fact is, though, my
ailment was worse.

•

One day my father told me that if I got my books appraised, he'd
buy them and give me the appraised value and give the books to
a college library. "They aren't doing you any good in storage, are
they?" No, and I wasn't able to pay the warehouse, either, not to
speak of the new divorce lawyers. It seemed like a good solution,
and with the help of some people from the Eighth Street Bookshop, I set about making an inventory of my collection.

As I did so, my life passed before my eyes. The Descent of the
Damned into Hell yet again. There was *The American Scene*, there
was *A Lume Spento*, there was *Pomes Pennyeach*, there was *Whoro-
scope*. . . . Collecting books seemed to have been my whole life.
There was *Women Have Been Kind*. . . . Collecting books and
loving women seemed to have been my whole life. Could that be
so? Was that what I wanted my daughters to think?

The appraised value of the books turned out to be three times
more than expected. My father was astonished, I was overjoyed.
I saw that I'd have enough money for the next couple of years:
enough to go on writing and not to have to take a job.

One of the people helping me from the Eighth Street Bookshop was a Hawaiian girl named Kathleen. I remember walking behind her on Third Avenue one day, thinking how beautiful her skin was, thinking how we'd look lying side by side. Like stripes on a striped awning. And I remember waiting with Kate (Kathy to everyone else) in a crowded movie theater. Keep an eye out for Haydee, I said to her. And Kate said, How can you keep an eye out for someone nondescript?

Haydee and I were going to Greece as soon as the books were done. Instead I went with Kate. Now I never forgot my malacca cane.

One memory I have of that trip is of smoking a Greek cigarette and thinking, with my first drag, The military dictatorship is over. Another is of being in Missolonghi and thinking, At last I am older than Byron was when he died. I'd acted badly with Haydee, worse with Susan. I wasn't going to act badly with Kate. I remember exactly where we were when I decided that: outside Meteora, on our way to Iannina. It was night, I was driving (having brought my own hand controls from the States). Kate was asleep, I felt resolute.

Back in New York, living with Kate, I learned how to balance my checkbook. This may sound like a small thing, but I'd never balanced a checkbook before. To me it was as momentous as learning how to massage his gums had been to Bertrand Russell when he found out that pyorrhea had caused the breakup of his love affair with Ottoline Morrell. After a year and a half, Kate left. *Come back! Come back!* I wanted to shout. *The man you're leaving isn't the same man you moved in with*, I wanted to say. *He can balance a checkbook.* I'd never been so unhappy. My heart was broken (time two). I'd acted well, hadn't I? I hadn't acted badly at least.

"I acted better with Kate than with any other woman I've known," I was saying to Steven Schneider. "Even so, she left me." I was weeping, thinking also that well as I'd acted, maybe it still wasn't well enough? "She said my parents had an *investment* in my being a failure. She said, she said—. . ." I couldn't go on. That stayed with me, though, that my parents had had an *investment* in my being a failure: which meant that I had an *investment* in being a failure, too.

Now I walked with two malacca sticks. I used to fall down in the snow sometimes.

Alice always liked saying we were close. "We're better friends now than when we were married," she liked saying, and she'd laugh as if to say, "I know it's a cliché, but still . . ." And we *were* close: at least from time to time. On the very day of our divorce, we went before the referee and held hands in the courtroom and laughed at the lawyers. We were close the way delinquents are close: close when arrested, but otherwise rivals, enemies.

Then little by little we weren't close. Against my will, I began to incline to my father's opinion of Alice, which had never been high. Indeed, even to have an opinion about Alice was hard for me. Or, if I had to have one, then let it be like my mother's: acerbic but not unaffectionate, with the children's good coming first. Soon the pleasure of defending Alice from the bad opinion of others was mixed with that of defending her from her bad opinion of herself. "You disapprove of me, don't you?" she'd say. No, I'd say, I don't disapprove. And I didn't. Asked to so often, how could I have disapproved? Besides, hearing from her of the "bad" things she did made me think better of myself. Once she gave me one thousand dollars. "Don't ask me where I got it," she said. "You don't disapprove of me, do you?" I said I didn't. But then I did. But then I didn't again. Anyhow, I took the money.

She got divorced from her second husband and began spending time in Barbados where her mother, who'd married money, owned a big house on the sea. She came back to New York only "for the children's education." One day she phoned and told me that a man had broken into her apartment and raped her. I went over there. It was true, about the break-in at least. Susy had been there. She'd had a fever and Alice had kept her home from school. Alice wouldn't go to the police. Instead, she told me later, she went to see an old lover. "He keeps an apartment just for me in the Volney Hotel. Just for me," she said. "Imagine!"

I said to my mother later, "I told her she was a fool."

"Why bother?" said my mother. "She's the type who if you spit in her face, she tells you it's raining."

One day Emma phoned and said Alice had been taken to Lenox Hill Hospital. I went over to the apartment. She'd injected some drug or other into the veins in her leg, diluting it with tap water.

I saw her legs later. They were scarred and tettered with sores. Tap water? "Endarteritis," she said. "*Acute* endarteritis."

One day my mother phoned and said Alice had "forced" her way into 19 Gramercy Park. She'd brought the children with her. "*Forced* her way past the butler," said my mother. "She told your father, '*Finally*, I've broken through.' "

And then one day Alice phoned me from Payne Whitney. She'd OD'd and committed herself, she said. This was her third OD. Susy had seen one, Emma the other.

I went over to the apartment.

"I can never forgive you for what you did to Stephen and Saidee," Emma said to me.

"You'll understand when you're older," I said.

"And I can never forgive you for what you did to Mummy."

What *I* did to Mummy? "You'll understand when you're older," I said.

Susy said that that other time when Alice came home from Lenox Hill, she'd said to Susy, They may have to amputate my leg. And Susy had said, "Oh great. Then I'll have two parents with one good leg between them."

"But she told us that she has *leukemia*," Emma said. "*Acute* leukemia."

"As if her real sickness weren't enough," Susy said.

"Well, I think you're being disloyal," Emma said.

I said nothing. After a time I left. Why didn't I do more? Why hadn't I done more all along? I can't account for why. My declared reason was that I was protecting the children, acting in their interests, but that wasn't it. I can only excuse myself by saying that like almost everyone around her, I had an *investment* in Alice's behavior.

And I got a rush from knowing her. Everybody did. After Kate left me, I went to Alice and she cut my hair. I wanted to go to bed with her, but she wouldn't let me. She said she didn't want me to see the scars from her back operations. Instead, she told me she would give a "singles" party for me.

MULTIPLE SCLEROSIS AND THE
SINGLE MAN

At the "singles" party Alice gave, the men she'd asked all wore suits and ties; I wore a suit and tie myself. They were art dealers, journalists, bankers. The pretty girls there were all models. The plain ones said things like, "I was an actress, but now I am a management trainee." A plain young woman I talked to said, "I was a netsuke expert, but now I am an auctioneer trainee."

Many of the men there worked at Sotheby Parke-Bernet, where Alice's second husband had worked as head of the Modern Paintings Department. She and her sister, Katherine, had had love affairs with a director of the auction house, and Alice had had love affairs with the heads of many departments at Sotheby's. Some of her ex-lovers were there. One of them said to me, "I am an ex-lover of your ex-wife."

Susy and Emma were carrying trays of canapés. I thought I'd wait until they went to bed, then I'd leave. The "singles" party had started to feel to me like a private view before an auction, and there was nothing I wanted to bid on. Also everyone there was going on somewhere, and I had nowhere to go.

Alice's bestfriend was at the party. She lived upstairs. A plain young woman who worked at *Newsweek*. Alice went everywhere with her because she was plain. She was funny, as plain bestfriends often are. "Oh, you're being bitchy. Isn't she bitchy?" Alice would say. And the bestfriend would smile and look self-satisfied as plain bestfriends will.

But the bestfriend's bestfriend (they all had bestfriends) was not Alice. The bestfriend's bestfriend was Sophie.

"I want you to meet Sophie," she said, "Sophie's about to leave."

•

My story ought to end here: more of the same, only different. And with increasing sickness and the death of my parents to come, not insisted upon, not narrated, but hints at, along with perhaps a success of my own: the sort of bittersweet ending comedies usually have.

But my story doesn't end here. Most of the humiliations predicted of MS had not yet come to me: I could still walk, if not for long distances; when I fell down, I could still get back up on my own; I could still have erections; I wasn't incontinent, not often anyway; I could still type and hold a pen. Also, I'd begun to see an analyst. For a "limited objective," for a "limited time." I was the same, only different.

And Sophie (not her real name) was different, if also the same. The same in that she was pretty and smart, but different in that, after we fell in love, she wanted to talk to my neurologist. Why hadn't anyone else wanted that? Why hadn't Kate? Why hadn't Helen? Why hadn't my mother? Another difference was that, with my father dying (his *catarrh* was cancer of the throat) I found comfort in telling Sophie my story and walking with her through the house. (An earlier version of *Lost Property* was dedicated to her.) With Sophie's encouragement, I started writing book reviews for *The Nation* and in the winter of 1977 I started to lecture at the Juilliard School. I'd never done anything like that before. I lectured to acting students about how to read plays. I wasn't a good teacher; I taught with a drier, more authoritative voice than I naturally had, and all I did was retail what I'd learned about the theater from Minos and Frank. Not wanting my students to like me: wanting them not to like me, in fact: I nonetheless lacked the skills to make my subject attractive. All the same, it was a new thing for me.

•

I'd managed to hold onto a few thousand of my books. All the dictionaries, most of the French books, many books of poems and plays. One day my father's accountant told me that I couldn't expect the full amount for which my books had been appraised. "You mean, he's going to cheat me of half of what he promised?" I said.

"You can't have expected him to give you more than the books are worth to him as a tax deduction," the accountant said.

But I still had a third edition of Johnson's dictionary (1765), I still had a seventeenth-century edition of Ben Jonson's collected plays, and I sold these together with some first editions of Genet and *Les Plaisirs et les jours*, Marcel Proust's first book. I used the money to go to Greece with Sophie in the summer of 1977.

In Athens I couldn't get up the stairs of a bookshop I used to go to. I couldn't go with Sophie to the Acropolis Museum. I had to wait for her in the parking lots of various temple sites. At Mycenae I was resigned to wait in our rented car (with the same hand controls I'd brought from the States when I'd traveled with Kate) while she went through the palace. I thought, I shall never again see the Lion Gate. But Sophie got the guard to let me drive to within sight of the gate.

There was an earthquake in Salonika when we were there. Sophie was terrified, I reacted as I would have when told the *Titanic* had hit an iceberg. "Well, *do* something," I'd have said to the steward. To myself I said, Our hotel is still standing, isn't it? Best not to do anything, best to stay put; someone will do something. Sophie insisted we drive out of the city and we drove for many hours down the Kassándra peninsula. I said to myself, I am the man you always see in news pictures taken as the earthquake strikes, as the volcano erupts, as the revolution begins. He wears a light-colored suit and he grins at the photographer. He is *there* for the camera, he is not *there* for the catastrophe. Not that I didn't see the destruction. Phlegmatic as I was, I still saw the exodus from the city of all who had cars (people driving in the same direction on both sides of the highway for miles). I saw the hundreds living under tents in the streets. But mostly I noticed my having been presented with another test, another end-of-the-world, which I'd failed.

Driving that night down the Kassándra peninsula, Sophie asleep beside me, I thought of how, when my father died, I wouldn't be *there* either; not for my mother, not for Helen. I wouldn't be *there* for Sophie when her parents died. I must say this to Sophie when we finally arrive. I'd begun to think about marriage with her, which I knew wasn't possible, and about having more children. I would say that to Sophie as well: a teasing warning against something dire that must not occur. I knew full well how hard to resist warnings like that always are. I stopped and got out to take a leak. Sophie said, half-asleep on the front seat, "Are you coming back to the car, baby?" And when we arrived, at who knows what hotel, I was exhausted and we fell asleep and when we woke up, I'd forgotten what I was going to say.

Bay-bee is how she pronounced it as in the popular songs she introduced me to.

We located Steven Schneider the next day. He had rented a little house on the peninsula. He and Toby had divorced and Steven was there with their fourteen-year-old daughter and a school friend of hers. Steven now lived in Bordeaux and was a shipper of Bordeaux wines. Not exactly an ideal trade for him. He told me he had had implants of Antabuse, the antialcohol drug.

"Stakhanovite shirkers!" he said of his daughter and her friend, meaning they didn't do their share of the housework.

I knew something of Steven's background, which I told Sophie. A granduncle of his had assassinated one of the Czar's ministers in 1905; his grandfather had been the Chief Rabbi of Odessa; and his father had been the first of a long line of eldest sons who didn't become a rabbi. Steven had put himself through Harvard by writing a handbook on dry-fly fishing. At Harvard he'd majored in Chinese and written his thesis on Yangtse River traffic. He quickly became an expert on everything he undertook. Fencing, fishing, photography, birds. Now, for example, he was reading Hobbes. He said, "I've been thinking of the proposition that every man is bound by nature to protect in wartime the authority by which he is himself protected."

Sophie said, "What about the war in Vietnam?"

She got stung by a yellow jacket before Steven could reply.

As we were leaving, Steven spoke of the Children of Darkness and the Children of Light. "I was one and now I'm the other," he said. Which sounded religiose and depressed me to hear.

"What are Stakhanovite shirkers?" Sophie said to me in the car. I don't know, I was going to say. "Well," Sophie said, "whatever they are, it's an odd thing to call your daughter when she's fourteen years old.

On our way back to Salonika, I remembered what I'd been going to say. I also remembered that Kate left me soon after I'd proposed marriage. This was going to end in tears, too, of course;

but not yet. So I said nothing. At the hotel I wanted to say, The way you care for me. Instead I said, Are you going to file a story about the earthquake? "I'm on my vacation," Sophie said.* We left the hotel, now empty of guests. The Mediterranean Palace: which, its name notwithstanding, was a small, well-run, family-owned hotel: Sophie and I were to be its last guests.†

•

Nineteen Gramercy Park was now given over to my father's being sick. "Unquestionably, the greatest house still remaining in private hands in New York," wrote the *New Yorker* at about this time. Going there has never been easy; I liked saying that. Its too-thick carpets impede my stride. And its too plentiful mass of things: passionately collected, lovingly assembled: left me with no space of my own; I liked saying that as well. Still, now that my father is dying, insolent though the house has been, my rage is gone, as Aufidius says when he learns that Coriolanus is dead. I liked saying that best of all.

On one of these visits my mother said, "You know, I can't help thinking about my own father when I told him that now there was money and he didn't have to wear the same shirt all week. I told him, *You can wear a different shirt each day.* And he said, *I suppose if I were very rich I could change my shirt two or three times a day? and if I were very very rich I suppose I could change my shirt every hour of every day?* . . . Now that he is on Thorazine, your father keeps getting dressed and undressed and lying down and getting up and getting dressed and undressed and dressed again, sometimes two or three times an hour."

One day the butler came in and announced to my father and mother that the car was downstairs. "I ordered the car," my mother said. "A drive in the country will do you good. Don't you remember? We talked about it yesterday and you agreed." To me, in his presence, my mother said, "He doesn't remember. He doesn't know what time of day it is. Talk to your father, why don't you?"

---

* Back in New York, an imbecile editor said: "When you work for *this* paper, you're never on vacation."

† I had stayed there a number of times. Which reminds me of a strain of this trip: my wanting to pretend to Sophie that I had never been to places where in fact I had been before.

As soon as we were alone, he said, "You know how I have always *adored* premeditated pleasures."

Another time when we were alone, he said, "If you ever have a son— . . ." We were in his bedroom, the bedroom was dark. He was in bed, I was sitting in a fine Sheraton wing chair. He was speaking very slowly, very thick of tongue, and pointing a finger to his head: "If you ever have a son— . . .": so slowly I was certain he'd lost his train of thought: "teach him to shoot."

•

Sophie and I went to Greece one last time, in the summer of '78. My MS was now more pronounced. "We'll need a bedroom on the ground floor," I once heard her say to a hotel clerk, adding awkwardly in French, "*Parce que mon mari ne marche pas.*" Intending, My husband can't walk, but signifying, My husband is broken.

"*Vous devriez bien l'échanger pour un autre, madame*" [You better exchange him for another], said the hotel clerk. How we laughed.

I myself never spoke Greek well. I spoke it with enough authority to elicit answers more complicated than I could follow. Greece was a country where, as I told Sophie, I was both understood and not understood. It pleased me to think that in Greece I was living in a condition of "fecund misunderstanding," as Eliot says somewhere, as opposed to the sterile understanding that obtained in New York. Then the smiles of the Greeks at my sickness didn't repel me as did the benignant smiles I was getting used to at home.

Minos was now head of the National Theater of Northern Greece. He was planning a series of plays to be performed in the huge stone quarries outside the cities of Northern Greece. One was the *Medea* with Melina Mercouri. At one of these huge natural, or anyway "found," amphitheaters, the one at Dodona, near where Persephone vanished on the first (or second or third or fourth) of her annual descents into the Underworld, I thought of telling Sophie that she was Persephone to me, for she spent half her life in the dark (she reviewed movies for a daily newspaper) and the other half with me: death and desire. But then I realized that, because of me, all Sophie's life was spent in the dark: all was desire mixed with death. And so I said nothing.

When we returned to New York, there was a city-wide newspaper strike. I started using a wheelchair sometimes. Not a wheelchair exactly, more a sort of motor-driven scooter. I could still get in and out of taxicabs and walk most places if there weren't stairs, with the help of my two malacca sticks.

My father died in September. A great deal was made of how *ironic* it was that he who had made his reputation as one able to get his clients into the papers almost at will should die at a moment when the presses were still. People went on television and said that.

With Alistair and Jane Cooke (the Jane White who had once painted my portrait) and with my mother, Sophie and I watched Alistair Cooke eulogizing my father on Channel 13. We were in the pine-panelled library. Sophie and I and my mother, watching Alistair Cooke watching Alistair Cooke as he talked about my dead father. And the room, the library, was where so many of his studied and repeated cruelties to me had begun: where I was always being asked to subscribe to *I sighed like a lover and obeyed like a son.*

PUBLIC RELATION

The house was soon put up for sale. I'd grown up there grandly, wanting to be either a gentleman burglar or a Man of Distinction.

My criminal life hadn't really been grand. I stole only new bills, but I stole them only from my father. I always made ready by singing a phrase from Hoagy Carmichael's "Ole Buttermilk Sky": "Oh, it'll be easy, so easy . . ." (in the song, about falling in love). And afterwards, *toujours debonair!* I bought charm bracelets for the maids.

And so to the Man of Distinction. Indifferent. Masterful. Saturnine. Rich. Drawn in part from the Lord Calvert whiskey ads, my pose had come mostly from guests. Some had made the cover of *Time.* Most would have rated a caption. A sobriquet (O press agent word!) handy to Damon Runyon.

Sometimes just to have been a guest was distinction enough. "Who's Thornton Wilder?" I asked as a child.

"He's been to the house."

Well, I mean to say, hadn't I *been* to it, too?

The servants were white. That had long been the rule in rich New York City homes. But when I was a child, "colored" help was the rule. White servants were an exception. Our English butlers and manservants: our Mearses and Spearses and Blanchards and Horns: made certain I understood that their antique deference cost too dear for it to be wasted on me.

Yet, along with the maidservants (is there a more erotic English word?), they'd made the house like a Cunarder. Even now I remembered the galas and forgot the seas. More Cunarderlike still was the consecration, in every room, on every floor, to a feudal notion of home. It came from the too-real deportment of a too-real English butler, the too-real look everywhere indoors of a great English country house. There were the "William and Mary" room from a famous castle somewhere; the Chippendale carvings and Adam swags; the coronets on the spoons and forks;

the charges and bearings, escutcheons and crests on practically everything else.

Yes, indeed. But the look was satirical, too, as showed soon after my father died. His very long will directed that the house and everything in it be sold, "with dispatch" and at public auction. So nothing of the "ancestral" and "dynastic" was going to last? Nothing of it was *meant* to! Satire flourished in that. To me at least the will declared the house had been not a simulacrum but a mass of quotations.

The will also said expressly that the house should not be preserved. And if *that* wasn't satire . . . ? For others maybe the house might become a monument, a showplace. *Without him?* said the will. *The very idea!* When he was alive, people used to suggest that 19 Gramercy Park be kept, like the John Soane House in London or the Merchant's House on East Fourth Street downtown, and he'd only jeer: Sardanapalus prepared to set his own pyre alight.

> So much for monuments that have forgotten
> Their very record!

I was sympathetic to both his arrogant trepidation and to the less esoteric plea that all, in the end, be seen, somehow, as having been *for* something more than for him: recondite, forceful and subtle and rich though his uses had without question been. And I was delighted by his words about public auction: a swipe at the many curators who'd visited over the years, unctuous and avaricious.

His records also were ordered destroyed. Conceit pure and simple, I thought. To be sure, he'd been rich, self-made, a success. Only who'd bother with the records? Who'd want to write a book? Who'd want to publish it?

The appraisers came; my mother moved; the servants were discharged. And, with the packers, a man was found to live in and caretake the house.

•

Much as I'd always hated the place, now a fascination of disenchantment prevailed over me. I visited more in the next several

months than in the years before. As Milton says somewhere in
Paradise Lost:

> . . . God attributes to place
> No sanctitie, if none be thither brought.

Inside, at times, I was able to walk without my malacca sticks.

I arrived at the house late one fall afternoon. The light was
evening. I pressed the doorbell and waited. I wasn't sure why,
but I wanted to feel I never had had a key.

Willson Powell opened the door with more ostentation than I
thought right. More than suited the dismembered house. He was
the young man found for it by the last of the butlers. That butler,
in his off-hours, affected a sort of Greenwich Village style, so to
me his choice of Willson Powell was both legitimating and anx-
ious, the apostolic stamp mixed with a jaded dissidence.

Good manners, a neat appearance, excellent references made
William Willson Powell ideal. So did his Southern accent. I
mean, if ever the house had struck a chord, it was Jewish money
and English taste. And doesn't a Southern accent bring agree-
ment to the two terms? The very effect which moreover had so
often eluded my father.

Each story I walked (there are six) was to ask how it explained
my life. My life was dissolute, pitted with debts: so that going
from floor to floor in this way, from room to room, inviting
answers,was also to see how to pay the debts off: to see in minute
detail. Each single object, vivid to me as no longer being there:
every framed "scrap," every Chippendale bench: was being
changed into cash.

The sureness of change, metamorphosis *back*, was eeriest on
the stairs.

I'd taken the lift to the top of the house, solely so I could drift
down, from the tiny cells of the servants to the big red room,
with the big movie screen, where the concert grand and Rent
Table had stood; to the three-room apartment where I'd grown
up. It was on the fourth floor. I lingered there. . . . Oh, the
luxury of remembered loneliness! The empty walls, the empty
floors, the spaces between the windows, the weight and width of
the high oak doors, all evocative of a more ample age, spoke to me

of anger and grief as well. Just to nurse the evening spell for a time was satisfaction indeed. Feeling entranced: disembodied almost: I descended to the next landing. Below were my parents' bedrooms.

I'd had a flashlight which I must have left on the mantel or someplace upstairs. It was in the dark, though, that I first was aware that I was missing a sound. All who grew up in such a house will remember how it sounded when one clock in particular struck, the sound deadened by a special sense of being at home and yet never at home, of the hours dropping away one by one in a place without interest or love. This absence was still more emphatic. For of the dozens of clocks in the house (wound for us every Thursday by Mr. Morriss of Morriss & Sasek), this clock had used to strike first. Now, from its silence, the others appeared to have all taken their cues.

Besides, each school morning for years I'd stood there waiting for it to strike, before going in, singing my song, thrilled to be robbing my father.

Well, so that too: changed to money, to cash. I felt elated. Then frightened. I clutched my elation and fled.

The broad, white stairs, now uncarpeted, gave back a *clickety-clack*, the brisk noise a new symbol of freedom. I remembered a phrase that I'd read about things, once transfigured through being collected, which the magazine-article writer declared were to be "relaxed to a merchandise state" by a fashionable auction. It was from one of those well-bred laments you got everywhere in those days. Big expensive collections as *ci-devant*. Yes, and the writer had just been a flack, not a child of the objects like me.

Relaxed, though: that was a powerful word. It made me stop in the hall. Was it possible I had a book? Could I break into print? I'd always been told I could write, after all. Maybe even by Thornton Wilder. Why not? Private lives were the rage just then. My own had its share of impressive names. Impressive values as well: rarities, not only dollars-and-cents . . .

But I was ignoring Willson Powell, who stood there holding a pad.

"Are you looking for me?" I said in a voice amazingly like my father's.

"At your service," the young man said.

"Where is the guest book?" My research could start. "Horn had several. Before Horn, Mears." (Before Mears to me was a season of mists.)

"In the wine cellar . . . ?"

Willson Powell returned; he was sorry, but it wasn't there.

"Are you quite sure? . . . Never mind, never mind." I could at least make a start.

•

Coming out of the house, that autumn night, I felt lighthearted and free. *Like a man of fortune greeting heirs.* I had money in my jeans, so to speak, and was in no hurry to spend it. A cab would be coming soon. A young woman came towards me from Gramercy Park, her high heels on the sidewalk making an alerting noise. She had on a white blouse and a yellow skirt and was walking a small white dog. *Snowdrop of dogs.* The dog sniffed at my shoes. I wanted to tell the young woman of "To Tartar, a Terrier Beauty," by Thomas Lovell Beddoes:

> . . . oft intensest looks,
> Long scrutiny o'er some dark-veined stone
> Dost thou bestow, learning darkest mysteries
> Of the world's birthday . . .

The young woman tugged the dog. At the corner of Nineteenth Street, she turned. A man with a big labrador was coming along Irving Place. The white dog strained to meet the new dog.

> . . . oft in eager tone
> With quick-tailed fellows bandiest prompt replies,
> Solicitudes canine, four-footed amities.

The young woman tugged again at the dog and the dog disappeared.

The cab came. I went home, thinking, I remember, *Oh well, a man knows only so many dogs in his life*, which is from Turgenev's *A Sportsman's Sketches*, and smiling to myself. Sophie had a dog, after all. My father always used to say if I weren't careful someone's husband would shoot me dead. However I died, I was sure there would be a dog there at the end.

•

The five-day, one-estate auction took place at Sotheby Parke-Bernet. Everything was on the block. The publicity everywhere, stressed how much *more* than mere art and antiques was being sold. The Rent Table went for many times the auction house estimate.

Robert Hughes remarked, in *Time* magazine, that 19 Gramercy Park had not been "comparable to the great mansions of Fifth Avenue at their height of extravagance . . . but [was] an astonishing survivor, a solid, heavy and opulent fossil." Too true. Our house had not expressed the wealth, power and pride of a "new" social class but instead was a genuflection towards, and a parody of, making money. And I was myself the offspring of "a solid, heavy and opulent fossil."

Then in October the house was bought. The very rich buyer wanted it for his perfume-bottle collection. He manufactured perfume. He renamed the place Evyan House and announced he would soon reopen Number 19 with a White Shoulders Ball. He was an Austrian baron, said to detest Jews. He lived somewhere else; so the house was to be a showplace after all, and now it belonged to a baron: rich, anti-Semitic, Viennese.*

Willson Powell stayed on in his job. However, Thornton Wilder was wrong. I could write, of course, after a fashion. A memoir though? Well, I mean to say, anyone *can* write a memoir. But the sort of memoir I might read myself was beyond my capacities. And to write about my father? . . . Well, I certainly couldn't do that. Having given up, I was somewhat perturbed to read in the Sunday *Times Book Review:*

> I am writing the biography of the late Benjamin Sonnenberg and would appreciate hearing from those with anecdotes and/ or letters.
>
> Willson Powell
> 19 Gramercy Park,
> New York, New York 10003

* Years later, after the baron's death, he was found to have been a Jew himself, his title was bogus, and he'd apparently stolen the formula for White Shoulders perfume.

The letter aroused the lawyers, which I found funny. They wrote to the *Times* denouncing the book: "unauthorized, contrary to the will . . ." I started to shape a story: not for publication but something to dine out on. It began, *I am a Collectors' Child.*

•

In the spring of 1978 Alice went with Emma to Taos, New Mexico, leaving Susy in New York to finish the school year. Our Trial Separation ended here. The real one finally began. Alice and Emma came back to New York at the time of the auction. Then, after the sale, in '79, Alice and Emma and Susy moved to Taos permanently. "She'd kept a careful record of the auction prices, though," Susy said.

There'd been an exhibition at the Royal Academy in London of paintings and drawings from the Sonnenberg collection, just before the New York auction. I'd gone with Sophie and we'd stayed at the Connaught in my old rooms. *Good to see you again, Mister Sonnenberg, sir*, and *Nice to have you back*. At the R.A. Show, I saw Donald Maitland, who cut me, and Gemma, who gave me a kiss on the cheek. But Sophie and I weren't getting on well. *Mon mari ne marche pas*, she had said to the room clerk in Greece. *Vous devriez bien l'échanger pour un autre, madame*, the clerk had said.

And then, when we got back to New York, Sophie met someone else. The brother of Alice's bestfriend (now no longer Alice's bestfriend): a marathon runner. So she did at last exchange me for *un mari qui marche bien*. (*Un qui court*, in fact.) All her young life, I remember thinking (mean of me, I know), she has shuttled between lovers who are healthy and dumb and ones who are smart and sick. I was sick, he was healthy. I began waiting for someone else: thinking, I'm too old to be insulted like this. Surely I must also have thought, Who's going to care for me now?

Then in December of 1979 my mother died. It's not true to say I felt nothing about my mother's death, but I didn't feel much, and the little I felt was exhilaration and relief, with maybe just a touch of guilt for not feeling, with Santayana, that this event was more important than any other in my life. For my sister's sake I regretted that so many details, of a boring, testamentary, yet also edifying, kind, were left to her alone.

Soon after (life happens at real-estate deals) I bought an apartment on Riverside Drive. Appearing before the co-op board, I sat next to this person, then next to that; each director began with something like "I once had the pleasure of visiting your family's exquisite home." (They always stressed the word *home*.) Brought by Mrs. Vincent Astor, brought by Brendan Gill; a benefit for the Pierpont Morgan Library, opening night of *The Skin of Our Teeth*; to hear Piatigorsky, meet Garbo . . . All how long ago!

I had tuned out completely when I suddenly heard "attended a party last Christmas . . ."

What?

". . . a guest of Willson Powell."

I sat up. What was going on? "You don't say?" What *was* going on? Had the house somehow *happened* to Powell? Had he gotten above his self-imposed role of hereditary retainer? Writing my father's life story, was he mimicking it as well? Was he possessed? In possession? What sort of a party? And where, oh where, was the actual owner of that night?

The answers I looked for would tell me whether I myself had gotten above my own hereditary role; whether I was free of the house. But the answer I got was the Ultrasuede back of a Madison Avenue matron. She had risen like someone reaching her stop with that air of a well-to-do woman in midafternoon which Americans frequently bring to the night.

Come back, madam! My questions were easy. They were all about Willson Powell. I mean to say, I knew he had made his adjustments. But was he still at my father's life? Was a publisher interested? Poor Willson (for now I so named him to myself fraternally)! My father's life story does not tell itself. Very far from it, in fact. Its complications of luck are too great. And how hard not to be distracted by its many vengeful displacements, its many recondite aims.

•

Then, from another quarter, Isadore Barmash, a writer on the business desk of the *New York Times*, batted out the very book to prove that, so far as the book trade goes, I'd been naïve and my father was right to want his records destroyed: a so-called celebrity life, pieced together from clippings and gossip, with every possible thrill suppressed and most of the details wrong.

"*Always Live Better Than Your Clients*": *The Fabulous Life and Times of Benjamin Sonnenberg, America's Greatest Publicist* wasn't remotely the baleful pleasure for which I was prepared. For one thing, it was remaindered almost as soon as published. For another, its method was corrupt. It first puffed up my father ("the era's greatest publicist . . . one of the times' great collectors of art . . . apostle of style, of grace, of a life style that had all but disappeared"), then it stressed his duplicity. What was that but to mix praise and praise? More seriously, the author missed the opportunity to describe my father's conspicuous role in a half-dozen partners' and proxy fights which a *Times* reporter could well have seized. The book also ignored his involvement with men of greater civic and political consequence than himself, such as Abe Fortas and the Washington lawyer Thomas Corcoran. Not to speak of the favors he got from, and did for, Senators Jacob Javits and Abe Ribicoff, Thomas Dodd and Brian MacMahon. The book's idea of sensation was to suggest that my father was sometimes a pimp: which, if indeed true, then why hadn't I ever met through him any but frumps and debs?

It was most disappointing not to learn more of the vulgar details of his practice of public relations. For example, my father's long relationship with the Philip Morris Company and its majority stockholders, the Cullman family: he worked hard for the tobacco industry and represented its interests so effectively as to cause the news show *60 Minutes*, not to cancel its program about smoking and lung cancer, but to schedule it opposite something like the Superbowl or World Series. His own throat cancer wasn't mentioned in the book.

All in all, though (poor Isadore Barmash!), what a bitch the public relations life is. How difficult even to contemplate, with its impoverished regard for the truth. With my father, the case is especially hard. For as long as I can remember, he was more often envied than liked, more often remarked than admired; and his control of it all was great: a triumph of public relations. But due to his cunning insistence on never being described except in terms that were minted and uttered by him, the public relations triumph was now (would this always be so?) an interested reader's defeat.

•

I went to Martha's Vineyard where Steven Schneider had rented a house. I took with me my electric cart (it was called an Amigo: "The Friendly Wheelchair"). Kate came and stayed with me for a while. I was feeling, not lonely exactly, but drawn in by loneliness. This was the pull of being sick. Steven said, "I was surprised when you and Sophie broke up, you and she seemed so well suited." I was surprised, too, and sometimes felt more bitter about Sophie and me than sad about my parents' deaths. (*N'est-ce que ça?*) Heartbreak number three.

"There'll be others," I told Steven. There already was one. "I'm never alone for long." Never *with* anyone either for long. "And the truth is," I told Steven, "it's not that Sophie and I were so well suited, but that our circumstances—she with her apartment, I with mine—suited me down to the ground." A lie, as "well suited' or not, Sophie had cared for me more than I was used to and she had changed my life.

Susy (now Susanna) came and stayed with her boyfriend (!) on her way back to prep school. She told me that Alice had been beaten up by the man she lived with in Taos. The atmosphere there, where Alice lived, sounded to be all violence and alcohol and cocaine.

I phoned and Emma answered. She sounded angry, as always when she spoke to me now, and defensive about her mother. I spoke to Alice and she sounded nuts. What was I to do? I spoke to the lawyers and the lawyers said, A private detective. I spoke to the welfare people in New Mexico. The idea was to "put Alice on notice," in the lawyers' phrase, that her behavior was being remarked.

I started writing a story about being married and being in debt. Then it turned into a story about getting sick. It was called "Our Politics." It was also about sickness taking the place of politics.

MY MONTPARNASSE

Déjà jadis.

G. *Ribemont-Dessaignes*

In the fall of 1980, while my parents' estates were being settled, and after Number 19 was sold, I moved into the big
apartment I'd bought, at 50 Riverside Drive. The building
lobby didn't have stairs. I could wheel in and out in my little cart:
to the street, to a cab, to Riverside Park. A life on wheels: *Make
way! make way!* . . . Inside as well, from room to room, I could
wheel in and out, in and out, in and out. . . . The sills to the
doorways had all been removed. A life without thresholds: downhill. . . .

Nineteen Gramercy Park had belonged to a "charitable" foun-
dation. When it was sold, Helen and I shared control of a fairly
large sum. A part of its income had to go to other so-called
charities. I gave some money to the Institute of Fine Arts, a
favorite of my father's, for a series of Marxian lectures ("The
Walter Benjamin Lectures") on the history of art. Hard for me to
attend, the lectures were also a little dull. To ginger things up, I
asked the Institute to invite Anthony Blunt to come and talk
about Poussin, about Picasso . . . about whatever he liked. The
Institute agreed, which astonished me, but Blunt, at the very
nadir of his fortunes, didn't reply. Next I thought about giving
money to the Bread and Puppet Theater, or to some other "dissident" theater group, but going to plays was no longer much
fun. Anyhow, from some Ruskinian well of revulsion in me at
the notion of undistributed capital (an attitude not unusual in
children of privilege), I wanted my share of the money to go, and
go quickly, to people, not institutions. All of it. What to do?

Lifelong habits of reading and writing, of maintaining cross
opinions, together with a too-long-suppressed wish to teach and
entertain, made starting a literary magazine a natural, perhaps
inescapable, choice. I was also bored with my attitudes of fastidious disengagement. Reading books, buying art, writing un-
produced plays, seducing women: not much of a life.

ST
Ben S. Sunday Jan 6 1991

My first thought was to do a magazine with Elizabeth Pochoda, my editor at the *Nation*, where parts of *Lost Property* were first published. A literary magazine, with politics in it, which for some reason I decided to call *Grand Street.**

But Elizabeth needed a well-paying job, so *Grand Street* was left all to me. I wanted *Grand Street* to look severe but for its contents to be fun, a mix of insolence and information. A magazine like one of those Fourth Avenue bookstores in New York when I was a child, where I used to find books by authors I'd never heard of, learned books on abstruse subjects, such as *Premature Burial, and How It May Be Prevented* by Tebb and Vollum, *Wolf Children and Feral Man* by Singh and Zingg, and *Seven Types of Ambiguity* by William Empson. A magazine like a bookstore where the owner: a smoker, a drinker, a cougher, foul-smelling, with filthy fingers: is unhelpful and rude until I say, truculently, "I don't suppose you happen to have *Faithful Only to One* by Stevie Smith?" After which the owner is kindness itself: courtly and handsome and helpful, even *bounteous*. A sudden Prince of Poetic Illumination.

In point of fact, in 1962, on a visit with Bill Davis to Cyril Connolly's house in Lewes, Sussex, I heard Connolly tell of having once wanted such a bookshop himself, one where he could scold the customers for not knowing Leconte de Lisle or Sir Richard Roos. "I soon realized that to earn money, I'd have to have *two* shops, the other across the road," he said. "So I could show people the door and point and say, 'And if you don't like it here, you know where you can go.' " Connolly's magazine, *Horizon*, which lasted from 1939 to 1950, would be one of my models, for its insolent reflection of only one man's taste.†

Another model would be the *Dial*, founded by Scofield Thayer, which lasted from 1921 to 1929 and was baffling and

* So as not to call it *Gramercy Park?* That was Murray Kempton's guess, in the introduction he wrote to *A Grand Street Reader* (1986).
† Connolly's collection of modern firsts, reposing now in the library at the University of Texas in Austin, was once ordered according to how the authors would look sitting naked on the shelf: Virginia Woolf next to Hemingway, Henry James next to Gertrude Stein. Or so he told me that time in Lewes. When I saw the collection, the books were all placed with the spines facing in: not to keep them from fading, as I supposed, but to keep his friends from stealing them. The mad look in his eye as he said that! I don't think I'd have stolen a book; I did covet a telegram framed on the wall. It read: MEET ME AT NOON EUSTON STATION. JOYCE. Connolly said, "As at the time I was trying to avoid a young woman called Joyce, I didn't go."

infuriating to many of its readers, and of which Marianne Moore, one of its editors, said, "Whatever character *The Dial* may have is the result of a selection not of writers but of writing." The *Dial* was also said by someone, I forget who, to have reflected Thayer's "intolerance of the merely good."

I began to interview designers. These were tasteful young men and women who'd done exhibition catalogues for the Pierpont Morgan Library, the Menil Collection, and the like. Many of them lived in Vermont. I had trouble getting across to them the kind of magazine I had in mind. Their good taste got in my way. My good taste, as well. Good taste! How to escape it? And wasn't the effort to escape the worst sort of good taste?

•

"The design is the thing. I always knew that. Decorous but not stuffy, formal but not stiff. Why can't I get the idea across?" Then Elizabeth suggests the designer Deborah Thomas and she sees at once what I want to do.

At the start, I publish my friends. A number of them are writers who know how to write for magazines. Then I begin asking for articles: "Is there any subject you *want* to treat? . . . *Grand Street* can pay." And the fees aren't bad: the money's supposed to *go*, after all. *Grand Street* gets known, and from then on there appear numberless (so it seemed sometimes) unsolicited stories, essays, poems and proposals. I reject many. I accept some. I respond promptly, and as a rule I pay upon acceptance. Soon I'm publishing Alice Munro, Glenway Wescott and Claud Cockburn. And I'm publishing Djuna Barnes, William Empson and Samuel Beckett.*

The famous names are draws for new work, as, like Ford

---

* Twenty-six years after our meeting in Paris, and a month after his death, I published what I believe is Samuel Beckett's last work: a poem called "What Is the Word," dedicated to his friend, the actor and director Joseph Chaikin, who had had a stroke the year before. I didn't get to write Beckett or to send him galley proofs; all my dealings were with his American publisher, Barney Rossett.

But after that issue came out, in the winter of 1990 (it was my next-to-last), I got a letter from a friend in Paris, a charming if not always credible chap. "I saw something of Sam [*sic!*] in his last days, and he told me, 'I've been trying to translate this joke into French: *A man goes into a bar where there's a piano player with a monkey . . .* ' "

Madox Ford, I make finds; like Art Blakey, I help young talent along. I suggest changes; most are accepted: gratefully, to my surprise. Together with Deborah and, occasionally, an assistant editor: Amy Wilentz, Susan Minot, Spencer Boyd, Suzanne Gardinier, Barbara Jones: and a superb copy chief, Helene Pleasants, I make a journal of which I'm proud. Each number has two hundred pages or more. Each has a rhythm, each has a theme (neither is obvious). Each number, read from beginning to end, or backwards, or from the middle, is a tour, a voyage, a career. The work I publish is all first-rate: "a selection not of writers but of writing": and Leon Edel calls *Grand Street* "our end-of-century *Dial* magazine."

•

For once in my life admired by those I admired myself, I was doing an exemplary thing; and I was, in a manner of speaking, laying out an education for my daughters, not to mention myself. Responsible, irreproachable, and with no zeal to revolt in disgust, I was happy, content and (as I say) proud. Not that it didn't occur to me that at last I was doing something my father would have liked: which should have spoiled it for me, instantly. And would have, had he been alive. I had trouble enough hearing praise with him dead, in particular for my "impeccable taste." Oh, for detraction from someone smart!

And, oh, for someone smart to see that I was in a prison. No one believed me when I shouted, *Help!* No one believed I wanted out. "You can't be serious," writers said when I asked for the liberating article on Judith Exner or Roma Furniture: just as in life no secret police had ever arrested me.* When I met the novelist Anthony Powell, at La Consula in 1963, he spoke of knowing someone with a lifelong compulsion to be searched by customs officers. I was like that someone in my drive for bad taste. I rationalized my compulsion by saying I wanted to up

---

* Judith Exner, once at one and the same time the mistress of the mafia chief Sam Giancana and President Kennedy, to whom she was introduced by Frank Sinatra, embodied to me the nexus of crime and politics in America, as brought about by entertainers. Her autobiography, *My Life*, is written with a most peculiar gentility of expression.

  Roma Furniture, on Grand Street, represents a peculiar gentility too, like that of Giancana's collection of porcelain figurines.

circulation. My readership, though loyal, wasn't large.* Surely bad taste would help get it up? First, in search of sensation, I commissioned from G. W. Bowersock, historian of the Late Roman Empire, an article on the scandalous practice of archaeology in Israel; next I got Steven Marcus, author of *The Other Victorians*, to write about the apostate psychoanalyst Alfred Adler; then I asked John Hess to write about the politics of the culture desk at the *New York Times*. Provocation like that got me only Zionists, cultists and Hilton Kramer, former art critic on the *Times*. *Kach*, cult and Hilton Kramer.

(Incidentally, the issue of *Grand Street* with Hess's piece was the only one I had to reprint, and it made the magazine many friends, especially on the *Times*.)

Grand Street's office was the dining room. Deborah was there every day, with at least one of my assistants. All of these being young women, an atmosphere began to grow, as of the old library in a good school for well-to-do girls: smelling of leather and light perfume. An air of serious purpose, with sounds in the background of laughter and chat. And there was I, Head Librarian, Boss: with my dog, Harry, a sometimes good-natured mutt, mostly terrier, who preferred women to men.

But *Grand Street* was bringing me into the world and it brought the world to me, on terms of respect which were new to me. Slowly I made a community, artistic and political, of which I (surprised) enjoyed being a part. I spoke daily on the telephone to writers and journalists; to editors, publishers, agents; I scanned other journals emulously: *I want something like that only better. . . . A story by her . . . A piece by him;* and I read the daily papers self-importantly, feeling newly connected to events. My dissident habits, once poses, became significant, so did my habits of mischief. All was my clay.

I truly loved being the editor of a magazine. In one respect, again to refer to Walter Benjamin (for maybe the last time), I now had in my own drawing room a private environment representing the universe, "a box in the world theater," where I gathered "remote places and the past." At my bidding people went farther than I'd ever gone myself: South Africa, Haiti, Nablus, Gettysburg, Pennsylvania. They went (for me! for *Grand Street!*) into

* Never more than five thousand.

the Past, sometimes (dark region) the Recent Past. Where before
in my life I'd been known by association with this or that young
woman or this or that older man, or as (detested appellation)
Young Ben: or as (at best) one who "consorts with the small poets
of the time," as Face says of Dapper in *The Alchemist*: now I was
on friendly and familiar terms with the likes of Arthur Danto,
Edward Said, Alexander Cockburn, Christopher Ricks and
Christopher Hitchens. Elizabeth Jolley phoned me up when in
town; Amy Clampitt visited me, so did Francis Steegmuller and
Craig Raine. With my old friends, too, my relations deepened. In
writing for me, Frank Hauser, Virgil Thomson, Ted Hughes,
Richard Howard, Michael Train, always cherished, became
more dear.

There was another reason I loved having a magazine. It began
with Susan Minot who came to me when she was twenty-six. She
was the first writer I worked with: word by word, line by line,
page by page, at her side. I was her accompanist: essential but
subordinate. *Her* performance, not mine, was the thing. It didn't
hurt that she was beautiful, young and very sad. What mattered
was this: that what I guessed of where she wanted to go, and
what I knew of how others had gotten there, was of help in
bringing her stories to life. Different from the magus-like role,
which some editors aim for. Different far from what I'd have
predicted for myself before I began. The end result was Susan's
first novel, *Monkeys*.

With more experienced writers, too (the more experienced the
apter to listen, I found), I was a good editor. Penelope Gilliatt, a
friend from London in the sixties (Siriol's successor as features
editor at *Vogue* and my neighbor in Mount Street when she was
living there with Kenneth Tynan), did a number of articles for
me and gave me two or three stories, including "The Nuisance,"
one of her best. Unlike most of her other stories "The Nuisance"
is savage and ends bitterly. I enjoyed sitting next to Penelope and
reading a piece of her fiction with her. What pleasure I had in
things well achieved, what thoughts I had about what was not,
what a miracle her faculty of prompt adjustment was. And what
satisfaction it was to assign "fact pieces" to her at a time when the
New Yorker, where she was on the staff, would accept only fiction
from her.

As a general rule, I avoided "special" issues, devoted to one writer. However, in the spring of 1983, I gave over three-fourths of an issue to Constantine Cavafy and dedicated it to George Savidis, Cavafy's editor and my friend of twenty years. To him, more than to anyone else, I owe my interest in Modern Greek letters, shown time and again in the magazine. From James Merrill I got translations of Cavafy's only known prose work, "In Broad Daylight," and of "Days of 1908," which may be Cavafy's best poem. (It is certainly the best translation of a Cavafy poem into English.*) And I published Yanis Ritsos, Takis Sinopoulos, Kostas Taktsis, as well as critical essays on Constantine Karyotakis, Alexandros Papadiamantis and Aris Alexandrou.

I'm sorry about a couple of things. I never found the right persons to treat the subjects of Genet and the intifada; Byron, the war of Greek independence and the intifada; Jewish-American intellectuals and the intifada. And I'm still annoyed by a couple of things (besides, my risible efforts to shunt aside good taste): hearing from people who said they admired the magazine but hadn't read it; and hearing from writers who'd read only their own work in an issue.

For nine years, absorbed by *Grand Street*, even as I got sicker, I felt my life change for the better. I put out thirty-five issues at quarterly intervals. I printed only what I liked; never once did I publish an editorial statement; I offered no writers' guidelines; and I stopped when I couldn't turn pages any more.

I stopped sooner than I wanted: rising costs, failing health, and the money had gone, most of it (at last!). But I wasn't too sad, having after all made a magazine that would have no successor.† Such sadness as I did feel had less to do with being sick than with the sudden disappearance of young women from the apartment. I thought of Susan Minot and wrote:

> They follow me. Me they used to seek
> Wanton, gentle, tame and meek.

---

* *Grand Street*, Winter 1987.

† Not strictly true. In 1990, I transferred the magazine, in name at least, to Jean Stein, who was also a Collectors' Child. When she and I were in our teens, my father said, "Why not marry Jean? It would bring about the merger of two great furniture collections." And the moment of the transfer looked something like a nuptial, a modern *Arnolfini wedding*.

They follow me but go to boys
Who make up in sex what they lack in poise.

What I lack in sex I make up in poise.
Still they follow, with little noise.
On naked feet they follow me.
If I but turn my head, they flee.

•

I don't care for much of what I read by people with MS. The truthful accounts lack style. The stylish ones are incomplete. A truthful and stylish telling of its onset occurs in Brigid Brophy's *Baroque-'n'-Roll*, published in London in 1987:

> That is the chief curse of the illness. I must ask constant services of the people I love most closely. . . . I cannot do any service to friend or stranger without passing on the burden of doing it to the people I love. . . .
> Sporadically it is, in its manifestations, a disgusting disease. Also sporadically, it has another anti-social result, wrapping one suddenly in an inexorable fatigue like a magic cloak of invisibility. . . .

A truthful and stylish telling of its progress occurs in the *Diary of a Disappointed Man* and *Last Diary* by W. N. P. Barbellion (nom de plume of Bruce Frederick Cummings), published in 1919:

> Even as I sit and write, millions of bacterium are gnawing away at my precious spine and cord, and if you put your ear to my back the sound of gnawing I dare say could be heard.

That was written in the epoch of *baffled*, *confused* and *mystified* notions of the cause of MS, when its pathogenesis was thought to be "possibly a case of orphan antigens in search of a disease." If today you put your ear to my back, no such metaphor will spring to mind. You won't hear a noise as of insects gnawing their way up a tree. You'll have to have a sixth sense for either the silent Virus or the still-as-stone Autoimmunity, which being long past ("genetically predetermined"), can be read, like Linear B, only by cryptoanalysts in the service of those excavating an ancient civilization. "Anyway," says one scientific friend, "as soon as a cure for the symptoms is found, no one will care what the cause is."

·

Soon after I started *Grand Street*, I met Dorothy Gallagher. *Don't marry me*, I was soon telling her. *I'm not going to get any better, I'm only going to get worse.* I wrote her warning letters, and I told her one night over dinner, "The good thing is, it's not painful . . . except if I have strong spasms and am thrown off my cart. But no one in her right mind ought even to *think* of marrying me. You have your own life, your own friends, your own work, your own beautiful loft on the Bowery. . . . And another thing, it isn't fatal. It's pernicious, but not fatal."

Dorothy Gallagher, at work on a life of the Italian-American anarchist Carlo Tresca who was murdered mysteriously in New York in 1943, lived on her own in a small, light-filled loft, on the corner of Rivington Street and the Bowery. I loved hearing her say of certain things, "I hate it worse than life itself." I loved her looks, which Susanna thought *mysterious and European:* like Anouk Aimée, I suppose. Also *coltish,* like Audrey Hepburn. I sang her the Song of One Frightened of Getting Involved Again, sung by me so often before. Alluring, warning, alluring again. "Marriage would mean so much more to me than to you," I wrote to Dorothy. I was seeing her every day and sleeping with her every night. Even so, I wrote her letters, as I always used to do. "You know what the problem would be, don't you? We are both so used to cherishing and not sharing our unhappiness. Say things go wrong, and they're bound to go wrong, would we cooperate? . . ."

But the words didn't sound as they used to.

·

Last year, for our ninth anniversary, I wrote this poem for
Dorothy:

>   Waiting for M. (or was it C.?),
>   I listened to Gymnopédies
>   by Erik Satie. Waiting for A.
>   I listened to Les Nuits d'Été.
>   The Mighty Sparrow waiting for K.
>   Waterloo Sunset waiting for J.
>   Other women I waited for were: I Care Not For
>   These Ladies by Thomas Campion, Pursue Thy
>   Conquest, Love, by Henry Purcell, Le Comte Ory by
>   Giacchino Rossini (two-record set) and Beechwood
>   4-5-7-8-9 by The Marvelettes, and so on
>   and on.
>   Don Schwann's catalogue.
>
>   I listened to no one waiting for you.
>   I waited
>   I waited.
>   I waited for you.

MY LAST FOOTNOTE "What happened finally with wife number one?"

"Survives," I say.

"And wife number two?"

"Flourishes, with our daughter. They live near Baltimore."

"Well, then," Alex Cockburn says, "that final stretch of the book's a bit rushed. It reminds me of your pal Cyril Connolly's review of Claud's first volume of autobiography, *In Time of Trouble*. He was unstinting in his praise but remarked that towards its end the book began to 'shamble forward with ungainly speed.' "

Surely mine doesn't *shamble?*"

"*Wheels* downhill, then, too precipitously. In tone too much like a post mortem note by the editor: 'Following his publication of *Grand Street*, the author reformed morally, married an intelligent and beautiful woman, amassed a select circle of loyal and delightful friends, received beatification from noted religious leaders, and basked in the love and admiration of his daughters.' More detail, more perhaps about sickness . . . ."

"Hand me down that anthology, won't you? Find that poem of Wedekind's where he says, 'It's ages since I got over being a sexual psychopath, and yet, I shall never forget it: those were happy days.' Read me the last four lines."

And Alexander reads:

> *Die sexuelle Psychopathie,*
> *Iche habe sie längst überwunden—*
> *Und dennoch, ich vergess es nie,*
> *Es waren doch schöne Stunden.*

I say, "*Es waren doch schöne Stunden.* . . . That's what I aimed for. The ending I got took me by surprise."

ACKNOWLEDGMENTS

I am grateful to Saul Steinberg for permission to reproduce the drawing on page 200 and on the back cover.

Parts of *Lost Property* first appeared in *The Nation, Paris Review, Raritan* and *Yale Review.*

The photograph on page 153 is by Stephanie Saia.

The following have read this book, or parts of it, and offered comments, encouragement and corrections, many adopted:

Sally Belfrage, Ernst Benkert, Georges Borchardt, David Bromwich, Sophie Zevon Clumber (Not Her Real Name), Alexander Cockburn, Sabina Dreier (NHRN), Penelope Gilliatt, Emma Hart, Frank Hauser, Christopher Hitchens, Richard Howard, Barbara Jones, J. D. McClatchy, Daniel Menaker, W. S. Merwin, Julie Middleton, Susan Minot, Agnès Nichol (NHRN), Jeremy Nussbaum, Eric Rayman, Edward W. Said, James Salter, Charles Smith, M.D., Susan Snodgrass, Saul Steinberg, Jean Strouse, Deborah Thomas, Michael Train.

And my sister, Helen; my daughters, my wife. . . .

INDEX

INDEX